Match the definition to the newly coined word

1. A noun that means: Self-advertising; the blazoning of one's name on hotels, casinos, and airliners; commercial graffiti.
2. An adjective for females only: Applied to a woman characterized by vainglorious physical daring, compulsive vigor, disregard for pain, eagerness to appear as strong and reckless as any male.
3. A psychological term: The mental state created when one is in one's vehicle headed for vacation and someone else in the car asks whether anyone turned off the stove.

A. **Vacanoia** *n* [vacation + paranoia]
B. **Trumpery** *n* [existing word meaning something without use or value, and by association with eponymous hero Donald Trump]
C. **Facho** *adj* [female + macho]

Our changing world needs new words as fast as we can make them up. These are the best of times and the worst of times . . . and neologisms give us a vocabulary to tell the tale.

IN A WORD
A Dictionary of Words That Don't Exist,
But Ought To

Answers:
1. B   2. C   3. A

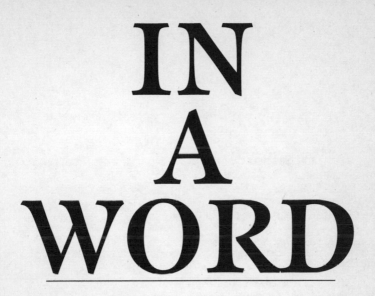

IN A WORD

A Dictionary of Words That Don't Exist, But Ought To

JACK HITT, *editor*

DEIDRE McFADYEN, *assistant editor*

A LAUREL TRADE PAPERBACK
Published by
Dell Publishing
a division of
Bantam Doubleday Dell Publishing Group, Inc.
666 Fifth Avenue
New York, New York 10103

ISBN: 0-440-50358-2

Printed in the United States of America

Published simultaneously in Canada

May 1992

10 9 8 7 6 5 4 3 2 1

RRC

To my mother and father, Ann L. Hitt and Robert M. Hitt, Jr.

Acknowledgments

Compiling a dictionary is a task that sounds like a great idea until one undertakes it. When I was in college, my english teacher had me read Samuel Johnson's introduction to his dictionary as an example of one of the great essays in the English language. Johnson's description of the lexicographer as a "harmless drudge" was always said, by my teacher, to be an example of the good doctor's rarefied sense of irony. But having worked on this inadequate and modest dictionary, I can assert without fear of error that Johnson's phrase is pure declarative description. The drudges who deserve all my thanks and pity are Richard Hicks, Matthew Butcher, Jennifer Barton, and Scott Anderson. I would also like to thank Lewis Lapham, the editor of *Harper's Magazine*, who indulged me when I first approached him with this idea.

Introduction

The idea of this dictionary dates back to a particular day during my freshman year in college when I stepped into one of the secluded alcoves in the school library. This one, paid for by an alumnus too rich merely to glue a silver name tag to the back of a chapel pew and too poor to build an entire edifice, was dedicated to the everlasting memory of the Venerable Bede. I had never heard of the Venerable Bede before that moment, but I noticed his name because his honorific seemed to suggest that he had fallen just a good work or two short of achieving sainthood. Before the day was over, though, I encountered the Venerable Bede three more times —in the title of a book, in conversation, and in an essay. I remember thinking how remarkable it was that I could pass eighteen years without coming across the Venerable Bede and then cross his path four times in a single day. And I wondered if there were a word, in the genus of "déjà vu" or "serendipity" or "coincidence," that adequately captured the sense of this phenomenon.

I soon learned that there isn't one, and I thought I had discovered a meaning in search of a word. Several years later, when I had taken a job as an editor of *Harper's Magazine*, I came upon the Venerable Bede once again, and I am certain we hadn't seen each other since my college days. The renewal of our acquaintance led me to write a number of writers and artists and ask them if they had ever had the experience of running across a meaning for which there is no word. If so, I asked, coin the word, provide an etymology, write out the meaning in standard dictionary form, and use the neologism in a sentence or explain the subtleties of the new usage. The resulting article ran in the February 1990 issue of *Harper's Magazine*.

With this book, I have expanded the letters of invitation to many more professions and many more people. I wrote the world's finest writers, actors, and filmmakers. I wrote musicians and cosmologists. I wrote academics and journalists. I wrote ecologists and quantum physicists. And I asked them all to coin a word they thought was missing from everyone's standard desktop dictionary.

The assignment both was and was not serious. Some wrote me back earnestly attempting a coinage for a meaning they thought missing. Others, mainly writers, couldn't resist trying all kinds of rhetorical and grammatical finesses within the confines of the peculiar literary form of the dictionary entry. Of all of these, I have chosen the best and published them.

For every ten correspondents who were pleased to contribute, one sent me a letter pleading that I call off this nefarious project. One writer penned a two-page jeremiad: "It seems to me that you are encouraging a pernicious trend in the English-speaking world—the irresponsible creation of new words. The truth is we are oversupplied with words. There are as many unused words stored away in the OED as the Pentagon has spare parts." Another, a noted scientist, wrote, "I'm afraid I can't endorse your pursuit of neologisms, because it tends to distract from the riches of the English language as we find it. It is worth remembering that Shakespeare was able to write entire plays with no more than a few thousand words of vocabulary, many of them being closely related by tense or case." You want to smack these people. Not only because they lack the modest gift of humor and goodwill necessary for this endeavor, but because their arrogance about our language is as excessive as their ignorance. The complaint about the debauchery of the language is as old as it is tiresome. By the time Shakespeare wrote, English had already been polluted by the Scandinavians, who added about 2,000 words to the Anglo-Saxons' 50,000. The Norman invasion had doubled the total number of "English" words to about 125,000. And the infiltration of Latinate and other learned terms in the Renaissance doubled the language again, to about 250,000. In a 1701 essay, Daniel Defoe fumed about "Roman-Saxon-Danish-Norman-English." In the century prior to Defoe, the language was in a fluid and creative state. Spelling was set by the mood of the writer, and neologisms flowed into the language. Shakespeare, who paradoxically is most often invoked by the guardians of the language as someone who would certainly be on their side, added more than 1,500 neologisms to the language. Perhaps Shakespeare felt liberated because at the time he wrote there was no standard dictionary.

The earliest attempts at something remotely resembling a dictionary of English date back to the Middle Ages when poor Latin students compiled lists of word translations, known as glossaries, to assist them in their homework. Perhaps it's fitting that today's dictionaries are descended from cheat sheets because dictionaries are, when you think about them, unnatural. Language is a mess—massive spontaneous and deliberate combustions born out of the jabbering and scribbling of millions. It obeys only the peculiar laws of chaos, which hold that extraordinarily high numbers of random acts actually betray, upon inspection, unlikely consistencies. These detectable patterns in language, distilled over the centuries, are called grammar and syntax. The dictionary is a further attempt to stop, examine, and quantify. If language is the leap of a frog, the dictionary is a pithing board with a hundred thousand little pins.

Because dictionaries are compiled by panels of highly credentialed experts, we readers invest in them an enormous amount of authority. But English, especially as we Americans have remade it, is probably the most untamed and untameable language there is. In the four centuries since Shakespeare died, leaving his language with roughly 250,000 words, it has doubled again. There is no one source that has dominated this period of lexicographic expansion. Rather, it's been fittingly democratic. There are only a few obscure languages in the world today that haven't dumped some old or new words into what we politely call the English dictionary. American English is less a tended garden than it is a junkyard of other cultures' castaways, imports, neologisms, and jargon.

Every year or so the newspapers run the obligatory story of the French academy "weeding" out new words lacking the pedigree necessary to refined French. The article always takes note of some bureaucrat charged with the task of imposing five-franc fines on Parisians corrupt enough to utter such bastard imports as "le weekend" or "le deejay." A professor from the Sorbonne or a minister of culture is called upon to boast that French has one word for, say, "death" and needs no other. This attitude seems pure and straightforward and appeals to the language marms on this side of the pond who see nothing but chaos in the meretricious surrender of English to new words.

But our stuffed junkyard contains some true beauties. While it is true that the French can always "dic" tidily with *"mort,"* the English speaker too can "die," if he wants to be plain and truthful; or be "deceased," if he is a bureaucrat with a form to fill out; or go "kaput," if he can afford to be flip; or "pass away," if he is a mortician in need of euphemism; or "expire," if he is a doctor with bad news; or "perish," if he wants a hint of drama; or "meet one's maker," if he needs more than a hint of drama; or "shuffle off this mortal coil," if he prefers Shakespeare's endorsement of the idea; or "cross the Stygian ferry," if he desires a trace of classical learning; or "kick the bucket," if he insists upon coarseness; or "push up daisies," if he wants an air of ironic carelessness. English has imported so many ways of saying the same thing, each with its own shading of connotation, that our dictionary is now twice, almost three times, the size of most continental languages such as French.

In English, as in all languages, vocabulary is a moraine over which the dictionary moves like a glacier, slowly absorbing new words and slowly sloughing off others. The dictionary itself is but a time-lapse photograph of this movement, always destined to be out of date. Very little might change from generation to generation, but a careful reader can see the history of a culture scattered through the pages of a dictionary. One needn't be either a historian or an anthropologist to examine the Anglo-Saxon words "sheep," "cow," "pig," and "lamb" alongside the Norman words "mutton," "steak," "pork," and "veal" in order to deduce just *who* in the era following 1066 were the aristocrats dining inside the big house and who were the servants working in the stables. A flip through Noah Webster's original *American Dictionary*, published in 1828, reveals a culture working largely within the vocabulary of agriculture. Today's dictionary would certainly show a world tuned to the advances of technology.

If the standard dictionary is a photograph of the entire language, then this dictionary is merely a snapshot of those most volatile areas. As the words came in, it became clear that many people were struggling to fill in similar lacunae. Like magic, the neologisms fell into a number of categories such as computer technology, new social roles in society, the relations between the sexes, and truth and falsehood in the era of television.

Many of the writers who sent in words chose to form their coinages by inventing compound or blend words (compounds simply push two words together, such as "birdcage"; blends interlace two words, such as "brunch" or "smog"). Curiously, many of the writers who sent letters complaining of this project insisted that the language was being ruined especially by cheap compound and blend words. Yet such words were commonplace in the sixteenth and seventeenth centuries when neologizing was at its zenith. Today we also hear language columnists complain about the hideous practice of making a noun from a verb or adjective. But consider Shakespeare's contemporaries who wallowed in the common practice of attaching a "th" to a word to give us nouns such as "strength" (strong), "wealth" (weal), "warmth" (warm), "growth" (grow), or "health" (heal). They had also tried

"greenth," "illth," and, later, even "coolth." For some reason, the capricious shears of usage clipped them.

There are older words whose compound or blended forms
are so old that we can no longer recognize their constituent
parts. The word "barn" seems perfectly Anglo-Saxon, short
and tough with a single, simple meaning. But "barn" is a
blend of "bere" and "aern," or "barley-place." And there are
many others: "lord" is "hlaf" and "weard," or "bread-
keeper"; "gospel" is "god" and "spell," or "good narrative";
"gossip" is "god" and "sibbe," or "good kinsman"; "don" is
"don" and "on," or "put on"; and "doff" is "don" and "off,"
or "put off."

Of course, the real reason most of the contributors to this
book participated was to have a good time. Few cling to any
hope that their word will make the more difficult jump to
Webster's. But what was Lewis Carroll thinking when he
shoved "chuckle" and "snort" together and gave us the necessary neologism "chortle"? Or did John Milton really think
the awkward "pandemonium" would survive outside of *Paradise Lost*? *Earlier in the century, Stephen Potter coined the word
"gamesmanship." But who would have thought that this seemingly
inelegant construction would spawn "one-upmanship,"
"brinkmanship," and even, in this age of foundation support of
nearly everything, "grantsmanship," or the ability to write a con-
vincing grant proposal? Not long ago, I learned that Joel Agee's
contribution to the original Harper's article, "Eurojive," was*
spotted in the January 1991 issue of (no less) the *Publication
of the Modern Language Association* (page 126).

New words come into the language by whatever means
necessary. They are often acts of spontaneous combustion
whose origins will always be marked "unknown." Or they
are as weird and deliberate as the human race. The number
"googol" or ten to the one-hundredth power was named by
mathematician Edward Kasner after he asked his young
nephew to think up a good word. The scientific term "quark"
is pulled from an unlikely source, James Joyce's *Finnegans*

Wake. And older words slowly metamorphose, putting on new meanings and taking off previous ones. Consider the word "terrific," from "terrify," an adjective meaning "scary" or "horrifying." Today it means "appealing" or "great." Is this the bastardization of the language as the newspaper columnists charge, or is this the inevitable movement of meaning in any living language? The *Oxford English Dictionary* not only acknowledges the mutability of language but exists solely to map these slight changes.

In Samuel Johnson's introduction to his dictionary, he didn't resist the ever-fluid state of his language, nor did he apologize for it. He realized that his work was fleeting because the language would eventually pass it by. He cautioned his readers on the changing meanings of the most common words: "If of these [words] the whole power is not accurately delivered, it must be remembered that while our language is yet living, and variable by the caprice of every one that speaks it, these words are hourly shifting their relations, and can no more be ascertained in a dictionary, than a grove, in the agitation of a storm, can be accurately delineated from its picture in the water."

But despite the apparent uselessness of dictionaries, of course, we need them if for no other reason than we need a stick of wood in a stormy sea. They are always inadequate and absolutely necessary. Lexicographers will go on compiling dictionaries of every description, including dictionaries such as this one, part exercise, part fun, part lexicon. A recent university study tried to determine just how adulterated the English language had become by the influx of so many new and foreign words. Thousands of English sentences from numerous sources were fed into a computer and analyzed. The results will no doubt be construed by many as alarming. The number of foreign or new words in the English language has completely overwhelmed words with Anglo-Saxon roots. English is now a minority in its own dictionary. Certainly this will trouble the kind of people who fret over immigrant quotas. But the same numbers spit out by the computer also uncovered another English. When configured to account for *frequency* of use, the computer revealed that of the one hundred most common words in English, all of them dated to Old English. Of the next hundred, eighty-six were of Old English vintage, and so on. One might conclude that neologisms work at the edges of the language, striving to enter into the ranks of permanent usage, while the core of English remains the same stubborn words of Anglo-Saxon, all of them brutish, nasty, and short.

JACK HITT
1991

A

ab•sti•stic *adj* [*abstract* meaning disembodied, divorced from the palpable world of our senses + *statistic*]: Of or pertaining to all conversation, writing, and argument that bases itself on theoretical principles, positions, political persuasions, on statistics devoid of the heart, voice, or poetry, on ideology rather than experience; includes the new "isms" that, in the name of statistics and theory, stereotype and group, erase particular characteristics into the inevitable and necessary fall from grace implied in "average," "norm," and "mean" as measurable by sociological, psychological, and scientific instruments and categories. "An African-American who condemns all whites, a Jew who condemns all Arabs or vice versa, a woman who in the name of feminism condemns all men, a man who in an act of male chauvinism condemns all women to underclass status and reduced respect in all cases, uses language we refer to as abstistic. The speakers of such high-mindedness are not themselves abstistic, because to label them as such would deny them of their humanity in precisely the same way that their thinking denies the humanity of individuals whom they insist on lumping together in a class. Human connection is absent in abstistic language since group identity with those of one's shared commonality has absorbed distinct personality traits such as a throaty voice or a rheumy eye." (ELIZABETH ANNE SOCOLOW, *poet*)

a•ca•dem•a•gogue *n* [*academy + demagogue*]: One who applies the methods of the demagogue to the problems of the academy. "Thanks to a group of shameless academagogues, the new epistemology now dominates many university departments of English, to the exclusion of all other views." (BERNARD LEWIS, *professor*)

a•ca•dem•ate *v* [*academy + accommodate*]: To imprison white-collar criminals in resort-like surroundings, a contradictory response containing aspects of both reward and punishment. "The Wall Street broker was taken into custody and academated in Florida, where he served two sunburned years at hard tennis." (BOB SHACOCHIS, *writer*)

academate

ac·count·out *n* [*accountant + out*]: A person in charge of paying taxes, setting up tax shelters, and paying for nonexistent people double what they didn't earn. "They're repossessing my house and I'm going to jail for 12 years because of my accountout." (Lou Reed, *musician*)

a·clone *adj* [*alone + clone*]: The feeling, akin to loneliness, that comes from being with people who always agree with you and never express original ideas. "At the board meeting, surrounded by two dozen smiling subordinates, Frank felt all aclone." (Richard Seltzer, *writer*)

a·cous·ti·cate *v* [fr. Gk *akoustikos* pertaining to hearing + *equivocate*]: To deny that one has been correctly heard, or overheard, when one is painfully aware that there has been no mistake, this denial being often supported by the hasty fabrication of a new utterance, similar in sound to the original, but more agreeable in sense. "I quickly acousticated 'fatuous ass' into 'anfractuous mass,' and nobody noticed a thing." (Richard Tristman, *professor*)

ac·quend *n* [*acquaintance + friend*]: Someone who is more than an acquaintance but less than a friend. "As a word, acquend takes the place of the introductory statement, 'I have this friend (well, she really isn't a friend, but someone I know) who . . .'" (Judith Kitchen, *writer*)

ac • quis • it *v* [*acquisitions editor + edit*]: To do the work of an acquiring or acquisitions editor. "In major publishing houses, those who acquire books are still spoken of as 'editors,' although they do almost no actual editing on manuscripts; thus describing their work as 'editing' is increasingly ludicrous, and yet 'acquiring' a book sounds as undignified as shopping. The word acquisit allows us to finesse the problem: A *New York* magazine article (December 17, 1990) explained that Bret Easton Ellis's first novel was heavily reworked by Joe McGinniss, evidently playing the old Max Perkins role, before it was acquired by Simon & Schuster. The statement that for acquiring editor Bob Asahina the book constituted 'his first real taste of editing fiction, and it was exhilarating' would seem less foolish—since it's obvious from the context that he did nothing traditionally considered editing—if the word acquisiting were substituted for editing, meaning not just buying, but also representing the manuscript within the company, passing it along to copy editors for hands-on work, negotiating changes with the author, and setting the engines of publicity in motion." "It wasn't until the copy editor mentioned it that Richard realized that the New Age telephone numerology book he'd acquisited was missing its last three chapters." (ELLEN GRUBER GARVEY, *writer*)

a • dead *adj* [fr. Gk *a*- not + *dead*]: Being dead while still remaining a subject of constant speculation and attention. "The numbers of adead Americans continue to swell: From John F. Kennedy and Marilyn Monroe to James Dean and Elvis, many of the dead continue to live active if unproductive lives long after their interment." (GEOF HUTH, *writer*)

ad • lift *v* [*advertise + lift* as in shoplift]: To co-opt anything of value in order to sell a product through advertising. "Within a week of the march, Madison Avenue was adlifting the protest slogans to push everything from deodorant to beer." (SCOTT RUSSELL SANDERS, *writer*)

ad • ver • size *v*
—ad • ver • size • ment *n* [fr. *adverse* hostile, opposed, and its root, L *adversus* turned opposite to + *advertise*]: To promote a commodity for sale, a corporation for unencumbered further activities, or a political candidate or administration for continuing or extended support, by aggressively touting the item or en-

tity's virtue in having remedied its defects in substance or abominations in behavior, once these negative features or activities have become widely known, while at the same time without admitting any culpability for those same crimes, errors, or flaws. "A simple example of adversizement is that label on a popular brand of white vinegar that declares 'New! Now made without petroleum!' Or, on a grander if no less obvious scale, there are those Exxon commercials from 1990 that adversized the corporation by profiling the brave, skilled men and women Exxon had hired to clean up the wildlife, landscape, and waters of Prince William Sound, fouled by a spill of several million gallons of Exxon oil for which no responsibility whatsoever is admitted in the course of the ad. And finally, of course, there are any number of scandals from the Reagan-Bush years to be adversized when and if they cannot simply be ignored into oblivion: the loan debacle at a time of increased economic hardship, the Iran-Contra scandal intruding on an administration known widely for its rhetoric of high moral purpose and respect for the law. 'We've done all we can,' this by-now more or less generic and utterly self-righteous adversizement goes, from the White House or Congress, Reagan to Bush to Henry Hyde, 'to make the facts known and resolve this situation. Now' —uplift of head, slight thrust of jaw, resolutely blameless blue-eyed gaze straight into the camera—'it's time to put this behind us and move on ahead. Next question, please?' " (FRED PFEIL, *writer and critic*)

aef•fec•tive *adj* [*affective* + *effective*]: Both affective (transmitting emotion) and effective (bringing about a desired response); effectively affective; affectively effective. "An aeffective speaker, Mr. Guynup was able to sway and move his listeners tonight." (GEOF HUTH, *writer*)

af•fleur•age *n* [*affluent* + *effleurage* to touch lightly in massage + *effloresce*]: Forced, insubstantial conversation intended solely to fill time. Usually occurs while awaiting something (an elevator, a luncheon guest). "Margot and Launce engaged in affleurage while Sir Geoffrey was in the men's. (JOHN J. MOELING, JR., *publisher*)

af•flu•en•tial *adj* [*affluent* + *influential*]: Having influence through great wealth; using wealth to exercise influence that may be disproportionate or dishonest. "Such an unsavory movement could not have become so powerful without affluential backing." (ALIX KATES SHULMAN, *writer*)

Afro-fraud *n* [*African-American* + *fraud*]: An individual who has been raised as a Caucasian person, yet seeks to be defined as an African-American in order to exploit affirmative action. "Two firemen who were promoted under affirmative action guidelines were discovered to be Afro-frauds." (ALVIN F. POUSSAINT, *psychiatrist*)

af • ter • graph *n* [*after* + *graph*; by association with epigraph, a cited passage that precedes the main body of a written work]: A quotation that properly appears following the text. "The series of poems collected in *The Escape into You* ends, not with a final poem, but with an aftergraph from the Talmud: 'It is not incumbent upon you to complete this task; neither are you free to desist from it.'" (MARVIN BELL, *poet*)

a • gen • cide *adj* [*agent* + *genocide*]: A booking by an agent into a very wrong place at an unusually wrong time—generally associated with great personal risk and humiliation. "My last tour was agencide." (LOU REED, *musician*)

a • glyph • i • cate *v* [fr. Gk *a*-not + *glyphe* carving]: To avoid or put off a writing assignment until the last possible moment. "The files had been rearranged, the bathroom floor cleaned, the public radio pledge mailed in, the dog petted, and the carefree people in the park below the window had been studied thoughtfully and at length. Unable to aglyphicate further, he reached out with a heavy sigh and turned on the computer." (TOM WOOD, *writer*)

air • ful • ness *n* [*air* + *full* + *-ness*]: A physical sense that the immediate surrounding space is saturated with an invisible presence or aura. "A visitor to Renaissance Italy could hardly fail to sense its airfulness of ideas and invention." (MARVIN BELL, *poet*)

al • gore *n* [fr eponymous hero *Albert Gore*, senator from Tennessee]: 1: A meaningless symbol, offered in token representation of debate. 2: An impenetrable blandness, capable of inducing a vast lassitude. 3: A smooth, generic surface, devoid of particular ethnic, regional, or intellectual origin. "The Democrats nominated the quadren-

nial algore, then went home."
"The algore droned steadily on
about competitiveness, until the
entire audience was sleeping or
insane." (KEVIN BAKER, *writer*)

a•ma•ri *n* [fr. Gk *a-* not + L
maritare to marry and by association with *amore* love]: Significant other, partner in intimacy
to whom one is not married.
"The word amari solves one of
the essential problems of our
age and can be used in formal
writing or in casual conversation, as in 'So nice to meet you,
let me introduce you to my
amari.'" (CYNTHIA MACDONALD,
poet)

a•ma•ter•ro•gate *v* [*amatory*
+ *interrogate*]: To engage in a
mutual questioning, covering
ex's, sexually transmitted diseases, birth control methods,
and expectations or hopes for
future commitment, conducted
by a couple before consummat-
ing their relationship. "Over
dinner, she amaterrogates David
with an adroit hardheadedness
that alternately amuses and irritates him." (ELIZABETH TALLENT,
writer)

am•bi•dove *n* [*ambivalent* +
dove]: A former antiwar pro-
tester with mixed feelings toward current military engage-
ments. "Ambidoves watched

the news of the latest U.S. military action with pride and hor-
ror." (ELIZABETH SEYDEL MORGAN,
poet)

am•bi•gu•phobe *n*
am•bi•gu•phob•i•a *n*
am•bi•gu•phob•ic *adj* [*am-
biguity* + *phobia*]: One who over-
defines terms and overdeter-
mines states of affairs out of a
compulsive fear of being misun-
derstood. "An ambiguphobe to
the max, Roderick's chief conversational project was always
the identification of his point:
'My point . . . no, no, *my* point
is that . . .'" "Almost anal in
its explications, his ambigupho-
bic recipe for yogurted veal occupies seven pages and four
schematic drawings." "Ambigu-
phobia often strikes our most
able politicians: 'Let me make
this perfectly clear'; 'I want to
make very sure that there's no
misunderstanding of what I'm
saying'; 'Well.'" (DAVID FOSTER
WALLACE, *novelist*)

a•mor•tal *adj & n* [fr. Gk *a-*
in opposition + L *morales* of
manners, customs; moral character, morality, mores + L *mor-
talis* death; the human, finite;
eventually to die + Fr *amour*
love]: The eternal, even un-
human, joy and grief experienced by lovers. Also, a disre-
garding of mores in the presence

of amour when all thought of caution, safety, or correctness flies out the window on behalf of an obliterating or liberating love. "The fixity of their obsession threw the rest of the world into an amortal chaos." Also, a noun: "The amortal is a phenomenon particular to the human being, particularly when the human being is erotically occupied." (DAVID BAKER, *poet*)

an•chor•sham *v* [*anchor + sham*]: To assume credit without any remorse, almost with arrogance, for another's work, especially as a TV anchor does for the dozens of off-camera people who actually research and write a news report that he merely reads. "President Reagan anchorshammed whenever he took credit for a serious thought in one of his speeches." (RICHARD ZACKS, *writer*)

an•dro•gy•greed *n* [*androgyny + greed*]: The concept that especially at the corporate executive level the genders will equally demonstrate avarice, savagery, unbridled competition, etc.; particularly, the notion that female lawyers and politicians are fit counterparts to their male colleagues. "The firm consisted of Sally, Luther, Mindy, and Rex: a quadrumvirate of androgygreed whose

grasp exceeded its reach by many millions." (ALBERT GOLD-BARTH, *writer*)

ang•ster *n* [*angst + gangster*]: An artist or writer who appropriates and capitalizes on the notion of angst. "Francis Bacon, Spalding Gray, and Karen Finley are consummate angsters." (BRIAN McCORMICK, *writer*, and CAROLE SEBOROVSKI, *artist*)

an•ni•la•tion *n* [*annihilate + elation + celebration*]: To welcome or celebrate large-scale disaster. "The girls in the apartment complex decided to throw a party in annilation of the approaching hurricane." (BOB SHACOCHIS, *writer*)

an•ti•gae•ic *adj* [*anti- + Gaea* earth goddess]: The quality of antagonism to the earth, its systems and biota; anti-Nature. "The Bush government stands in a long antigaeic tradition in America." (KIRKPATRICK SALE, *writer*)

an•ti•se•man•tic *adj* [*anti- + semantic*]: Of or pertaining to statements whose deliberate purpose is to mean nothing while sounding as if they express a significant point. "The Pentagon issued today another antisemantic explanation of its weapons procurement policy.'' (ELTON GLASER, *poet*)

an·ti·sum·mi·tism *n* [*anti-* + *summit* + *-ism*]: An attitude of fixed antagonism, suspicion, or hostility toward gatherings of important national or international political figures; it is often manifested in denunciations in the public press, and in degrees ranging from apparent scorn for summits as follies or public relations stunts to fear that the summits might bring some real, perhaps dangerous, results. ''Drug czar William Bennett's widely quoted remark at the Education Summit ('There was . . . standard Democratic pap. There was standard Republican pap . . .') exemplifies the summit-as-folly form of antisummitism.'' (ALBERT SHANKER, *educator*)

anx·ni·ci·ty *n* [*anxiety* + *ethnicity*]: 1: A late form of racial neurosis characterized by long, latent periods of lethargy and silence—even episodes of goodwill—broken by eruptions of confusion and betrayal, not unlike hysteria. 2: The tendency in people of all races to deny or suppress strong racial feelings and thus be all the more prone to them. 3: Any subconscious racial atonement, often characterized, in blacks, by a sense of being victims and, in whites, by

a vague sense of being both beyond the historical statute of limitations and also guilty. ''Whereas God, for Emerson, was a circle whose center was nowhere and whose circumference was everywhere, anxnicity in a society is like that ball, or certain retrograde stars, everywhere and nowhere.'' ''Just as Paul McCartney's song 'Ebony and Ivory' was an early and especially insipid form of anxnicity, the phrase, 'It's a Black Thing,' a later form, slams the door before it's had a chance to open.'' (BRUCE DUFFY, *novelist*)

aph·o·rec·tum *n* [fr. Gk *aphorismos* aphorism + L *rectus* behind + vulgar Yid *aphorectush*]: A peculiar subphylum of asshole who loiters near life's little crossroads, armed with a homily designed to denigrate your chosen path. ''At the office party, Pete was about to slip into the john for a quick knee-trembler with Valerie, the inebriated redhead from purchasing, when an envious aphorectum remarked, 'It's not wise to shit where you eat, Pete.' '' (TIM KAZURINSKY, *screenwriter*)

a·pod·i·a·bol·o·sis *n* [*apotheosis* + L *diabolus* devil]: An act of making a devil of someone, especially someone undeserving. Antonym of deification.

"Kevin Phillips's book, *The Politics of Rich and Poor*, marks another chapter in the apodiabolosis of Ronald Reagan." (R. EMMETT TYRRELL, JR., *editor*)

ap•plic•tion *n* [*appliance* + *addiction*]: A compulsory, physiological reliance upon or attachment to household appliances, especially television sets. "He called me in a state of near-hysterical appliction, asking me if I knew any good TV repairmen." (DARREN HABER, *literary agent*)

ap•pro•ccive *v* [*appropriate* + *apperceive*]: To view an artistic work, in a broad sense; not only to view and read, but to hear, feel (with mind and body), and even smell and taste a work of art; to experience fully a type or example of art. "It's impossible to approceive the *Mona Lisa*, trapped as it is behind glass, guards, and viewers." (GEOF HUTH, *writer*)

ap•pu•cious *adj* [onomatopoetic]: Disgusting, sickening, nauseating, causing revulsion. (WOODY ALLEN, *director*)

ars•in•ine *adj* [*assinine* + *arse* + *Arsenio Hall*]: Acting in an animated but pointless manner, jumping, gyrating, pointing, and shouting with apparent purpose but not meaning. "Give my husband two beers and he acts like an arsinine two-year-old." (DANIEL B. BOTKIN, *environmentalist*)

ars•sur•di•ty *n* [fr. L *ars* art + L *surd* deaf, mute, voiceless, incapable of expression]: The unexplainable or irrational in art, especially as regards the exchange and commerce of art. "The decadence of the '80s is summarized in arssurdities such as the price paid for late-19th-century French masters." (ROY GARY, *critic*)

ar•ti•fract *n* [*artifact* + *fracture*]: A poorly made object often manufactured in great quantities by corporations. "To be successful, the profit margin of an artifract must exceed the lawsuits it causes." See TECHTOID. (GAHAN WILSON, *cartoonist*)

art•ing *v* [fr. the noun *art*]: To inquire about art without following any specific guideline; analogous to "fishing for art." "To go arting in New York is to visit studios and galleries for a grapevine update." (LUCIO POZZI, *artist*)

ar•tion *n*—**ar•te•tic** *adj* [*art* + *-tion*]: Commercial (often anonymous) art that because of its different purposes is not considered legitimate art; examples are advertisement and magazine illustration. "The artion of Madison Avenue is often more affecting than the art of any serious painter or poet today." (GEOF HUTH, *writer*)

a•scu•di•fy *v* [fr. *SCUD* a Soviet-made missile + a south Missouri locution, *skud* or *skut*, an acronym for "something kind-uh dealie" or "some kind-uh thing," referring to any device or object of unknown or unexplainable name or origin]: To send terror into an unprepared or unwitting populace; to distribute fear randomly; to disseminate an unnamed force or object into the wider world. "The report of widespread measles completely ascudified the parents of the grade school." "When the members of the motorcycle gang strode into the burger joint, the glee club president looked askance, ascudified." (DAVID BAKER, *poet*)

a•sex•is *n* [fr. Gk *a-* not + *sexuality* + *axis* signifying an intersection, a conjoining of conditions; not to be confused in meaning or etymology with *asexual*]: That girllike quality often found in the early adolescent male; that state of anima and animus locked in full struggle, if not conflict, before a definite "bent" is established. "The word is best defined by its usage in the poem, 'Asexis Ceremony': She brushed through mirrors, he danced in naked light/ flashing his metal phallus/ in upturned pipes and sissy bars/ Turning twice in entrechat/ she felled the ancient blade,/ slipping skin around its tip while/ the girl in him slipped slowly away." (WALTER GRIFFIN, *poet*)

as•so•hol•ic *n* [*jackass* + *alcoholic*]: A person who behaves habitually and excessively like a jackass; a chronic asshole. "His wife divorced him on the grounds that he was an assoholic." (BOB SHACOCHIS, *writer*)

ass•ho•list•ic *adj* [*asshole* + *holistic*]: Characterized by insensitive excess in the use of New Age jargon or assumptions. "Bill found the therapy group somewhat assholistic and went back to Jim Beam." (JACK COLLOM, *poet*)

as•tic *adj & n* [fr. Gk *asky* city; asky refers to the physical city, the houses and streets; the more common root, polis, refers to the city dwellers and their municipal government.]: Being in or practicing a culture wherein farming and herding are efficient enough to produce a surplus of food, to be traded to nonfarming city dwellers for specialties and luxuries; as specialists, these urbanites can make tools, ornaments, and other merchandise more skillfully than a farmer, who must be a jack-of-all-trades; the term refers to cities and their culture before the Industrial Revolution. "In Mexico, Native Americans passed from georgic to astic culture around the beginning of the Christian Era." See DYNATIC. (L. SPRAGUE DE CAMP, *writer*)

ath•dive *n* [*athlete* + L *dives* riches + *diva* prima donna]: An overpaid ballplayer. "Whatever happened to our national pastime? It used to be played for fun and with spirit; now it's a bunch of athdives checking their investments." (DANIEL B. BOTKIN, *environmentalist*)

aud•i•con *n* [fr. L *audire* to hear + Gk *eikon* likeness, image]: 1: A highly charged piece of sound information pertaining to a particular political, social, or economic event. "One of the most significant audicons of World War II is the sound 'Heil Hitler.' " 2: A graphic image of a recorded sound file that is logged into a computer's memory for reference. "The audicon for the Gettysburg Address is 'Four score and . . .' " 3: In music, a short audio section of a larger work that expresses the

meaning of the work. "The first sixteen notes of Beethoven's Ninth Symphony, fourth movement, is an audicon for the entire piece." (CHRISTOPHER JANNEY, *artist*)

au•to•ha•gi•o•gra•pher *n* [fr. Gk *autos* self + *hagiography* writing of the lives of the saints]: One who speaks or writes reverently of his own life and achievements. "In the new season, lecture agencies and publishers again present competing offerings from the autohagiographers of sport, entertainment, and politics." (BERNARD LEWIS, *professor*)

au•to•strap•per *n* [fr. Gk *autos* self + *strap* as in "pull oneself up by one's bootstraps"]: One who, addicted to self-help advice and therapies, works obsessively on one's real or supposed problems by means of constantly changing strategies. "Santa Fe has become a haven for autostrappers, with healers and quacks and fix-it parlors operating around the clock." (SCOTT RUSSELL SANDERS, *writer*)

au•to•ton•so•ri•al•ist *n* [fr. Gk *autos* self + *tonsorial* pertaining to a barber or his work]: One who cuts his own hair or, more frequently, one who looks as if he cut his own hair. "The preeminent autotonsorialists of our day are musician David Byrne, Supreme Court Justice David Souter, and film director David Lynch." (CHRISTOPHER COR-BETT, *writer*)

a • za • le • ate *v* [*azalea + commiserate*]: To commiserate needlessly with a visitor upon his missing some dubious seasonal distinction of the host's town, region, or country. " 'Pity you weren't here last week,' said the lady who met me at the airport. 'The azaleas were in bloom.' " "In another part of the country I was similarly pitied for missing the fall colors at their height. 'Do please stop azaleating,' I grumpily said, and was instantly understood." (HOWARD NEMEROV, *poet*)

B

bam *v* [fr. the acronym *B.A.M.*, the Brooklyn Academy of Music]: 1. To be so bored with an entertainment such as theater, concert, or opera that one wants to stand up and scream. 2. To bombard an audience with your own ego to the point where they wish they were dead or armed. (EMILY PRAGER, *novelist*)

bam • bi • fy *v* [*Bambi + modify*]: To imbue animals with cartoon-like bourgeois Judeo-Christian attitudes and morals. "Having gleefully bambified the family spaniel, Sparky, in a costume of an oxford cloth button-down shirt, Ray Bans, and blue zinc cream, the Cooper children then watched in confusion as Sparky proceeded to romp across the lawn with a confidence gathered from his makeover and molest the neighbor's border collie." (DOUGLAS COUPLAND, *writer*)

bam • boid *n* [*Bambi + android*]: One whose world view derives from the fervent belief that all animals, except Homo sapiens, are cuddly, Disney-cute, and exempt as subjects of rational discourse. "Just as the prairie dog shoot was getting under way, a Honda full of bamboids pulled up, protest signs sticking out the windows." (JOHN CALDERAZZO, *writer*)

bank verse *n* [variant of *blank verse*]: Poetry written to make money. "His bank verse epic of Afro-American lesbian migrant poppy pickers in Colombia won Trender a $50,000 grant from the New Traditions Foundation." (X. J. KENNEDY, *poet*)

bard • bash *v* [*bard* + *bash* + *bark* + *party* + *crash*]: 1: To criticize federal support of the arts. "Jesse Helms bardbashed the National Endowment again today." 2: After a poetry reading, to come uninvited to the reception. "I want Robert Bly to sign a copy of his new book, so I'm going to bardbash the reception at the 'Y'." (MICHAEL J. BUGEJA, *poet*)

ba • tho • snick • er *n* [*bathos* + *snicker*]: Tittering as an inappropriate response to serious emotional display, in order to avoid a deeper feeling or to avoid the realization that one *has no* deeper feelings, as when one titters at violence or nobility in a movie. "The love scene in *Romeo and Juliet* was touchingly done, although it elicited bathosnicker from a few of the hard-of-thinking." (ALBERT GOLDBARTH, *writer*)

ba • tho • sphere *n* [*bathos* + *bathysphere*]: The compartment, made of language, in which we descend to the "depths" of our private fears, our personal history, and our incurable sense of being cheated by life. " 'I was never really allowed to play with my toys as a child, not really, I mean not the way I wanted to,' he said, safe and warm in the bathosphere of his confession, while the others in the workshop listened with apparent sympathy and silently rehearsed what they would say when it was their turn to speak." (SCOTT SPENCER, *novelist*)

bee • zle *v* [*beg* + *weasel*]: To speak evasively and meaninglessly, especially in response to a boss, creditor, or anyone who's "got the goods." "Beezling often occurs in conversations such as the following: Boss: 'Why isn't that report completed?' Employee: 'Is that the report we discussed last week?' Boss: 'Of course it is. Quit beezling!' " (KEN BOSEE, *publisher*)

bel • li • cist *n* [fr. L *bellus* war + *publicist*]: Republican spokesman who argues that any president of the U.S. is entitled to *make* war, while the Constitution empowers Congress only to *declare* it. "Whenever hostility is in the air, the bellicists tend to occupy the chairs on the Sunday morning newscasts and the MacNeil-Lehrer program." (JOHN LUKACS, *writer*)

bel•lie *v* [fr. eponymous hero *Alexander Graham Bell* + *lie*]: To lie (excusably) on the telephone, used particularly for telling telephone solicitors and canvassers that you are not home, that you are your brother or sister, and that you will not be home until very late that night. "John gets at least ten calls a month, always at dinnertime, and bellies them all." (HOWARD LEVY, *poet*)

berr•en•gel *n* [fr. eponymous heroes *Yogi Berra* and *Casey Stengel*]: An apparently meaningless remark that nevertheless contains a kernel of wisdom that is beside the point. "Berrengels include the following: 'I don't remember the feller's name and even if I could, I doubt it would be him.' 'She was always buying you something you didn't want and then forgetting to give it to you.' 'You ever notice when you can't find something it's always in the last place you look?'" (WILL STANTON, *writer*)

be•rump•tot•freude *n* [fr. G *berumpt* famous + *tot* dead + *freude* happy]: Lurid thrills derived from the deaths of celebrities. "It was a smidgen too much berumptotfreude for me when Dominick arrived at Stacey's Favorite Dead Celebrity party dressed as the half a

ham sandwich that choked Mama Cass." (DOUGLAS COUPLAND, *writer*)

bi•den•ize *v* [fr. eponymous hero *Joseph Biden*, United States senator from Delaware, 1973—present. In the 1988 race for the Democratic presidential nomination, Senator Biden concluded a Democratic debate with the following summary: "Why is it that Joe Biden is the first in his family ever to go to a university? Why is it that my wife . . . is the first in her family to ever go to college? Is it because our fathers and brothers were not bright? Is it because I'm the first Biden in a thousand generations to get a college and a graduate degree that I was smarter than the rest? . . . My ancestors who worked in the coal mines of northeast Pennsylvania and would come up after twelve hours and play football for four hours . . . It's because they didn't have a platform upon which to stand." Soon it was revealed that British Labour Party leader Neil Kinnock regularly finished his speeches with the following peroration: "Why am I the first Kinnock in a thousand generations to be able to get to university? Why is Glenys (Mrs. Kinnock) the first woman in her family in a thousand generations to be able to get to university? Was it because all our predecessors were thick? . . . Was it because they were weak, those people who could work eight hours underground and then come up and play football? Weak? . . . It was because there was no platform upon which they could stand." When confronted with these striking similarities, Senator Biden first claimed that the controversy was "much ado about nothing," and then made the argument: "In the marketplace of the political realm, the notion that for every thought or idea you have to go back and find and attribute to someone is frankly ludicrous." Biden also suggested that he had made the statement only once, but other videotapes were brought forward. This revelation, in addition to the senator's inability to explain the awkwardness of the "thousand generations" reference from an American and the fact that Senator Biden could not name a single relative who had ever worked in a coal mine caused him to withdraw from the race.]: To plagiarize so publicly, wantonly, and brazenly as to reveal the plagiarist as living in a fantasy, which, in the late 20th century, American public life had become. (R. EMMETT TYRRELL, JR., *editor*)

Big Chill *n* [by association with the cosmological theory known as the Big Bang; first used by David N. Schramm in a lecture at Les Houches, France, in July 1979]: The ending of the universe if the present expansion continues unabated and the entire universe dilutes itself to zero density and zero temperature. "If the average density of the universe is sufficiently small, the end will not be with another bang but with the whimper of the Big Chill." (DAVID N. SCHRAMM, *physicist*)

Big Crunch *n* [by association with the cosmological theory known as the Big Bang; first used by David N. Schramm, Beatrice Tinsley, James Gunn, and Richard Gott, physicists, in 1973 while writing a collaborative research paper for the *Astrophysical Journal*]: The catastrophic ending of our universe if the present expansion eventually stops and the whole universe collapses upon itself. "If the average density of the universe is high, we will all be crushed in the Big Crunch to near-infinite density in about a hundred billion years." (DAVID N. SCHRAMM, *physicist*)

black-cat story *n* [*black cat* traditional symbol of bad luck + *story*]: A news story that will lead to others that end its subject's career. Antonym of a "strange new respect story." "Robert McFarlane had assumed the Iran initiative top secret, and reacted with shock to the black-cat story that appeared in *The New York Times* days later." (R. EMMETT TYRRELL, JR., *editor*)

blan·di·ose *adj* [*bland* + *grandiose*]: Relating to entertainment or spectacle that doesn't live up to its advance publicity and is too dull to achieve pomposity. "Critics rated the new 3-D, Smellorama, Supercolor, stereo, touchy-feely film as blandiose." (SANDRA VAGINS, *editor/writer*)

bloaf *v* [*buy* + *bloat* + *loaf*]: An often nocturnal, usually postprandial, wandering through shopping malls, discount stores, or fast-food strips in pursuit of extraneous, sweet, savory, or unsavory objects, foods, or activities. "To properly bloaf, one should have eaten within the past hour so that the hunting and snarfing down of personal comfort foods can lead to the requisite feeling of bloat. However, the quality of 'bloat' can also be attained by the purchase of objects of which one already has one too many, as when the bibliophile with full bookshelves buys the OED on impulse.

Bloafing is primarily an avoidance activity occasioned by quotidian tasks with impinging deadlines, such as the prospect of filing tax returns, cleaning the cat box, writing letters of recommendation, hand-sewing a wedding dress, laying 1,000 feet of soaker hose, or painting the perennials with an ecologically correct bug juice." "We were supposed to draft our wills last night in preparation for our trip to the Amazon rain forest, but we wound up bloafing the night away in Meijer's Thrifty Acres instead." (ALICE FULTON, *poet*)

bloa·toc·ra·cy *n* [*bloat* + *aristocracy* + *bureaucracy*]: An extremely self-satisfied, overweight, or overwrought leadership. "The Democrats' Tom Foley-George Mitchell leadership team, which seemed a 'modest, respectable' contrast to George Bush's Ralph Lauren presidency, was even more modest and respectable compared to the Democrats' own Jim Wright-Ted Kennedy-Jesse Jackson bloatocracy." (JOE KLEIN, *writer*)

blook *n* [*book* + *block* or *blockbuster*]: A thick block of paper imprinted with a novel designed to sell. "Have you read Marge Crawlins's latest blook, about the TV star and the corporate takeover artist?" (X. J. KENNEDY, *poet*)

blun • dit *n* [*blunder* + *pundit*]: A pundit who always gets it wrong, one who professionally offers false predictions and wrong explanations, always with an air of certitude and authority. "The usual blundits of the media and the academy, undeterred by their failure to predict or explain the latest war, are back to ply their trade in peacetime." (BERNARD LEWIS, *professor*)

blur • bon • ic plague *n* [*blurb* + *bubonic plague*]: A disease of literature characterized by the appearance of suppurating blurbs on the skin of a book, feverish half-quotes, and regurgitation, leading to rapid film adaptation and hallucinations of grandeur, thought to be transmitted from author to author via their shared agents. "Tom Wolfe's *The Bonfire of the Vanities* contracted blurbonic plague, and, in its final tragic stages, the book suffered even more than did its author." (BRIAN MCCORMICK, *writer*)

body • wit *n* [*body* + *wit*]: The subconscious mind of the body itself as distinguished from the undertow of knowledge in the much-touted mental subconsciousness. "Bodywit is that suave, svelte part of us that knows without knowing how to evade a bureau in the dark on our way to the bathroom in a strange house, that makes curvatures in the bent-away flesh to avoid collision, or that makes the forearm twitch at the approach of a fly or the gnat-haunted eye blink involuntarily at an unseismic sound. Bodywit is the true knowledge of the body's persistence, the sixth sense of its preservation, sans fact, sans logic. It is the course of poetry that runs its hawthorn-embroidered way along the paths of the almost unrealized, the felt but unseen, bred awareness, product of the millenia. Bodywit is the marvelous fears and fantasies of the body itself. The word may be used in such sentences as: 'The hummingbird's cold coral feet told my bodywit, before I looked, that I was being visited by a nuncio from another world.' " (GEORGE A. SCARBOROUGH, *writer*)

boot • scaf • fle *n* [*bootstrap* + *scaffolding* + *baffle*]: The end result of an evolutionary process that throws away the scaffolding that is necessary for it to occur, giving the impression that the process is impossible. "Bootscaffle is the use of iron tools to mine for iron ore, and the use of robots to make robots." "The chicken-egg business is just a load of bootscaffle." (IAN STEWART, *mathematician*)

bork *interj* [fr. eponymous hero *Robert Bork,* retired court of appeals judge, and perhaps onomatopoeia from the sound of retching]: An exclamation of political disgust. " 'Bork,' like 'yuck,' can be used either by itself or in such phrases as 'Oh, bork—I can't believe they actually reported that bill out of committee!' " (PAUL BICKART, *chemist*)

bot • er • i • um *n* [*bottom line* + *bacterium*]: A disease, apparently incurable, suffered by those addicted to the phrase, "the bottom line is . . ." It especially afflicts those who have never realized how poorly gathered statistics (or good tax lawyers) can camouflage bottom lines, and speakers who do not know the word *conclusion.* "According to the pollsters, the bottom line was that Tom Dewey would defeat Harry Truman in 1948." (WALTER LAFEBER, *historian*)

bo • vel • ou • sy *n* [*bovine* + *jealousy*]: Anger at a neighbor's unexpected good fortune, as when a neighbor receives a free cow. "Although Fred realized that his feeling of bovelousy over Jane's unexpected good fortune was a bit childish, he could not shake the desire to kill her." (HAROLD J. GOLDBERG, *historian*)

bo • vis • fac • tion *n* [*bovine* + *satisfaction*]: Happiness for a neighbor's unexpected good fortune, as when a neighbor receives a free cow. "Aware of Jane's hard work, Fred felt a genuine bovisfaction when he heard that she had received the promotion he had been hoping for." (HAROLD J. GOLDBERG, *historian*)

box • gig • gle *v* [*box,* by association, *gift* + *giggle*]: To use repeated acts of kindness, with the knowledge that they'll never be returned, employed solely to prove over and over again an ex-lover's worthlessness. "His Christmas present to her was, of course, the best of ruses— boxgiggled, beribboned, and bowed." (ALEXANDER THEROUX, *novelist*)

bre • fe • ca • tion *n* [fr. eponymous hero *Bret Easton Ellis* + *defecation* + *publication*]: The publication of inferior works by, of, or related to Bret Easton Ellis and writers of his ilk. "Vintage Contemporary's decision to go ahead with its newest brefecation confirmed Freud's theory that lucre is filth." (BRIAN MCCORMICK, *writer*)

bridge・word *n* [*bridge* + *word*]: A kind of euphemism that acceptably spans the chasm between what is written and what is spoken, in order to satisfy the disparate criteria between the two forms of expression, and without diluting the intended earthy quality or meaning of the word it supplants. "In the sentence, ' "that prof is full of crap," the disgruntled student remarked,' *crap* is the bridgeword that would most likely survive the editor's blue pencil for a family-oriented publication (like this one, perhaps)." (BILL WALTON, *athlete*, and PAUL THERRIO, *writer*)

brown・speak *n* [*Brown University* + *speak*]: A manner of speaking in which all statements are expressed as questions; detected first in the speech of graduates of Brown University in the late 1980s but spread to graduate schools all over the country. "Jane Austen unquestioningly accepted many of the values of her class and era?" "I went to the movies last night?" See DISQUERIFY. (FRANK CONROY, *writer*)

bub・ble・gaf・fer *n* [*bubble* + *gaffer*]: One who destroys ill-prepared adversaries or small, virtually defenseless ideas with undue vehemence. "The only bubblegaffer in the bunch got promoted to principal, of course." (WALLACE E. KNIGHT, *professor*)

buch・wald *v* [fr. eponymous hero *Art Buchwald*, derived from the contract in which Paramount promised Buchwald a share of net profits, which even on a $300-million hit was claimed to be nothing]: To offer someone a complicated lawyer-crafted formula for payment, which in almost all cases results in no payment. "Hollywood buchwalds idealistic young writers who often turn into cynical drunks churning out jingles for Barcaloungers." (RICHARD ZACKS, *writer*)

bulc・naf *n* [*fan club* spelled backward]: A loosely knit group of individuals having in common only their dislike for some celebrated figure. "For whatever reason the members of a bulcnaf simply can't stand some personage who may be admired or even revered by the majority. Members correspond and put out a monthly newsletter mostly comprising quotes and photos of the subjects saying 'between you and I,' spitting, or scratching themselves in indelicate places, that kind of thing." (WILL STANTON, *writer*)

bull•roar *n, adj & v* [*bull* + *roar*]: An acceptable BRIDGEWORD (see above) for the common, earthy, conversational term that would otherwise not survive the more genteel, restrictive criteria used for written material. " 'That is pure, unadulterated bullroar,' exclaimed the irate center to the referee when a foul was called on him for goal tending." " 'That ref made a real bullroar call,' the center complained to his coach." "He bullroared his way into the referee's job with no knowledge of the rules of the game." (BILL WALTON, *athlete*, and PAUL THERRIO, *writer*)

bul•ly•mi•a *n* [*bully* + *bulimia*]: The process of gorging a petty tyrant on weapons and then purging him of those weapons by means of war. "No doubt a future letter to the editor will read: 'If the lily-livered author of "Another General, Another Case of Bullymia?" (Op-Ed, November 19, 1995) has so little respect for our President and the valiant fighting men and women currently risking their lives, perhaps he would like to try writing his treasonous, pusillanimous swill as a human shield for one of the Maximum Leader's ill-gotten Patriot missiles.' " (STEVE MESSINA, *editor*)

bu•reau•cra•de•mi•a *n* [*bureaucracy* + *academia*]: 1: A procedure-ridden, rule-dominated, formula-funded organizational system acting as a filter on the wisdom of the ages. 2: A social system wherein innovative ideas, discoveries, and scholarship are judged by bottom-line accountants. 3: A cloistered grouping of individuals characterized by conflict in direct proportion to contemporary political sensitivities and in inverse proportion to the ultimate importance of the issues at stake. "Members of bureaucrademia were found squabbling in committee over the multicultural implications of quantum mechanics." (HANS MARK and SHELDON EKLAND-OLSON, *educators.*)

bu•reau•cra•ni•ac *n* [*bureaucrat* + *maniac*]: A person who zealously tends to overinstitutionalize and overorganize things better left alone, hiring a consultant when a few moments of reflection would do, creating a committee when hiring a consultant would suffice, establishing an agency when creating a committee would do, and then issuing a report when a press release would handle the job. (VINE DELORIA, JR., *professor*)

bushed *adj* [*pushed* + eponymous hero *President George Bush*]: Converted to a conservative position by insistent force of persuasion or the pressure of prevailing opinion. "He managed to retain at least vestiges of his radical chic all through the 1980s, but then he got bushed during the Persian Gulf War." (AGNIESZKA OSIECKA, *writer*)

C

ca•ca•dem•oid *n* [fr. L *caca* feces + *academe* + *oid*, fr. Gk *eidos* form or shape]: The lowest creature in higher education; typically, a sexually repressed, humorless, and self-impressed professor or administrator afraid of the real world, incapable of teaching and producing useful research, and hostile to new ideas; found in every kind of academic institution, cacademoids love to serve on committees, despise students, and venerate their inferior superiors. "Professor Freddy Cavity claims there are no dialect terms for genitals in American English. What a cacademoid!" (REINHOLD AMAN, *editor*)

ca•co•sco•py *n* [fr. Gk *kakos* bad + Gk *skopein* to look at]: Visual din; eyescream. "Perhaps because human beings lack earlids, most of us find sonic noise more painful than the visual variety. But sensitive, synesthetic persons respond to the colors of sound—'tonal coloration' in a concrete sense. So, too, the eye may be deafened by sights: the shriek of subway graffiti, the yammer of discordant typefaces, the croak of piles of rusted-out car bodies." (PAUL BICKART, *chemist*)

can•ker•tone *n* [*canker* + *tone*]: 1: An enthusiastic singer without talent; one who delights in singing despite the pain it inflicts upon others. 2: By extension, any performer who overestimates his abilities. "We were afraid to attend the wedding for fear some cankertone would sing 'Oh Promise Me.'" (DANIEL MARK EPSTEIN, *writer*)

ca•reer•sma *n* [*careerism* + *charisma*]: Spectacular but essentially bogus facility for career advancement, especially in the cultural, academic, and intellectual fields but not limited to these. "As a critic of the moral decadence of our universities, that writer has tremendous careersma." (GERALD GRAFF, *professor*)

care•less•ful *adj* [*careless + careful + purposeful*]: Of or pertaining to an action initiated with careless abandon while gambling on one's ability to recover in time to produce the desired results; the smooth outcome of an action started recklessly or haphazardly; serendipitous control over chaos. "The carelessful stunts performed by Buster Keaton in his early silent films have kept audiences on the edge of their seats for seventy years." (MICHAEL HOLMAN, *filmmaker*)

ca•ta•me•nial *adj* [*catamenia* menses + *menial*]: Of or pertaining to a menstrual period that is not terribly painful and/or does not interrupt the menstruating female's daily activities. "Mary Lou Retton informed a reporter that discipline, good nutrition, and catamenial cycles allowed her to compete athletically all month long." (DEBORAH MARGOLIN, *artist*)

cathy *v* [fr. Gk *katharos* pure, or the attempt to be pure by purgation or sacrifice]: To appease a parent subconsciously, usually by behavior, often by gifts, in order to avoid hating him or her; self-delusion. "She cathied her father with gifts the same week he walked out on her mother." (ALEXANDER THEROUX, *writer*)

cha•ce•bo *n* [*chaser + placebo*]: A nonalcoholic beer. "A chacebo for me, please. I'm the designated driver." (MAXINE KUMIN, *poet*)

cha•grim *n* [*chagrin + grim*]: The expression on the face of someone who, say, has gone to the checkroom of the Grolier Club to which he had been kindly invited for the first time by a famous young novelist only to be told that his wonderful long wool scarf from Christchurch College, Oxford, had evidently been preempted by some louche barfly of low moral degree. "Senator Pantagruel's usually vibrant face was marked by a look of bitter chagrin when he realized the member of the Senate Contradictions Committee physically held a copy of the brief note he had sent about Norb Whimster's trial to the chief prevailing judge of the state hanging assizes court. Who had leaked it? Why does poisonousness always escape even double-hulled containers?" (LIONEL TIGER, *professor*)

chair • per • daugh • ter *n* [by language-desexing evolution from chairman to chairperson to chairperdaughter]: The female head of any organization that wishes (a) to stamp out longstanding words and parts of words that have recently been discovered to be sexist and oppressive, and (b) not to have its leader called chair and thus identified, after long and hard work and struggle, as having attained the position of an article of furniture. "The chairperdaughter of the literary society introduced a resolution to call 14-line poems written in iambic pentameter 'daughternets' when such poems are composed by females—rather, people of femininity." (MARK J. ESTREN, *writer*)

Char • lie syn • drome *n* [eponymous hero obscure and perhaps best left that way]: The disappointment felt by certain decent liberal humanitarians who should, in fact, feel relief when they discover that one of the outrages they previously assumed to have been perpetrated on certain vulnerable populations turns out to be a myth.

"Despite all my proof to the contrary of his assumption, my friend suffered a fevered attack of Charlie syndrome when he snapped, 'What do you mean, they're not performing psychosurgery on black prisoners against their will in hospitals?' " (WILLARD GAYLIN, *M.D.*)

chaz • ze • ra • ti *n* [Yid *chazzerai, schweinfleisch, trafe,* junk + *literati* the educated class, men of letters]: Those who indulge in dim-bulb literary exercises, punsters, poetasters, anagrammatists, palindromists, neologists. See LITERAI. (DANIEL PINKWATER, *writer*)

cheese-dip rev • o • lu • tion • ary *n* [*cheese dip* a common often cheap hors d'oeuvre at cocktail parties and receptions + *revolutionary*]: One who while cocktailing and cheese dipping vociferously proclaims one's backing of any guerrilla group, no matter how murderous, so long as it calls for humaneness and liberation. " 'Sure, they kill people. How else can they make a revolution?' shouted the cheese-dip revolutionary, all the while careful not to stain his two-hundred-fifty-dollar denim jeans with Zabar's best wine herring." (WILLIAM HERRICK, *novelist*)

chef • let • ter *v* [*chef* + *letter*, inspired by one of this lexicographer's favorite *Fawlty Towers* episodes, in which Basil, as chef for the night, reads a "letter from the chef" to his disgruntled patrons who have just been served wretched food]: To announce, sometimes to apologize, either by public notice or by private whisper, that the talents or services of someone on whom you are currently depending will simply be mediocre or worse. "Anyone who travels a lot is frequently cheflettered by hotels that are undergoing extensive and loud repairs that often require the use of a jackhammer and typically are taking place near my room, or by restaurants whose menu bears no resemblance to what the cook is capable of preparing. One often finds that the symptoms of cheflettering easily spill over to other circumstances such as one's dealing with a mail order house, or a girlfriend with whom your relationship is getting ever shakier, or a colleague who is on the verge of moving on." (DON MCLEAN, *musician*)

chick • ty *n* [*chicken* + *empty*]: The sinking feeling one gets when going to collect eggs in the chicken coop and discovering that there aren't any. "After assessing the failure of his latest investments, Fred realized that he was chickty and would have to declare bankruptcy." "When Fred's wife left him unexpectedly, he felt an overwhelming sense of chickty." "I'm chickty, man, can you spare some change?" (HAROLD J. GOLDBERG, *historian*)

chim • punc *n* [*chimpanzee* + *punctuation*]: The habit of saying "quote unquote," accompanied by the crooking of a pair of fingers on either side of the head as if scratching two imaginary monkeys. "A chimpunc is the use of inclusive punctuation marks that don't include anything in the hope of giving significance and stature to an otherwise empty-handed remark. It is based on the idea that a weakness can be given strength by underlining it." (WILL STANTON, *writer*)

chro • no • cen • trism *n* [fr. Gk *chronos* time + *centrism*]: 1: A habitual, if usually unconscious, tendency to judge ancient peoples or cultures by the standards and practices of one's own time. "To suggest that the civilization of Ancient Egypt, with its rigidly institutionalized religion, oppressive and inflexible administrative bureaucracy, and brutal professional army, was generally more 'advanced' than the ancient cultures of Africa or America is a clear example of chronocentrism." 2: A tendency to view ancient peoples or cultures with patronizing nostalgia or romanticism, thereby reducing their complex humanity to mere decorative motifs. "The main modern appeal of archaeological restorations such as Colonial Williamsburg, Knossos, Pompeii, and Luxor lies not in their historical value but in their chronocentric power to inspire modern fads and fashions and to sell exotic souvenirs." (NEIL ASHER SILBERMAN, *writer*)

cla • pre • hen • sion *n* [*clap* + *apprehension*]: A feeling or condition of extreme anxiety expressed during a concert or other serious musical performance, when one is desperately unsure about the correct moment to applaud. Claprehension is usually accompanied by a combination of personal insecurity and deep boredom. "During the presentation of 16th-century Christmas carols at the museum, he was overwhelmed by waves of claprehension, and his hands, lacking instructions as to when to come together, froze in the air before him as if they were made of stone." (ROGER ROSENBLATT, *writer*)

cle • men • vy *n* [fr. eponymous hero *Roger Clemens* + *envy*]: The pangs of distress or envy experienced by a person when he or she reads about the enormous salaries pulled down by modern-day baseball players. "He turned to the sports pages and cringed with clemenvy." (LOUIS PHILLIPS, *writer*)

clit • er • a • ture *n* [*clitoris* + *literature*]: Any writing by a woman which deals solely with women's issues, or is likely to appeal only to women; also applies to women's pornography."Judith Krantz's novels make delightful cliterature." See MASTURPIECE. (BRIAN McCORMICK, *writer*)

cloin *v* [*coin* + *cloying*]: To coin useless or forgettable words and phrases simply for the pleasure of hearing oneself speak. "Motor-mouthing Valley girls cloin at least as many words as East Coast intellectuals, but who can begrudge teenagers their sophomoric delight?" (LAWRENCE E. JOSEPH, *writer*)

clos • et • hang • er *n* [*closet* + *hangman*] sometimes **clos • et • cohn** [*closet* + *queen* + *Roy Cohn*]: One who consistently and publicly obstructs gay rights and attacks gay people while privately having same-sex affairs. "If I hear one more fag-bashing joke from the closethanger, I'm going to out him." (ELLEN GRUBER GARVEY, *writer*)

club-heart•ed *adj* [fr. a malady first diagnosed by Groucho Marx when he said he "wouldn't want to be a member of a club that would have me as a member"]: Losing interest in another person once that person has become interested in you. "When Rodney finally began to fall for me, I quickly grew clubhearted." (JONATHAN ALTER, *journalist*)

co•al•lu•sion *n* [*coalition + collusion*, first used by Congressman Roy Weir of Minnesota in the early 1950s to characterize the combination of Republicans and southern Democrats who together acted to obstruct the passage of civil rights legislation]: A hybrid form of cooperation; a portmanteau word that combines, with proper shading and modification, the meanings of coalition, an acceptable political relationship, and collusion, a somewhat less respectable kind of cooperation. (EUGENE J. MCCARTHY, *politician*)

cog•i•tall *n* [*cogitate + all*]: A person who thinks of everything; a detail person. "We've got the basic concept; now we

need a few cogitalls to flesh it out." (ELIZABETH SEYDEL MORGAN, *poet*)

com•pu•gi•list *n* [*computer + pugilist*]: A hater of automation, especially one who repeatedly bangs fists on computer keyboards. "I knew he had pluck, but I didn't know he had it in him to be a compugilist." (DON SHARE, *poet*)

com•pu•talk *n* [*computer + talk + doubletalk + doublethink*]: A new form of jargon, consisting of computer terms applied to business and human relations, especially in the use of nouns as verbs. "The sentence 'We'll have to interface George before we can implement this new form of architecture' is computalk for 'Let's talk to George before using the new order form.'" (RICHARD SELTZER, *writer*)

com•pu•tis•tic *adj* [*computer + -istic* possessive of certain traits]: To have the attribute of approaching problems, whether technical or those of normal living, as if everything had a direct logical solution, the steps of which merely need to be correctly plotted out; often includes the tendency to use expressions from computer languages in everyday conversation, such as using "if-then-else" constructions and "while" loops. A classic computistic assertion is: "I will be home by six if I finish my work by five, else seven." (ROGER C. SCHANK, *professor*)

con • cras • ti • nate *v* [fr. L *contra* against + L *crastinus* tomorrow]: To avoid with passion, to put off an especially onerous task even further than tomorrow and quite consciously; to avoid with great purpose in protest against something; to act oppositely with exceeding fervor and feeling quite contrary in order to avoid a task, even to the point of performing equally onerous tasks. "Rather than grade a stack of poorly written exams, the professor concrastinated for two weeks by calling committee meetings and holding evening office hours." (IMOGENE BOLLS, *poet*)

con • cre • tin *n* [*concrete* an extremely hard substance known for the single property of almost never yielding to pressure + *cretin*]: An urban dweller who has not the slightest sympathy or interest in nature or the countryside, often used as a put-down of those whose hardheadedness can be found at the root of much of today's environmental havoc. (DON MCLEAN, *artist*)

con • flat • u • la • tions *n* [*congratulations* + *flatulence*]: Congratulatory statements made by false friends. "Iranian President Hashemi Rafsanjani sent Iraqi President Saddam Hussein his conflatulations." (BRIAN MCCORMICK, *writer*)

con • float *v* —**con • float • a • tion** *n* [*confuse* + *conflate* + *float*]: To send forth or publicize a false definition as an ideological maneuver: "When William Safire claims in his column that the useful neutral term for noncelibate, 'sexually active,' really means 'promiscuous,' he is engaging in an unusually heavy-handed confloatation. A subtler confloatation is the theft of the term 'politically correct' from leftists, among whom it carried a cheerfully ironic ring, by the right, who use the term to claim that the left is all-powerful, and to represent themselves as a tiny insurgent group battling those 'politically correct' orthodoxies that have for decades prevented conservative versions of Western history and literature from being taught on college campuses." (ELLEN GRUBER GARVEY, *writer*)

cong *n* [by shortening from *congress*, a U.S. legislative organization]: Unit of measurement of costs incurred or increased by the failure of leadership to lead. Equivalent to one billion dollars. "Far from being insulted at being dubbed 'king cong,' Congress was delighted with the new unit of measurement, since the cost of cleaning up the S&L mess seemed much smaller when said to be 500 congs than when stated as 500 billion dollars." See STEALTHBOMBER. (MARK J. ESTREN, *writer*)

con•geal•i•ate *v*
con•geal•i•a•tion *n* [fr. *congeal* to form into a thick mass + -*iate* suffix fr. the Latin that means, well, it doesn't really matter what it means because the etymology has no bearing on the meaning of this word and its possible uses]: A little of everything and a lot of nothing. "This word actually has no meaning whatsoever; it only seems to have meaning, it only sounds as if it should have meaning, which is its attraction. It is a word as necessary to language in these parlous times as any I can think of. Congealiate simply sounds as if it means something, which, when you think about it, is a word right in step with the world in which we live. The great appeal of this word is its applicability to almost any situation. When you are in doubt, when the enemy is using five-dollar words, resort to congealiate, as in the following examples. Legal: 'During the testy interrogation, the district attorney suddenly turned on the suspect and said, "If you don't answer the question, I will have you congealiated immediately." ' Romantic: 'Honey, all my life I have felt a congealiation when you are near.' Financial: 'If you do not pay up, sir, I am afraid we will begin congealiation proceedings tomorrow.' Sports: 'Pete Rose congealiated his career yesterday.' Politics: 'In response to the crisis, the president congealiated with his advisers in secret session this morning.' " (LARRY KING, *radio host*)

con•nounce *v* [fr. L *contra* against + L *nuntius* messenger]: To alter the way one pronounces a word for reasons lacking historical or etymological basis. "What sort of anal compulsive decided to say we should connounce the seventh planet, U-r-a-n-u-s, 'YOO-ren-us' instead of 'yoo-RAIN-us'?" (MARK J. ESTREN, *writer*)

con•pose *v* [antonym of propose]: To make the opposite of a motion. "Mr. Chairman, rather than give the outgoing president a million-dollar bonus, I conpose that we make him pay the shareholders some of the millions of dollars that his bungling has cost our company." (MARK J. ESTREN, *writer*)

con•sum•as•sault *v* [*consume + assault*]: To explain to neighbors or visitors, in relentless detail, why and how one's latest household acquisition such as a rotisserie ('50s), electric knife sharpener ('60s), Crockpot ('70s), or wine Cruvinet ('80s) was worth the money. "They consumassaulted us for an hour when we stopped by their house." (ANNE EISENBERG, *professor*)

con•tor•ture *n* [*convenience + torture*]: The distress suffered in arranging for comforts and pleasures. "I'm sure our vacation in Tuscany will be great, but we'll have to go through major contorture to make it work just right." (EVA HOFFMAN, *writer*)

con•tra•scha•den•freud•e *n* [fr. L *contra* against + G *schadenfreude* the malicious enjoyment of the misfortune of others]: The ability to play upon another person's joy at your possible misfortune for your own satisfaction; to turn another person's schadenfreude back on himself. "Peter's barely concealed joy that my book might not be published led me to engage in a scheme of con-

traschadenfreude: I pretended the book was being turned down by one publisher after another, lifting his joy to almost unbearable heights, when in fact it was already about to appear in print; then I mailed him a copy of the book, thus dashing him into greater depths of envy than if I had just sent him the book in the first place." (HENRY S. F. COOPER, *writer*)

con•vi•vor *n* [fr. L *con* with + L *vivere* to live]: A fellow inhabitant of the living world; a fellow survivor of the evolutionary process. "Each species feeds upon the wastes of its convivors." (FREDERICK TURNER, *professor*)

co•pa•noia *n* [*copacetic + paranoia* or *coping + annoy*]: The terrible fear that everything is all right; intense discomfort caused by the sudden realization that there's nothing to worry about for the moment. "It was a beautiful sunny day and a strong feeling of copanoia overwhelmed me, so I went back inside and sat in the dark." (RODGER KAMENETZ, *poet*)

cop•o•lyte *n* [*copy + acolyte*]: A journalist, especially one whose eagerness to receive answers supersedes his willingness to ask questions; a member of the press who delights in the dissemination of prepared copy, especially that which emanates from government sources. "The pressroom at the White House was packed this morning as over 200 copolytes gathered to receive instruction from the press secretary." (TIMOTHY FINDLEY, *novelist*)

cop•u•les•cence *n* [*copulate + excrescence + essence*, by way of "boudoir"]: The healthy afterglow that attends successful sexual intercourse. "For years, people who observed other people emerging from bedrooms, clos-ets, under desks, behind cars, inside bathtubs, and on top of chandeliers knew these people were on to something because of their copulescence, the peachblow on their cheeks and the Cheshire smile on their lips." Antonym: **coputank** *n* [*copulate + stank + tank*]: The heavy weight of failed sex. (LEWIS BURKE FRUMKES, *writer*)

corp•eye *v* [*corpus + eye*]: To eye compulsively one physical attribute in others—such as width of hip, thickness of hair, roundness of butt, depth of paunch, straightness of back—

copanoia

and compare it with oneself. "In her youth she corpeyed her friends' thighs, but when she aged, she corpeyed the other ladies' postures and the slope of their backs." (ANNE EISENBERG, *professor*)

corp • o • bab • ble *n* [*corporation + psychobabble*]: The discourse of touchy-feely management consulting, in which reliable and ever-increasing profits flow from communication theory, motivational hype, and, of course, synergy "Corpobabble pioneer John Naisbitt has been surpassed of late by a clutch of niche-burrowing organizational pseudoseers." (EDWARD SILVER, *editor*)

cor • poc • ra • cy *n* [*corporation + bureaucracy*]: The condition that develops when a business grows so large that it begins to resemble the government bureaucracies that conservatives love to hate yet assume only exist in the public sector. "It is ironic for J. Peter Grace to find hundreds of billions of dollars of supposed waste in the federal bureaucracy but to neglect the comparable hierarchies and inefficiencies of his own corpocracy." (MARK GREEN, *politician*)

cor • por • a • do *n* [*corporation + desperado*]: 1: An unfettered corporate executive, a laissez-faire zealot, an Adam Smith fundamentalist. 2: A rare but increasingly evident business leader who tends to believe that the Cold War was misguided and that regulatory bureaucracies and bureaucrats are the true enemies of capitalism. "The business roundtable during the 1980s fell under the sway of corporados." (MARK DOWIE, *journalist*)

cor • por • o • nu • ga • city *n* [fr. L *corporare* to make a body + L *nugae* trifles or worthless objects]: Business for the sake of busyness, involving self-deception and obsession with the trivial, trite, and inane due to the lack of a purpose or agenda; form over content, which in the final analysis accomplishes or produces absolutely nothing. "Although it required a vast amount of energy, the semiannual board meeting resulted in nothing more concrete than several hours of corporonugacity." (MARK D. JONES and THOMAS P. LUCE, *business executives*)

cor • rect • nik *n & adj* [*correct + -nik* Slavic suffix meaning one who belongs to or has the attribute of; a formation on the evident analogy of the American-Yiddish ALLRIGHTNIK, a driving opportunist dedicated to transcending immigrant status and succeeding in the new society]: One who scrupulously observes and ostentatiously enforces the attitudes, gestures, and above all the language of political correctness; frequently implies smugness, moralism, and pious conformism. "The correctnik roundly reproved the Pope for failing to refer to God as 'He or She.' " **correctnik** *adj:* "He encountered the usual correctnik hostility to courses in philosophy that began with Eurocentric hegemonists like Plato and Aristotle." (ROBERT ALTER, *professor*)

cor • vo *v* [fr. eponymous hero *Frederick, Baron Corvo* (1860–1913), whose *Chronicles of the House of Borgia* argued that all criticism of the Borgias was calumny, and whose *Hadrian the Seventh* showed an obscure, impoverished English writer—like Lord Corvo himself—being named pope]: To construct elaborate fantasies in which one passionately believes. "Conservatives corvo that tax cuts for the rich invariably trickle down to the poor, while liberals corvo that poverty can be eliminated if we keep spending more money on social programs." (MARK J. ESTREN, *writer*)

cos • met • o • faux *n* [*cosmetic* + Fr *faux* false]: Constant attention to a personal unsightliness long ago remedied by artificial means. "He kept on self-consciously combing his toupee over the bald spot it covered in a gesture of pure cosmetofaux." (ALBERT GOLDBARTH, *writer*)

cos • mo • pos • i • teur *n* [*cosmopolitan* + *posit* + *poseur*]: One who renders judgment on haute society through stilted observation; one who fobs off with great affectation his social observations; an ingenuous but misguided gadfly. "The cosmositeur gleefully mingled with the pseudo-Schnabel mishmash spangling the Pyramid Club atrium." (MICHAEL GLOBETTI, *journalist*)

cos • mo • sis *n* [*cosmos* + *hypnosis*]: A state of dazed awe or intellectual vertigo caused, in the previously uninitiated, by exposure to the wonders of fundamental physics or cosmology. "As I read Stephen Hawking's *A Brief History of Time*, my head began to spin and I fell into a state of cosmosis." (MICHAEL LOCKWOOD, *philosopher*)

couch•ant *adj* [*couchant* heraldic term meaning "lying down with the head raised"]: Of or pertaining to something that is about to break out, but has not yet done so, typically used in conjunction with the word "rumor"; couchant rumors stand in antonymous relation to rampant rumors, meaning that they are on the verge of becoming known. "Whereas history once relegated whispered gossip to oblique references cast deep within the most soporific footnotes, today's pop history such as the kind written by Kitty Kelley has elevated couchant rumor to the very substance of contemporary history." (EUGENE J. McCARTHY, *politician*)

cre•ac•tive *adj* [*creative + proactive*]: The attribute of both being creative and actually doing something about it; most creative ideas are ignored or worse, and true creativity requires not only thinking up something new but figuring out how to put a new idea into play. "It was very creactive of John to design such a radical building and get someone to pay him to build it." (ROGER C. SCHANK, *professor*)

crew•ci•fy *v* [*crew + crucify*]: To tease or deride a person for having Ivy League or similarly elitist affiliations. "The party on Charles Street seemed to be composed entirely of graduates of the University of Kansas, and sure enough, a few young men in multicolored down vests took it upon themselves to crewcify Winkie, but she never let them know that, yes, this caused her pain." (TOM DRURY, *writer*)

crool *adj* [*cruel + cool*]: Characteristic of someone who is so cool that his or her mere presence demeans those around him or her. "Winona Ryder is so crool to me." (BRIAN McCORMICK, *writer*)

cryp•tych *n* [*crypt + triptych*]: A painter's memorial to the three principles in a ménage à trois that ended in a double murder and a suicide. "As Pierre 'Gavroche' Gagnier gloomily surveyed the assembled celebrants at the service, he was silently exultant that he had so quickly been able to create a work of art, this cryptych, which so cogently memorialized the passion and yet the firmness of this turbulent affair—such a gorgeous disaster to the cadre of artistic copains who dined at their home, sunned in their flame, and now scanned the thwarted painted faces perched atop their three akimbo coffins." (LIONEL TIGER, *professor*)

cube *v* [fr. *cubism* a period of art in France when people tried to act like certain artists]: To imitate someone unconsciously and thereby distort him or her; to copy someone's behavior in a way that belies your misunderstanding of the person and of yourself. "I don't like being with him because I get the feeling he is always studying me in order to cube me later." (EDWIN SCHLOSSBERG, *artist*)

cy•ber *n* [fr. Gk *kybernan* to steer, govern]: Any device, from a vending machine to a robot, that uses computers for self-regulation. "Between rising from bed and settling into his chair at the office, he dealt with exactly fourteen cybers, beginning with his alarm clock and ending with his talkative desk." (SCOTT RUSSELL SANDERS, *writer*)

cy•na•ïve•té *n* [*cynicism* + *naïveté*]: 1: Extreme cynicism to the point of utter credulity. 2: The state of believing so readily in nothing that one believes in everything, particularly common among sophisticated industrial cultures and their media representatives. "In their cynaïveté, the press believed Ronald Reagan to be nearly senile, with natural brown hair." "In their cynaïveté, the American people believed only in astrology, glowing extraterrestrials, and magic crystals." (KEVIN BAKER, *writer*)

D

dan•daid *n* [*Dan* first name of eponymous hero Vice-President Dan Quayle + BAND-AID, especially in its metaphorical sense of hasty, temporary, emergency relief]: Quick damage control applied after any misstatement notable for its earnest, forthright idiocy. (WILL BAKER, *writer*)

dark•nat•ter *n* & *v* [*dark* + *natter* an analogue of "dark matter," which some astrophysicists speculate may constitute as much as 90 percent of the uni-

chatter, whether in direct discourse, by way of the electronic media, or in print. "A lethal cloud of darknatter formed above Washington, D.C., and was not dispelled, as optimists hoped, by Hurricane Rita as she flung gale-force winds off the Atlantic Coast." **darknatter** *v:* "He was darknattered to death by department colleagues." (JOYCE CAROL OATES, *novelist*)

da • ta • cloud *n* [*data + cloud*]: The dense and rapidly expanding cloud of uncollated digital data that obscures the pockets of valuable information that lie embedded within it. (JOHN PERRY BARLOW, *musician*)

de • bel • li • cized *adj* [fr. L *bellicus* warlike + prefix *de-* undoing or reversing]: Rendered entirely unwarlike; pacifist in attitude and action without being rooted in a principled or ideological opposition to war. "Among the other questions to be considered in the aftermath of the Persian Gulf crisis is whether anything has really changed since Vietnam, or whether our defeat in that war has left us capable only of flyswatting operations like Grenada and Panama but otherwise permanently debellicized and forever unmanned by the idea

(which Friedrich Nietzsche saw as the mark of a slave) that nothing is worth fighting and dying for." (NORMAN PODHORETZ, *journalist*)

de • car • bu • late *v* [originally runners' slang referring to the initial phase of carbohydrate loading during which one purposely depleninshed the body's store of glycogen resulting in later enhanced absorption and superior muscle performance]: 1: To strategically release available energy (military, political, economic, etc.) to enhance later strength; term is particularly favored by formerly virulent pacifists suddenly experiencing a release of previously suppressed righteous rage. "We're going to decarbulate Iraq." 2: The expulsion of violent wishes by acting upon them. "You will feel better when you decarbulate your fantasy." (MARCO LEYTON, *writer*)

de • ci • co *n* [*decimate + cohort*]: The substitution by sportscasters of fabrications and solecisms for standard English. "The word 'decico' is fabricated from two of the most common solecisms. The habit of its use can be traced to the secret societies formed by small boys who create passwords and secret codes in the hope of making special and exciting something that doesn't amount to much. Hence, with what passes for reason in the sports world, it has been decided that calling teams or towns by a different name will make them better. Instead of reporting that the White Sox beat the Tigers, they say the Pale Hose from the Windy City trounced the Bengals from Motor Town. The Pirates have become successively the Buccaneers, the Bucs, and finally the Buckos. Nicknames, which are customarily a shortening of the familiar, here become longer, alliterative, and obscure: The Manassa Mauler, the Splendid Splinter and the Galloping Ghost. From the Big Apple to Chocolatetown, the highly mannered and frantic style of sportscasters is based on the peculiar notion that a multibillion-dollar sports empire could be built on a fan population that was capable of boredom." (WILL STANTON, *writer*)

de·hu·man·ism *n* [back-formation fr. *dehumanize*]: The belief that hatred of one or more demonized others is the sole requirement for a moral life, currently the state religion of the United States. " 'Secular dehumanism? No, I don't think that's a threat to our moral fabric,' the reverend remarked as he emerged from a meeting with the President." (STEVE MESSINA, *editor*)

dé·jà vous *interj* [fr. Fr *déjà* already + *vous* you]: An expression of disgust occurring when a person has reappeared once too often. "Déjà vous!" "Déjà vous can be applied in a variety of informal situations in the context of seeing someone again: 'When he showed up after I told him to get lost, I said, "Look, I can't take the déjà vous." ' " (GLADYS SWAN, *novelist*)

de·lec·ta·ti·o·bell·um *n* [fr. L *delectatio* entertainment, amusement + L *bellum* war]: 1: Entertainment warfare. 2: Specifically, a strategic American military, think-tank, or philosophical doctrine that holds that it is wasteful and counterproductive to build costly conventional and nuclear weapons systems and risk lives in mortal combat when America almost always conquers its adversaries with pop culture years after any conflict. "The best example and inadvertent use of delectatiobellum was in Vietnam where the American government spent billions of dollars bombing that country 'back to the Stone Age,' yet lost the military war anyway, only to discover years later that most bars and discos in Ho Chi Minh City were now playing capitalist American pop, disco, and rap music for their communist customers. Delectatiobellum doctrine states: 'Why wait until after a military conflict to see an enemy embrace our pop culture when we can hit them with it before a war and win them over without a shot fired?' Early examples of possibly unintentional strategic entertainment warfare campaigns include the leafleting of the Vietcong by U.S. Army helicopters that also blared pop and rock music from loudspeakers; the underground popularity of Frank Zappa, the Plastic People, and the Velvet Underground in Czechoslovakia is said, by President and playwright Vaclav Havel, no less, to have been as responsible for the collapse of communism in his country as the velvet revolution in 1989. During the Panama invasion, U.S. troops blasted the Vatican embassy in Panama City, where General Manuel Noriega had taken asylum, with loud heavy metal rock music. U.S. troops used the same delectatiobellum strategy in the Persian Gulf, where it has been reported that soldiers opened fire with a few Guns N' Roses tunes before following up with more traditional ammunition. It might be worth considering that we set up a Strategic Entertainment Warfare Agency in the government, a top-secret, unofficially recognized bureau responsible for designing, developing, and deploying strategic entertainment weapons systems. Consider the possibility of dropping battery-powered VCRs and cassette re-

déjà vous

cordings of any of Madonna's music videos. In the Middle East, this simple strategy would provoke more cultural revolution than a warehouse full of cruise missiles. It's known, for example, that other agencies of the government have researched the psychological and emotional impact on sensory-deprived test subjects of the videotape of James Brown singing 'Papa's Got a Brand New Bag' live on the T.A.M.I. Show. The results are classified, but one research scientist on the code-named project 'New Bag,' who would not give his name, stated that 'the sensory-deprived subjects simply fell on their knees and stared agape at the screen as soon as James Brown started his act; the test subjects wept instantly, wrung their hands together, and tried to form words with their mouths that wouldn't come. We're guardedly optimistic about the project. That's all I can say.'" (MICHAEL HOLMAN, *filmmaker*)

del•fer•i•or•i•ty *n* [*delusion + inferior*]: A feeling that one is inferior to another when one is not; a delusion of inferiority. "Many people are swept by feelings of delferiority when meeting Prince Charles." (BRIAN Mc-CORMICK, *writer*)

de•mock•er•a•cy *n* [fr. Gk *demos* people + Gk *kratos* rule + ME *mokken*, fr. MF *mocquer* to ridicule by imitation of speech or action, from a root *mok* imitative with residue of laughter; by rhetorical trope tmesis with a little help from a friend (see etymology for PASTRIOTISM), the insertion of the virus of an almost silent *k*, causing the "mock," like some parasitical monster, to exit the belly of the word, making it gape.]: 1: Government utterly not by the people. 2: That form of government in which the sovereign power feigns and imitates residence in the people and whose exercise by them is hollow form. 3: Imitation of democracy with an ulterior motive, pseudodemocratic discourse in a venomous language, replete with laughter. "The composite elements of a demockeracy were described in a conversation with Bill Moyers by linguist Noam Chomsky: In a capitalist democracy, you have the problem that the general population participates in the decision-making by participating in politics. The state is not capable of stopping them. You can't shut them out, you can't put them in jail, and you can't keep them away from the polls. It's striking that this has always been perceived as a problem to be overcome. It's called 'the crisis of democracy'—too many people organizing themselves to enter the public arena. That's a crisis we have to overcome. . . . Even the mainstream democratic theorists have always understood that when the voice of the people is heard, you're in trouble, because these stupid and ignorant masses, as they're called, are going to make the wrong decisions. So, therefore, we have to have what Walter Lippmann, back in 1920 or so, called 'manufacture of consent.' We have to ensure that actual power is in the hands of what he called a specialized class—us smart guys, who are going to make the right decisions. . . . From a point of view that perceives democracy as a problem to be overcome, and sees the right solution as being far-sighted leaders with a specialized class of social managers—from that point of view, you must find means of marginalizing the population. Reducing them to apathy and obedience, allowing them to participate in the political system, but as consumers, not as true participants. You allow them a method for ratifying decisions that are made by others, but you eliminate the methods by which they might first, inform themselves; second, organize; and third, act in such a way as to really control decision

making. The idea is that our leaders control us, we don't control them. That is a very widespread view, from liberals and conservatives. And how do you achieve this? By turning elected offices into ceremonial positions. If you could get to the point where people would essentially vote for the Queen of England and take it seriously, then you would have gone a long way toward marginalizing the public. We've made a big step in that direction." (MARSHALL BLONSKY, *writer*)

de•plhor•rence *n* [*deplore* + *abhorrence*]: 1: A state of rich and gratifying disgust manifest not in a grimace of revulsion, but rather in an all-knowing-cat-that-just-ate-the-canary or more - in - pity - than - in - anger smile, or a smug expression of august condescension or benevolent disdain. In all its forms, unabashed self-satisfaction is its common ingredient. " 'Oh, what a pity,' he said as he handed her his napkin. He then leaned back and added with ingratiating deplhorrence, 'I myself have never spilled ketchup on my formal attire.' " 2: A state of unsmiling, justifiable, and ruthless disdain. "Hearing her dinner companion's priggish remark, she arose from the table without a word, and in a state of utter deplhorrence, stalked out of the restaurant, stained ball gown and all." (R. BRUCE MOODY, *novelist/playwright*)

de • prel • der *n* [*depression* + *elderly*]: Feeling of intense guilt at warehousing an elderly parent in a nursing home, often in a faraway place long ago left by the child, which is not ameliorated by reasonable questions from helpful friends like, "What else could you do?" and culminates in an inability to speak of one's parent in any context whatsoever without crying. (ANNE EISENBERG, *professor*)

de • prove • ment *n* [*de-* + *improvement*]: 1: Backward-moving progress. An invention that makes things worse. "The invention of the car phone is a clear case of deprovement in modern life." (MOLLY IVINS, *journalist*) 2: A new or altered product or feature designed to make things better that actually makes things worse. "Deprovements include loud beeping noises on vehicles in reverse gear; car alarms; 'colorization' of movies; air fresheners; PACs." See IMPRAVEMENT. (KIRKPATRICK SALE, *writer*)

der • i • va • sa • tion *n* [*derivative* + *conversation*]: A conversation that is derivative of other people's opinions. (BRIAN MCCORMICK, *writer*)

der • ri • do • lo • gy *n* [fr. eponymous hero *Jacques Derrida*, French philosopher + *teratology* the medical study of the malformed, of monsters]: The study of texts that permit so many deconstructions that they remain forever ineffable. "Texts such as the following by Howard Fast in the October 15, 1990, issue of the *New York Observer* provide fertile ground for aspiring derridologists: 'Nothing good came from the Civil War. The emancipation of the black slaves, an afterthought when the Union had almost lost the struggle, was hardly a reality.' " (GERALD WEISSMANN, *M.D.*)

der • vi • ant *adj* [*dervish* + *deviant*]: An irresistible, untimely urge to dance or frolic. "A derviant tends to whirl when he or she should worry." (HAROLD JAFFE, *editor*)

des • i • tive • ly *adj* [*definitely* + *positively*]: Without a doubt, most assuredly. "Desitively is an old New Orleans musicians' phrase that is seeping into the general population. The first written use of the word appeared on the album by Dr. John aka Mac Rebennack entitled *Desitively Bonaroo*." "I will desitively show up for the gig by ten." "I don't know about you, but I feel desitively bonaroo (real good)." (JOE NICK PATOSKI, *editor*)

dex • ag • ger • ate *v* [*de-* + *exaggerate*]: 1: To shrink below the limits of truth; understate. 2: To exaggerate smallness, shortness, or slowness. " 'Okay, so I have 98 percent of the voters' support. That leaves my opponent with, whatever, Barbara does the math, three percent. But a front-runner, me? Whoa, you reporters, going too far. Wouldn't be right. I'm no front-runner. Just an underdog with a darn lot of that big mo,' dexaggerated President Bush." (MARK DOWIE, *journalist*)

di • ag • ol • ways *adv* [*diagonal* + *ways*]: Cutting corners in problem solving, especially a problem for which linear reasoning doesn't work. "He solved the Rubik's cube by thinking diagolways." (MARGARET H. HAREN, *writer*)

di • cate *v* [back-formation fr. *abdicate*]: To return to a throne one has relinquished. "Ex-King Michael of Romania has said that he might like to dicate. Ex-King Constantine of Greece made an unsuccessful try at dicating. As Eastern Europe splinters into linguistic and ethnic shards, an orgy of dication may be expected." (PAUL BICKART, *chemist*)

dic • to • crat *n* —**dic • toc • ra • cy** *n* [*dictator* + *democrat* or *democracy*]: A dictator who, by virtue of an alliance with the United States, is considered someone who believes in democracy, in fact, loves democracy, but has simply forgotten to hold a popular election in his own country. "The greatest practicing dictocrat, who invented the idea and perfected the art of transforming himself before the CNN gaze of millions, is Mikhail Gorbachev. Dictocrats are liberal and progressive and don't have to worry about being thrown out of power, and therefore are our natural allies. The Al-Sabah family in Kuwait and the Saudis in Saudi Arabia (a country named after the family is a fairly reliable sign of a strong dictocracy) are both stellar examples. The ideal dictocrat should be presentable, smiling, affable, and speak decent English for those occasional *Nightline* appearances when he will be called upon to reaffirm how much he loves democracy in the face of, say, a massacre he has ordered or the revelation that he has been siphoning his country's wealth into an account in

Monaco. General Pinochet of Chile was one of our favorite dictocrats, as were the ever smiling, sometimes singing, Ferdinand and Imelda Marcos. King Hussein of Jordan is a great dictocrat, as is Yasser Arafat. A sure way to spot a dictocrat is to see if the adjective 'popular' is part of his official title, as in, Oliver Tambo, 'the popular head of the African National Congress.' When affairs get testier than he can handle, the dictocrat often becomes a madman, a fate that afflicted Manuel Noriega and Saddam Hussein. Citizens of a dictocracy can discover the level of dictocracy by asking the question, 'Who elected you?' and listening carefully to detect the amount of sarcasm and irony in one's voice needed to get the words out. If the ruler responds by putting a bullet through your head, the transition to madman may be well under way." (MICHAEL ROSENBLUM, *journalist*)

dic • trai • tor *n* [*dictator* + *traitor*]: A dictator who betrays those who have put him into power or helped keep him there, often applied to a dictator who turns against the country that supplied him with weapons in order to prepare him and his army for war against sundry "guerrilla" groups. Dictraitors

are most easily identified by their tendency eventually to treat those outside their country the same way they have always treated those inside their country. "The Middle Eastern dictraitor promised to destroy the world if other countries opposed his territorial annexations." (ROBERT J. STERNBERG, *professor*)

dig • a • bah *interj* [*dig* with a tail for emphasis]: A somewhat impatient response to another person when he or she sees the light or gets the point. "A man in a restaurant beckons the waiter to come over and taste his soup. The waiter says, 'Is there something wrong with your soup sir?' 'Please, just taste the soup.' 'How can I taste the soup?' the waiter says, 'There's no spoon.' The patron nods with disdain, saying, 'Digabah!' " (ANNE BERNAYS, *novelist*)

di • gre • dote *n* [*digress* + *anecdote*]: A story that includes tangents, asides, superfluous details, and ruminations on the part of the teller about his powers of recall ("at least I'm pretty sure it was blue, but who knows, the ol' eyes aren't what they used to be"), and frequent questions about the authenticity of his facts ("Was it Danny Stern or Manny Stern?"), to the extent that the teller seems eventually to have forgotten the point of the story, though he continues to talk, and the listener, though nodding vigorously, is in fact contemplating the perspiration on the speaker's upper lip, or wondering whether to have fish or chicken for dinner. "Five minutes into Fred's digredote, Sharlene had mentally balanced her checkbook." (BERNARD COOPER, *writer*)

di•gres•si•vism *n* [*digress* + *progressivism*]: The belief that history is not going forward or backward but is constantly getting hopelessly, pointlessly sidetracked. "Having studied history for many years in the hope of discovering the master plan, the graduate student decided in despair that he believed in digressivism and became an accountant instead." (ELLIOTT RABIN, *editor*)

dis•an•thro•py *n* [*dis* black slang for "insult" or "taunt" + *philanthropy*]: 1: Spending money in a manner designed to arouse resentment in others. 2 a: A blatantly sociopathic acquisition. b: An organization founded on disanthropy (e.g. Lincoln Savings & Loan). "In the 1980s, Leona Helmsley, Donald Trump, and Michael Milken managed to turn disan-

thropy into a kind of performance art." (RODGER MORROW, *writer*)

dis•clu•di•fy *v* [*disqualify* + *exclude*]: To be removed from consideration; to be made ineligible. "If you pilfer petty cash, you are discludified from handling any cash transactions." (ANN LANDERS, *columnist*)

Dis•ney *v* [fr. *Disneyland*]: To prettify and simplify the world; to turn animals and landscapes and cities into benign caricatures. "No matter what facts I threw at her, she blithely Disneyed them, refusing to acknowledge the gravity of our situation." (SCOTT RUSSELL SANDERS, *writer*)

dis•quer•i•fy *v* [*disqualify* + *query*]: To omit the interrogation mark (?) from a rhetorical question. "Why do so many people do this nowadays." See BROWNSPEAK. (IAN STEWART, *mathematician*)

dis•six *v* [*dis* + *disrespect* + *disempower* + *sixties*]: To attempt to discredit an action or event by suggesting that it only repeats something that happened in the 1960s, or as a Charlie King song puts it, is "vaguely reminiscent of the sixties." "When asked to give her opinion on an article about the demonstration for more funding for AZT (or for housing for the homeless, or for money for crack addict rehab programs), a perceptive reader might say, 'Not terrible—only a couple of dissixing paragraphs and then a snide bit about how the good weather created a picniclike atmosphere, but in the final paragraph, the reporter quoted one of the speakers.' " (ELLEN GRUBER GARVEY, *writer*, and JANET GALLAGHER, *attorney*)

do•mes•tic non•in•ter•ven•tion•ism *n* [*domestic policy* + *noninterventionism*]: A domestic policy based on the intentional neglect of the problems of one's own country, usually accompanied by foreign adventurism. Synonyms: *autoisolationism, intraphobia, self-abuse.* " 'We are not guilty of domestic noninterventionism,' the President asserted from his vacation home. 'We simply believe that the burning of the capital is a problem best dealt with by the private sector.' " (STEVE MESSINA, *editor*)

dom•i•naut *n* [*domino* + *double naught* the lowest number on a domino + *cosmonaut* one who believes he has achieved dominion over the cosmos]: Global commentator who uses the domino theory to explain why the U.S. lost China, Korea, Vietnam, Cuba, Nicaragua and (eventually) the Middle East. "The dominaut is convinced that if it were not for the eggheads, do-gooders, and the bleeding hearts in Washington, all of these countries would be democracies and all dominoes would naturally stand on end." (WILL STANTON, *writer*)

doom•gress *n* [fr. *doom* + L *gradi* to go; by association with *progress*]: Change, or changes, often mistaken for "progress," which can lead to psychological, cultural, political, economic, or environmental degradation, and even global disaster. "The word 'doomgress' counteracts the uniquely Western belief that most changes, especially those emanating from the realms of science and technology, lead in near-linear fashion to ever higher stages of civilization, quality of life, and human fulfillment. This belief, based on the idea of progress, first appeared in Western culture in the 17th century and was reinforced by the process of industrialization that transformed Europe. Doomgress articulates the perspective of contemporary environmental movements that holds that many innovations touted by scientists and other experts may well lead to a future imperiled by drought, famine, acid rain, the 'greenhouse effect,' nuclear catastrophe, and other forms of ecological ruin. Western culture boasts that one 'can't fight progress.' The concept of doomgress implies that sometimes we must. Chernobyl demonstrates conclusively that nuclear power represents nothing less than doomgress. Examples of doomgress are manifold, ranging from our automobile addiction to television violence to the 30-second political spot to the swimsuit issue of *Sports Illustrated*." (BILL SCHECHTER, *teacher*)

do•re•mi *n* [fr. the first three notes of the musical scale sung by schoolchildren]: An endeavour that is neither very good nor very bad, but is at least a start. See FASOLATIDO. "Philip Roth's first novel was very doremi." (BRIAN MCCORMICK, *writer*)

do•ri•an•gray *adj* [fr. *The Picture of Dorian Gray* by Oscar Wilde]: Aged yet suspiciously youthful. "After noticing the septuagenarian film star's hands —wattled and flappy like boiled hen's claws at a Chinatown dim sum lunch—Nora couldn't help but boggle at the film star's smooth, dewy doriangray face." (DOUGLAS COUPLAND, *writer*)

driv•u•let *n* [*drivel + rivulet*]: A small but constant stream of fatuous talk. "The MP's so-called explanation constituted nothing more than a well-articulated drivulet calculated expressly to obfuscate the issue and discourage serious discussion." (BARRY GIFFORD, *novelist*)

dron•age *n* [*drone* to talk on monotonously + *bilge* the putrid water in the bottom of a boat + *drainage* detritus and excess and dregs that have spilled out beyond the levees]: Any of the time-consuming bursts of blather one is forced to endure in the modern technological age, but especially any voice-mail menu that wastes a good minute or two, enumerating all the possible options available, every time one calls an institution; but most especially a recorded message on a personal answering machine that takes more than ten seconds; dronage of the latter variety also includes "clever" messages of any length that cease to be clever after the first hearing. "Dronage comes in several varieties: **grand dronage** stretches well into minutes in length and, on an answering machine, often involves music meant to suggest that the person not home is in possession of a subtle sense of cultural irony. **Gross dronage** takes the next step; the parties not at home have composed their own song and sing it to you every time you call, such as, 'Amy and Ted are not here right now/ But they'll be back with you/ As soon as they get home from work/ They have so much to do/ So please leave them a simple message/ Be sure to tell it all/ If they don't have the information/ They can't return the call.' The **petit dronage** is one in which the message is, by now, painfully ingenuous—'Hi, I'm not here to talk to you now (obviously), but you can leave a message here (obviously), after the beep (obviously)'—and seems to be directed to any Ashanti warrior relatives who have happened to find a quarter and a pay phone in the bush and would be bewildered to encounter an answering machine on the other end of the line." (MICHAEL ROSENBLUM, *journalist*)

dude•ism *n* [*dude* slang term suggesting a regular guy + *-ism* the ideology thereof]: A behavioral dogma that advocates: sports fanaticism, maudlin displays of patriotism, shouting "YES!" in victory, mild misogamy and misogyny, homophobia, emotional high-five hand slapping, and other forms of collective, sophomoric behavior, with the intention of inspiring camaraderie and group-bonding, specifically among insecure, young American males. "Advertisers of the cheaper brands of beer and inexpensive sports cars depend heavily on dudeism in their television commercials to reach that lucrative target market." (MICHAEL HOLMAN, *filmmaker*)

du•raws *n* [*duration + awful moment*]: The lapse of time, perceived only by the speaker, between the casting of a veiled insult and its recognition by the recipient. "Malcolm waited for his opportunity and then let the insinuation slip into the conversation; Bendrix was slow, and the duraws extended itself to a near-eternity." (SVEN BIRKERTS, *writer*)

dust•belt *n* [*dust bowl + rust belt*]: Silicon Valley, after the Japanese take over the manufacture of computer chips; the region of the United States once famous for production of computer chips and other computer products. "I can make more money farming in Fresno than I can as an engineer in the dustbelt." (DANIEL B. BOTKIN, *environmentalist*)

dy•na•tic *adj & n* [fr. Gk *dynatos* powerful]: Being in or practicing the culture resulting from the Industrial Revolution of the 18th and 19th centuries in Europe. "Third-world countries, while embracing dynatic culture, are often dismayed by its unanticipated side effects." See GEORGIC. (L. SPRAGUE DE CAMP, *writer*)

E

east • urb • in • ver • sion *n* [*east + urban + inversion*]: The vaguely held notion, particularly prevalent in the midwest, that New York City is north of Boston. "Thrown off by easturbinversion, Jim's search for Radio City Music Hall took him as far north as the windswept province of Prince Edward Island." (TOM DRURY, *writer*)

ea • sy • ace *n* [fr. an episode of a popular radio show of the 1940s entitled *Easy Aces*, in which Jane Ace, asked by her husband why she was using red ink to keep her books if she was in the black, answered that were she obliged to purchase black ink she would be in the red]: A situation such that the fulfillment of the conditions necessary to achieve a result causes its failure. "A sobering easyace was reported in the paper under the headline, 'Two in sex change die of breast cancer.'" (ALIX KATES SHULMAN, *writer*)

ec • ce • den • te • si • ast *n* [fr. L *ecce* behold + *dentes* teeth]: A person who simulates a smile by stretching open the mouth and displaying both rows of teeth, used frequently on television talk shows. "Farrah Fawcett found a way to be even more friendly in an already neurotically friendly nation by becoming America's leading eccedentesiast." Synonyms: *crocodile, corpse.* Antonym: *a secure person, usually a foreigner.* (FLORENCE KING, *writer*)

e • co • fraud *n* [*economics + fraud*]: An economic theory so patently contradictory that to assert it is to commit a kind of fraud. "Recent ecofrauds include the claim that a reduction of taxes will increase tax revenues and the idea, perpetrated in the 1980s, that the country's economic ills could be traced to the belief that the rich were unproductive because they didn't have enough money and that the poor were unproductive because they had too much.'' (JOHN KENNETH GALBRAITH, *professor*)

e•co•la•cy *n*—**e•co•late** *adj* [*ecology + legacy*]: A form of analysis in general and ecological analysis in particular that takes into account time and its consequences; an analysis that turns on the key question: And then what? Or, what further changes occur when the treatment or experience is repeated time after time? "Time and the web of life thwart many attempts to remake the natural world nearer to human desires. We thought we could wipe out malaria in Africa and Southeast Asia by spraying mosquitoes with DDT. In fact, after an initial apparent success, we found we were selecting for DDT-resistant mosquitoes. Malaria is now increasing in those areas. The tunnel vision of enthusiasts seldom encompasses either time or the reticulated web of organisms and causes. The ecolate critic, with his irritating question, 'And then what?' is not welcomed by enthusiasts, whether they be profit-minded promoters or altruistic reformers. The commercial promoter wants to make a fortune selling something, e.g. pesticides. The reformer wants to diminish human suffering through single-minded attention to only one of the factors involved: for example, through increasing food production in a poor country in which the environment is being ruinously exploited by an overfertile population. Such a reform increases the number of people, which in turn has one of two effects: either the amount of food per capita ultimately decreases, or the population becomes increasingly dependent on donations of food from the outside. A cautious approach to innovation is the mark of a true conservative. With respect to the things he understands best, an ecologist is clearly a conservative (whatever may be his attitude in other areas). But is this not the behavior of genuine experts in every field? Anticonservatism (under whatever name) is more often associated with ignorance than with knowledge. Prudence, an essentially ecolate virtue, is not popular with enthusiasts. In summary, different kinds of analysis ask different questions: Literacy asks, 'What are the words?' And numeracy asks, 'What are the numbers?' But ecolacy asks,

'And then what?' " (GARRETT HARDIN, *ecologist*)

e•co•logue *n* [*ecology + ideologue*]: A humorless fanatic on toxic wastes, global warming, oil spills, acid rain, and ozone depletion. "Let's invite that ecologue friend of yours to dinner with my friend the oilman." (SUEELLEN CAMPBELL, *writer*)

e•co•nau•se•a *n* [*ecology + nausea*]: The sick apprehension caused by learning yet another piece of bad news about the environment. "Wiping the oil from her NIkes after a run on the beach, blackening one paper towel after another, she suffered a wave of econausea." (ELIZABETH TALLENT, *writer*)

e•con•tri•vance *n* [*economics + contrivance*]: An economic concept designed not to enlarge knowledge but to serve particular interests. "Supply-side economics in the Reagan era or reduction of the capital gains tax in order to increase employment in the Bush era are two econtrivances that nearly qualify as ecofrauds." See ECOFRAUD. (JOHN KENNETH GALBRAITH, *professor*)

e•co•phist *n* [*ecology + sophist*]: One who pretends to know a lot about the environment, but

feels good only about environmentalism. "The ecophists would have us believe that science has no role in the solution to environmental problems." (DANIEL B. BOTKIN, *environmentalist*)

e•co•porn *n* [*ecology + pornography*]: Useless or harmful products sold as though they were beneficial to the environment. "Examples of ecoporn abound, such as products that boast they 'contain no chlorofluorocarbons known to harm the ozone layer,' yet the replacement propellants cause smog. Or, claiming that a container is 'made of recyclable paper,' without explaining how one recycles a plastic-coated, ketchup-stained hamburger box. In Toronto, not too long ago, one could buy a cute little baby seal doll made of real baby sealskin." See GREEN- SPEAK. (PAUL BICKART, *chemist*)

e•co•pre•neur *n* [*ecology + entrepreneur*]: One who organizes, operates, and assumes the risk of ventures oriented toward the advancement of ecology or the enhancement of the environment. "An ecopreneur combines the economics of business enterprise with goals which are enhancing the ecological future of the planet." (EDWARD P. BASS, *investor/rancher/entrepreneur*) e•co•ste•ry *n* [*ecology* + *monastery*]: A small community of men and women dedicated to the restoration and protection of an ecosystem or part thereof, modeled in part on the monasteries that grew up after the collapse of another great civilization. (KIRKPATRICK SALE, *writer*)

ec•to•the•ism *n* [fr. Gk *ecto* outside + *theism* belief in a god]: The maintenance of the trappings of religion, such as going to church, without internalizing religious teachings (especially ethical or moral ones). "Brutalizing my family and co-workers during the week, then praying every Sunday for forgiveness of my sins, doesn't make me a hypocrite—just an ectotheist." See ENDOTHEISM. (MARK J. ESTREN, *writer*)

e•cu•i•cide *n* [*ecology* + *suicide*]: The conscious and willful destruction of the world's ecosystems to the point of death, including that of the species perpetrating it. (KIRKPATRICK SALE, *writer*)

el•e•feign *n & v* [*elevator* + *feign*]: An insincere gesture of holding open an elevator door for an onrushing passenger. "I saw my boss trying to catch the elevator, so I elefeigned him." "Not wanting to travel with my boss, but not wanting to offend him either, I chose an elefeign." (JONATHAN ALTER, *journalist*)

el•o•quate *v* [*eloquence* + *aerate*]: To express a premeditated thought loudly in a public place in order to be overheard, usually with the intention of creating a certain positive impression. "Charles would spend hours at home concocting bons mots and pithy remarks so that he could better eloquate at the fashionable restaurants he frequented." (GARY KRIST, *writer*)

e•mall•grate *v* [fr. L *e-* out of + *mall* + *migration*]: To migrate toward low-tech, lower-information environments that contain a lessened emphasis on consumerism. "Joey and I were going to emallgrate to Vermont but then we found radicchio for sale in a grocery there and we changed our minds." (DOUGLAS COUPLAND, *writer*)

en•do•the•ism *n* [fr. Gk *endo* inside + *theism* belief in a god]: The internalization of ethical or moral teachings of religion without obeisance to external practice. "Endotheism looks to the casual observer like atheism, is therefore rarely used, and is considered by lexicographers as a noun best described as 'obscure'." See ECTOTHEISM. (MARK J. ESTREN, *writer*)

en • dow • a • ger *n* [*endowment* + *dowager*]: An artist, especially a writer, who lives year after year on grants and awards, usually at the expense of gainful employment or any real-world experience. "This poet I knew in grad school, she moved to Minneapolis and turned into an endowager." (JOHN CALDERAZZO, *writer*)

en • gy • no • cize *v* [*en-* + Gk *gynos* woman + *-ize*]: To render unfeminine; mentally or emotionally to undermine the essence of being female; the female counterpart of emasculate. "Feminism, by seeking to force women to play male roles, will only engynocize them." (ROBIN FOX, *professor*)

en • vi • ron • nui *n* [*environment* + *ennui*]: Listlessness and vague despair resulting from hearing too many tales of environmental woe; a malady peculiar to the last two decades of the 20th century. " 'More dead seabirds,' she sighed, writing her largest check yet to the Sierra Club to compensate for the environnui that had been descending over her for some time." (JOHN CALDERAZZO, *writer*)

en • vi • ro • pre • neur *n* [*enviro* about + *preneur* bold initiator]: A person who initiates practices to protect and promote a clean environment, especially an industrial or business leader who understands environmental protection is an economically sound investment. "I'd like to introduce the CEO of Textiles U.S.A., a leading enviropreneur, who will speak to us today of corporate innovations beyond the minimum regulations and how those practices resulted in the invention of a new treatment technique that prevents toxic waste products." (WILLIAM K. REILLY, *environmentalist*)

ep • i • stem • ic hap • pi • ness *n* [fr. Gk *episteme* knowledge + *happiness*]: Confidence in the redemptive character of knowledge, based on an equation of the salutary with the comprehensive, the coherent, and the complete. "The epistemically happy man generally regards the spectrum of human knowledge encyclopedically, that is, as one large, ultimately consistent body of lore; and his favorite provinces of knowledge are apt to be those displaying the highest degree of rationality and mathematical abstraction. In philosophy, he is a rationalist—speculative and systematic; in science, he is a physicist." Antonymous to *epistemic gloom:* "The epistemically gloomy man tends toward skepticism or at least toward empiricism; the various fields of knowledge are for him discrepant and even antipathetic, and his favorites among them are apt to be those that include a large measure of exploration and description and rather little in the way of a priori conceptualization. Until the advent of molecular theory and genetic codification, biology was a science unusually hospitable to the epistemically gloomy." (RICHARD TRISTMAN, *professor*)

erd • mensch *n* [fr. G *Erde* earth + G *Mensch* man]: Someone excessively rooted in reality. "A *luftmensch* is someone with inadequate ties to reality. An erdmensch is the luftmensch's antipode: someone too busy making money to have time for art, philosophy, or humor." (PAUL BICKART, *chemist*)

er • nes • ty *n* —**ernestine** *adj* [*honesty* + *earnest* + *Ernest,* from Oscar Wilde's play *The Importance of Being Earnest*]: An attitude that substitutes moral earnestness for honesty. "Many professional persuaders—salespeople, performers, proselytizers, media personalities, politicians—wear the ernestine demeanor habitually." "American ernesty combines corn bread sincerity with the presumption of personified virtue; it is compatible with conscious duplicity but innocent of irony. Ronald Reagan and Pete Seeger are pure examples of ernesty." (JOEL AGEE, *writer*)

es • tro • gen poi • son • ing *n* [analogue to *testosterone poisoning,* a term coined by Alan Alda to describe males prone to over-aggressive, macho, combative behavior characterized by a taste for blood sport, kick-ass philosophies, and delusional idolatries, often involving the worship of the self]: A condition, usually found in females, characterized by chronic passivity, vicarious expressions of aggression, simpering, large personal contributions to the cosmetic and clothing industries, and delusional idolatries, often involving the worship of a male or males. Many victims fanatically embrace cultural values such as beauty contests and cheerleading. "Tammy Faye Bakker's cloying, mascara-laden attempts at fund-raising for Jim and Jesus is an example of estrogen poisoning. But an extreme case in the United States involved a mother who wanted her daughter to be on the cheerleading squad. Thinking that her daughter's rival might make the

squad instead, she was con-
victed of trying to hire a hit man
to kill the rival's mother. She
thought the murdered woman's
daughter would be too upset to
compete." (ALICE FULTON, *poet*)

eth • alp • ian *n* [*ethics + Alps*]:
One who lives on the moral
heights or who speaks of himself or herself as if he or she did
live there. "Ethalpians do well
in times of confusion, as they
seem to be possessed of cer-
tainty and perseverance in cultural matters. Their final reference, however, is to behavior,
not to dreams, and their attempts to prove that God is an
ethalpian always fail, and may
be resented by God." (DONALD
FAGEN, *musician*)

eth • i • co • ter • ra • tro • pism
n—**eth • i • co • ter • ra • tro • pist**
n [*ethics* + L *terra* earth + *tropism*
to bend toward in search of
nourishment]: The tendency to
bend toward the moral high
ground and to feel its attraction.
"Ethicoterratropism is manifested deep within subnuclear
physics, in the realm where an
almost imaginary event is said
to 'display charm.' The moral
high ground is like the quark or
the black hole, something no
one can see but that we have
evidence of by way of its effect
on what we can see. Scientists

working under a generous grant
have discovered the "ethicotro-
poblast," a layer of cells, often
cancerous, from which the
ethicoterratropist takes his
strange nourishment." (DONALD
FAGEN, *musician,* and GEORGE
TROW, *writer*)

eth • noid *n* [*ethnic* + *-oid* risible
enclitic; see etymology of FAC-
TOID]: A person who sees ethnicity as the root of all behavior.
"The new owner modified the
paper's ethnoid editorial policy
to one that acknowledged the
possibility, though not the cer-
tainty, that other races and
groups might be as worthy of attention as his own." (JUDITH MI-
CHAEL, *writer*)

eth • o • ple • gic *n* —**eth • o •
ple • gia** *n* [fr. Gk *ethos* custom,
character + Gk *plegia* strike, as
used in quadriplegia]: A mid-
level management person or
bureaucrat or well-connected
figurehead incapable of making
moral judgments. "Ethoplegia
may be congenital or the result
of administrative amputations.
Often articulate, persuasive, and
well-groomed, the ethoplegic is
nevertheless easily identified by
its sympathetic half smile, flip-
perlike gestures over a bare
desktop, and characteristic cries:
'If I had hands, they'd be tied,'
or 'I've argued for this all my

life,' or 'What I can do is shoot this upstairs.' " (WILL BAKER, *writer*)

eu•pho•nism *n* [*euphony + -ism*]: Substituting an impressive-sounding expression for one that, though more concise, fails to communicate the user's sense of self-importance; also: the expression so used. See SUPERFLUNYM. "Peppering the press conference with such phrases as 'eleemosynary institution' and 'fungible commodity,' the senator demonstrated his mastery of euphonism." (RODGER MORROW, *writer*)

Eu•ro•jive *n* [*Euro + jive* defined in Wentworth and Flexner's *Dictionary of American Slang* as "ordinary, tiresome, or misleading talk or actions; anything that should be ignored; baloney; bull"]: Jive in the European tradition of intellectual abstraction often found in educated comments on popular culture. "A university professor's wistful recollection of New York subway graffiti as 'splendid exercises in deconstruction' is an exercise in Eurojive. A rock critic's comparison of the Fine Young Cannibals' rhythms to those of Richard Strauss in *Die Frau ohne Schatten* is jiving *à l'Europe*. Theodor Adorno's impenetrably erudite critique of jazz, a subject he knew nothing about, is unadulterated Eurojive at its most pompous." (JOEL AGEE, *writer*)

ex•as•pe•rats *n* [*exasperation + congrats!*]: A word used as the opposite of the colloquial "congrats," indicating extreme displeasure, mixed with exasperation or frustration, at the actions or language of another person. (NORMAN COUSINS, *writer*)

ex•er•cist *n* [*exercise + masochist*]: Anyone who exercises excessively and then complains about the difficulty, pain, or effort involved in said exercise, thereby expecting sympathy from less fit peers. "Oh, damn, I have to run another marathon on Sunday," grumbled the exercist. (SALLIE TISDALE and KAREN KARBO, *writers*)

ex•fil•trate *v* [fr. Gk *ex* out, from + *filter* to pass through]: To quietly withdraw from any voluntary organization for the express purpose of avoiding labor or responsibility, usually after one has already benefited from association with that organization. "Jack exfiltrated the soup kitchen as soon as the prints from the group photo were returned." (GEORGE THRUSH, *architect*)

ex•pec•u•lat *v* [*expectorate +
speculate*]: To spit out an idea
or opinion without careful
thought, thereby offending
some or all of the listeners, and
often revealing a prejudice on
the part of the speaker. "Several
TV sportscasters have gotten
into trouble when they expecu-
lated on the abilities of black
athletes." "Mary walked away
in disgust when John expecu-
lated, 'They had no business
giving a man's job to a
woman.' " (ROBERT M. HAZEN,
writer)

Ex•xon•e•cu•tion *n* [*Exxon
+ execution*]: Destruction through
pollution. "The Exxonecution
of the wildlife along the Alaska
coastline has not yet stopped."
(SANDRA VAGINS, *editor/writer*)

eye•drop•per *n* [*eye + eavesdropper;* not to be confused with
the obsolete home health care
device known by the same
word]: One who oversees something not meant for him; a visual eavesdropper, especially
when used in the context of
reading upside down across
someone's desk. (ANDREW TOBIAS,
writer)

eye•lie *n* [*eye + lie*]: To pretend
not to see someone. "Passing
me on the street, my old college
roommate Skip gave me the
eyelie again." (DON SHARE, *poet*)

eyedropper

F

fa•cho *adj* [*female + macho*]: Applied to a woman; characterized by vainglorious physical daring, compulsive vigor, disregard for pain or discomfort, eagerness to appear as strong and reckless as any male. "She was so facho she skied the steep chutes all day without an avalanche beeper; that night she drank them all under the table; next morning at the campfire, she turned the bacon with her finger." (DAVID QUAMMEN, *writer*)

fac•tion *n* [*fact + fiction*]: Any literary work portraying real characters or events, as a biography, history, or social commentary. "Faction is stranger than fiction." (WITOLD RYBCZYN-SKI, *writer*)

fac•toid *n* [*fact + -oid* suffix suggestive of such words as void, spheroid, and Mongoloid, connoting qualities of emptiness and simulation]: Any fact that has no existence other than that it once appeared in print as a purported fact and has been treated as fact ever since. "It was part of Marilyn Monroe's genius to recognize that not only did the public prefer fac-toids to the real article, but newspaper editors did as well, and public relations people would come to adore them." (NORMAN MAILER, *novelist*)

fac•tu•al•ize *v* [by association with *fictionalize*]: To make into fact or regard as fact. "The minute we factualize our fantasies, we feel that anything is possible in reality. The visionary factualized what she imagined nature to be." (TODD SILER, *artist/ writer*)

fan•dy *adj* [contraction of Fr *fin de siècle* end of the century]: Suffering from late-twentieth-century malaise; jaded, bored, world-weary, yet vaguely troubled by a lack of a future; a posture toward life somewhere between that of Samuel Beckett and that of Sid Vicious. (PAUL TOUGH, *journalist*)

fan•tas•ma•gor•bi•a *n* [*fantasmagoria* + eponymous hero *Mikhail Gorbachev*, president of the Soviet Union, 1985–present]: Whatever the hell the Soviet Union is in the process of becoming these days. "That the capital of the Russian republic might be renamed MacMoscow in the coming years seemed a minor point in the overall fantasmagorbia enveloping the Soviet empire. (BRIAN McCORMICK, *writer*)

far•land *n* [*far + land*]: 1: A country so remote and unimportant as to be of no current interest whatsoever, that is, any country that has not been mentioned for three months straight on any page, including the classifieds, of *The New York Times*. 2: Any country that, having become an INTERVALAND (see below), quickly reverts to its former status of invisibility. Also, **far-lander** *n*: A person so uneventful that nobody ever recalls him or her. "My wife's sister was such a farlander that I didn't even realize she had a sister until one evening a year after we began going out together I sat down on the couch and it was the sister I was sitting on—and not the couch." (ARIEL DORFMAN, *writer*)

fash•i•mite *n* [*fashion + imite* indicative of a group of followers]: A slave to fashion. "Black and white is what all the fashimites are wearing this season." "He's nothing but a fashimite: he was a hippie in the

fantasmagorbia

1960s and a superannuated yuppie in the 1980s." (MICHAEL LOCKWOOD, *philosopher*)

fash•ist *n* [*fashion* + *-ist*]: A person who endeavors to turn people into FASHIMITES. "The trouble with the advertising industry today is that it's dominated by fashists." (MICHAEL LOCKWOOD, *philosopher*)

fa•so•la•ti•do *n* [fr. the last five notes of the musical scale sung by schoolchildren]: An endeavor that was neither very good nor very bad, but at least it's over now. "Philip Roth's last novel was fasolatido." See DOREMI. (BRIAN MCCORMICK, *writer*)

fa•tu•ate *v* [*fatuous* + *infatuated*]: To cause someone, by guile or calculation, to fall in love violently; to create amorous spells that render the victim stupid. "She took great pride in her ability to fatuate men." "Richard's taste in cheap music and meaningless small talk nevertheless fatuated Helen." (CHARLES BAXTER, *writer*)

fa•tu•lous *adj* [*fat* + *you* + *louse*]: 1: Acting complacently stupid or inane about the details of one's diet; used to describe endomorphs obsessed about losing weight. 2: Of or pertaining to, in the immortal words of Dylan Thomas, "fat poets with thin volumes." 3: Used also to describe certain critics who fatten on the oeuvre of dead and hence, mute, poets. "Fatulous is thought to have been coined in a last desperate moment by poet Percy Bysshe Shelley, who had grown exasperated by his friend and fellow Romantic George Gordon (6th baron Byron of Rochdale, called Lord Byron; 1788–1824). Byron, stout, short and limpish with a clubfoot, yearned to fit the stereotype of his black-caped hero Don Juan, reputed to have been rapier-thin—'except where girth was wanted.' 'My dear George,' declaimed Shelley one blustery day on Lake Como, 'if you say one more fatulous word about your interminable diet, or the best shop in Italy for herbal purgatives, I shall certainly scuttle the *Aurora*.' When Byron persisted, Shelley jumped overboard and sank immediately, thin of shank and bony as he was. A still babbling Byron retrieved the body and towed it back to shore, where he personally supervised its immolation—thereby depriving literary scholars of all evidence of the first poet thought to have been literally bored to death." (LLOYD VAN BRUNT, *poet*)

fauxl•tru•ism *n* [fr. Fr *faux* + *altruism*]: A charitable interest in others' welfare fueled by self-interest and the need for recognition. "When the foundation for pothole repair bearing his name increased its annual stipend, Donald's fauxltruism was once again saluted by the mayor's office." (MICHAEL GLOBETTI, *journalist*)

fawn•et•ics *n* [*fawn* + *phonetics*]: Simpering, insincere prose meant to suggest politeness, especially in a letter to someone not well known to the writer. " 'I hope my qualifications are of interest to you, and I thank you very much for your attention to this letter,' Steve wrote, then added, 'I look forward to hearing from you.' Steve wondered: 'What would Orwell have said about this bilious fawnetics?' " (STEVE MESSINA and LYDIA BUECHLER, *editors*)

fax•raff *n* [*fax* + *riffraff*]: 1: Those individuals who have such an infatuation with facsimile technology that they must fax every piece of business they conduct even if there are six months to complete the correspondence. "The pertinent pages sent by faxraff are usually preceded by a hand-scrawled note that reads 'FYI—hard copy to follow Fed Ex.' " Or, "That

company is crawling with faxraff. Tell them our machine is down." 2: Unsolicited fax transmissions sent overnight and found in the morning, i.e., sales fliers, dating services, uninvited manuscripts, and magazine articles people you don't know think you will enjoy. "I didn't see your memo in all the faxraff this morning. Would you mind sending it again?" (TOM BODETT, *radio commentator*)

fe *pron nominative*—**fis** *possessive* —**fim** *objective* [fr. *Fe* the symbol for the chemical element iron, fr. L *ferrum* iron]: The metal, or nonorganic, person in question. "It would be impolite to make assumptions about the sexual preference, if any, of an intelligent, autonomous machine, but downright insulting to refer to one as 'it.' To forestall any mech lib rhetoric about 'carbon chauvinism,' we should adopt an appropriate pronoun in discourse about or with Metallo-Americans. Use of epithets such as 'rustback' should be made a penal offense. It is never too soon to be politically correct." (PAUL BICKART, *chemist*)

feb•rish *adj* [back-formation fr. *February*]: Symptoms of imminent illness accompanied by dry skin, fatigue, and depression. "This year I felt febrish until the end of March." (ELIZABETH SEYDEL MORGAN, *poet*)

fec•tor *n* [back-formation fr. *defector*]: One who flees back to the country from which he has fled; whirlcoat. "Recent fectors include the Taiwanese rock singer who defected to China during the thaw and fectored in the freeze, and the KGB agent who, dining at Au Pied de Cochon with his CIA handler, got up to go to the bathroom and was next seen at a press conference in Moscow. Svetlana Alliluyeva, the daughter of Joseph Stalin, is the current record holder, a trifector." (PAUL BICKART, *chemist*)

fed•po *n*—**fed•po•ex•po** *n* [*federal* + *poetry*]: Poetry written or published with the help of a government grant; beyond a certain threshold, this becomes a fedpoexpo. "There wasn't much art shakin' here in Squalid Corners, but now that the grant came through, we've got a regular fedpoexpo of sonnets and haiku." (ALBERT GOLDBARTH, *writer*)

fe•li•feign *v* [*feline* + *feign*]: The strategy observed in cats as they wait with seeming innocence for you to leave the room in order to leap up onto the forbidden love seat for a nap. By

extension, the cold violation of a trusted relationship that yields nothing but profit for the abuser. "He felifeigned his clients out of $5 million!" (JOYCE CAROL OATES, *writer*)

fer•ro•lunk *v*— [fr. L *ferro* iron + *spelunking*]: To pursue any arduous communal effort of self-discovery made by many educated white-collar males: "To ferrolunk involves sitting or standing in crowded auditoriums for long periods, with sporadic weeping or chanting; includes also private individual meditation (posing nude with bone ornaments and drum, mythic breathing, practicing a wise, faraway look) or informal small-group rites (bear hugs, long-distance chats with former buddies, purchase of camping gear, covert observation of sons)." Also, **ferrolunker** *n* [ibid with interesting shift of derivation, probably from slang *lunk* or *hunk*]: A large, sometimes muscular male, with a maddening urge to manifest sensitivity and sincerity, particularly toward smaller beings; notable for apologetic demeanor, glistening eyes, crushing handshake. (WILL BAKER, *writer*)

fer•ver•sion *n* [*fervent* + *forgive* + *perversion*]: A newly adopted morality on the part of a disgraced public personality or deposed dictator that allows him to regain public office or favor by means of a growing, unrecognized fanaticism of a voting or consuming public. By extension, any extreme act of forgiveness. "Ivan Soveral's protean career began with years of atrocities as the ruler of Guanau, followed by his overthrow, years of seclusion and the embrace of evangelism, and finally, defying the expectations of all but the church, his appointment as the nation's ambassador to the United States." (ROY GARY, *critic*, and TOM SPACCARELLI, *professor*)

fic • to • ry *n* [*fiction* + *victory*]: 1: The successful management of a military campaign by skilled Pentagon PR teams. 2: Any advantage through the substitution of optimistic imagery, media blitz, etc., for unpleasant statistics (i.e., body counts, number of refugees, interest rates, unemployment figures). "Spokespersons scored an easy fictory by quoting the letter from the crippled eight-year-old black girl who supported the President's new taxes." (WILL BAKER, *writer*)

fitch *n* [*fit* + *itch*]: A maddening yet familiar itch. By extension, a person or event that relentlessly irritates. "After more than a decade in office, Mayor Ed Koch was a fitch that most New Yorkers decided they would rather live without." (EDWARD HOAGLAND, *writer*)

flaf • fy *adj*—**flaf • fer** *n* [fr. Fr *faire laugher* or *faux laver* a false wash or *foutu élève* an abortion on horseback]: The quality of expendability raised to an exponential extreme. "Flaffy should be pronounced with maximum disdain, heavy emphasis on the first vowel, and some time spent on it too, almost yawning. A histrionic word, this, unlike 'worthless' and 'jejune,' although it signals what these words say, but without the imputation to the *flaffer* of base motives. The word stigmatizes the pointless product of a hopeless mind or gift, although, especially in Scotland and Canada, it almost seems to imply a quality of gentle befuddlement in the flaffer. Flaffy refers to works or products that cannot be praised for anything, not even by hired hacks out on the cutting edge of hypocrisy. Essentially the word invokes a dead work, one of the curious effects of its application being that no one ever remembers the object of the scorn, even though the scorn was merited. Thus flaffy should be seen as one of the words in our language that not only condemn but efface as well, lately dubbed 'detergent adjectives,' or more 'vulgarly, wipe-words.' Once you have been called flaffy, you are doomed to be thought irrelevant to every human enterprise thereafter. This lexicographer will provide no examples, of either works or people, of course; but the death-dealing sentence often reads: '———'s latest is totally flaffy' or 'Flaff, flaff, flaff.' " Also **flaff** *v*: To execute something as poorly as possible, but without deliberately seeking oblivion for doing so. (PAUL WEST, *writer*)

flaunt • law *n* [*flaunt + scofflaw*]: A person who observes a local ordinance in an ostentatious manner. "A flauntlaw is someone who puts a coin in a parking meter with an unnecessary flourish when a meter maid is in view, or a nighttime dog walker who speaks to his pet at greater length and in a louder tone than normal to indicate to householders that he has a legitimate reason for skulking in the vicinity of their garbage cans, or someone who hurries to place a gum wrapper in the recycling bin." (WILL STANTON, *writer*)

fled • u • ca • tion *n* [*education + flagellation*]: The process by which students are sent to school and made to do repetitive work consisting of endless drills and memorization of irrelevant terminology, dates, and formulas until they succumb and behave. "Little Johnny has been a bit difficult in kindergarten, but he will be fleducated in first grade." (ROGER C. SCHANK, *professor*)

flin • ti • ma • cy *n* [*flinty + intimacy*]: A stern or abrasive affection exhibited by one or both partners, often as a barrier to deeper emotion. "Alexandra silently bemoaned Manfred's flintimacy when she opened his tenth wedding anniversary gift to discover another handy kitchen gadget." (MICHAEL GLOBETTI, *journalist*)

floit *v* [*flaunt + flirt + floozy + exploit*]: To flaunt sexually. "The other guests considered her series of nude grand jetés across the room and into Jack's lap, out-and-out floiting." (LEWIS BURKE FRUMKES, *writer*)

floop *v* [*flop + droop*]: To droop from failure. " 'This never happened with my last girlfriend,' Jenny's date from hell said pointedly as he flooped on the bed.'' (MARGO KAUFMAN, *journalist*)

flount v [*flaunt* + *flout* + a wee bit of *flounce*]: To scorn, mock, or defy in a particularly conspicuous, egregious, or melodramatic manner. '' 'Flount' ends the confusion of 'flaunt' and 'flout' once and for all. 'He flounted the rules of the club by walking up to the bar completely nude.' '' (DANIEL SCHORR, *journalist*)

flu • sion n ⌊*film* + *allusion* + *confusion*⌋: A modern form of malapropism in which the speaker alludes to a film or television show without being familiar with the book or historical event upon which the film or show is based or the time period or area of the world in which it is set. This also includes confusing Hollywood portrayals with historical fact. ''Did you hear Mary's latest flusion? She thinks Hal Holbrook was president sometime between Lincoln and Reagan.'' (RICHARD SELTZER, *writer*)

flus • trate v [*fluster* + *frustrate*]: 1: A state of panicked discombobulation that brings together in one, often hilarious, unity all the confusion born of furious haste with the complete surrender of common sense associated with the intense frustration at the collapsing world around you. ''The rookie quarterback, totally flustrated, scrambling backward in that familiar but still painful to see dance as the defense poured in over his line, finally fired the ball directly into the hands of the popcorn vendor.'' (LESLEY VISSER, *sportscaster*) 2: To produce a state of nervous tension through confrontation with something that does not function; usually denoted by the biting of lips and the making of fists. ''This birdhouse kit has left me so flustrated I could spit nails!'' Also **flustration** n: ''After the cursor had jammed for the nineteenth time, Allison was reduced to a state of utter flustration.'' (TIMOTHY FINDLEY, *novelist*)

foe • tish n —**foe • tish • ize** v [*foetus* + *fetish*]: The fetishized fetus; the symbolic fetus as distinct from the biological one, roughly paralleling the distinction between phallus and penis. ''The foetish is typically iconographic, usually represented as floating in space, or conversely, sensationalistically dismembered. (The fetus, in contrast, might be experienced through internal kicking, through morning sickness, etc.) Unlike the fetus, whose mother may, for example, find basic prenatal care unavailable, the foetish carries tremendous social power as an instrument to control women; the foetish is invoked when pregnant women are jailed for drug use, when they are attacked entering abortion clinics, or when potentially pregnant women are barred from high-paying jobs." "How do I like being pregnant? All I have to do is put a can of beer in my shopping cart, and some crazed foetish protector comes over to yell at me." (ELLEN GRUBER GARVEY, *writer*)

fon•da•noi•a *n* [fr. eponymous hero *Jane Fonda + paranoia*]: Tendency, especially among certain U.S. war veterans, to view actress and calisthenics instructor Jane Fonda as the root cause of all ill fortune. "Sgt. C.'s fondanoia was perhaps best expressed by his remark, 'Where's my screwdriver? I can never find it! Has Jane Fonda been in my toolbox again?' " (TOM DRURY, *writer*)

frab•ble *n* [*fracture* a part broken, a break caused by violence + *rubble* debris + *rubbish* + *rabble* a noisy crowd or mob, especially of the lower orders]: The aesthetic result of an intellectual preference for chaos and violence. "The visual incoherence of the museum's addition had been carefully planned; this frabble was put forth as though our world already made too much sense." (GEORGE THRUSH, *architect*)

Fran•ken•stein fac•tor *n* [*Frankenstein + factor*]: The exaggerated concern about the dangers posed by a new piece of high technology at the neglect of the dangers of far more devastating aspects of low technology. "The Frankenstein factor acknowledges the terror of technology and its inflated influence on popular opinion and accounts for the frenzy of worry about electrodes implanted in the brain and the indifference to third-rate teachers in our schools or the advent of the eight-hour-a-day nursery school." (WILLARD GAYLIN, *M.D.*)

frue *adj*—**fruth** *n* [*true + false*]: Not quite true, not quite false. "Every news report Americans receive from places around the world where we have soldiers stationed, watching, defending, or fighting is so censored and rewritten for reasons of 'national security' that it is safe to assume only that the reports we hear are whitewashed, fitting into an area of news situated somewhere between what is said and what remains silent, an area we

should call frue or the fruth."
(ROBIN M. KOVAT, *journalist*)

frus・tu・late *v* [*frustrate* + *ululate*]: To emit a defeated high-pitched wail, especially by, say, an anxious high-school calculus student who will never, never understand any of it, ever— "Why don't I just kill myself now and get it over with?" "Cheeks bloated in rage, face apoplexy-red, 17-year-old Sharon's homework frustulating was silenced when neighbors hit the walls complaining of the noise." (ELLEN ABRAMS, *writer*)

fug up *v* [fr. Norman Mailer's use of *fug* as a substitute for a well-known Anglo-Saxon obscenity in *The Naked and the Dead*; possibly related to *fug*, the stale air of a crowded room]: To bastardize the English language by inventing euphemisms, especially ones that are never fully accepted by the public and seem pretentious or silly less than one generation later. "Whoever called the Korean War a 'police action' really fugged up." (MARK J. ESTREN, *writer*)

funk・tion・lust *n* [fr. G *Funktion* function + *lust* morbid pleasure in]: The pleasure that a physician or surgeon derives from performing an operation or carrying out a therapeutic act that is more important than the financial reward. "Medical insurance auditors suspected that the hospital was doing unnecessary lab work in order to generate extra income. In fact, the culprit turned out to be a young lab technician with a funktionlust for elaborate quantitative chemical tests on the blood." (FRANCIS D. MOORE, *M.D.*)

fu・si・fix *v* [fr. L *fusus* spindle + *fix*]: To be able to gauge a person's real attitude toward you by considering only the movement in his face; implies ignoring speech. "Ali fusifixed the Hindu judge's face and knew he was doomed to the gallows." (ALEXANDER THEROUX, *writer*)

fus・sion *n* [*fission* + *fusion*]: 1: A simultaneous melting together and breaking apart. 2: In language, the fusing together of two disparate words, and their straining toward separation. "Any city is always in a state of fussion, its underlying infrastructure seeming to unite people who are thrown into conflict from their close proximity to one another." (GEOF HUTH, *writer*)

G

ga • cho *adj* [*gay* + *macho*]: Loud and assertive homosexuals, usually male, and often of Argentine origin. Generally pejorative. "She came in all leathered up with spike heels and a nose ring. What a gacho little bitch." (WILL BAKER, *writer*)

gai • ed *adj* [fr. Gk *Gaia* Mother Earth]: Screwed by Mother Earth. "For the proper effect, the word should be pronounced 'guy-ed.' Its meaning is well known to anyone who has worked closely with the Earth." (DANIEL B. BOTKIN, *environmentalist*)

gal • lup • ism *n* [fr. eponymous hero *George Gallup*, American pollster, 1906–1984]: A political ideology where policy is dictated by the latest opinion polls. "The president was a firm believer in gallupism. He would make his decisions by carefully noting what was popular in today's opinion polls." (DAVID N. SCHRAMM, *physicist*)

ga • lub • cious *adj* [*glorious* + *lub* + *luscious*]: The sensation of the tongue wrapping itself around the first mouthful of a chocolate dessert covered with whipped cream. (KATHARINE HEPBURN, *actress*)

gangst *n* [*gang* + *angst*]: 1: The complex form of dread felt by white liberals on seeing groups of minority youths on a street or subway. The sufferer of gangst experiences purely physical fear as well as intense guilt for that fear, which he sees as shameful and racist. "Hello, Evan, I'm sorry I didn't come to your party. I had an attack of gangst at the 104th Street station, so I just went home and watched Cosby." (JAMES GORMAN, *writer*) 2: An exaggerated fear of or anxiety about violence, particularly urban gang violence. "Gangst gripped the Jeppersons when they learned that Harry's job transfer from Omaha to Manhattan didn't mean Kansas after all." (JOHN CALDERAZZO, *writer*)

gar • page *n* [*garbage* + *paper* + *page*]: The unwanted arrival of paper in one's life by means increasingly more insidious than traditional junk mail. "Had junk mail stayed as it was, the word garpage would never have been necessary. But accompanying the labyrinthine paths blazed by information, garpage now routinely assaults us through every portal to our lives, no matter how small: unsolicited fax transmissions, menus slipped under the front door, leaflets 'disguised' as dollar bills meant to catch our attention in the urban litter, preprogrammed productions by the computer printer advertising its own virtues, the various cards that drift languidly from every magazine, junk mail hidden inside of legitimate mail, and advertising printed on toilet paper in public bathrooms." (DEIDRE MCFADYEN, *journalist*)

gas•light *v* [fr. *Gaslight*, the 1944 George Cukor movie]: To engage in any number of acts or to make statements designed to prove that your spouse is crazy in his or her assumption—which is correct—that you are having an affair. "Gaslight captures the most cruel aspect of marital infidelity, which is not the sexual act, but the lengths to which the unfaithful partner will go in order to protect his or her innocence at the expense of the aggrieved spouse's sanity. When a suspicious wife tells her husband, 'I smell perfume on your collar and it isn't mine,' typically the husband has to gaslight her by snapping, 'Are you paranoid?' or by asserting, 'I don't smell anything. Are you okay? Maybe you should see a doctor.' " (WILLARD GAYLIN, *M.D.*)

gaulle *n* [fr. eponymous hero *Charles de Gaulle*, president of France, 1958–1969]: A French metrical unit measuring the arrogance of a French official or elected officeholder—a quality that, as all the rest of the world knows, is virtually part of the job description in the public life of France. "A self-important customs official might be said to possess 300 *millegaulles;* the mayor of a medium-size commune might check in with 10 *centigaulles;* and the current president of the republic a healthy 8 *decigaulles.* There have only been two officeholders in French history with a rating of 1 *gaulle,* Louis XIV and its namesake, President Charles de Gaulle, although St. Louis gives them both a run for their money." (L. J. DAVIS, *journalist*)

gen *pron nominative;* **ger** *possessive;* **gen** *objective* [abbreviation for *generic person*]: The third-person personal pronoun when referring to people of both sexes; a proposed substitute for the words "he" and "she," "his" and "hers," and "him" and "her." "With the use of 'gen, ges, ger,' which should be properly pronounced 'jen, jes, jerr,' we will no longer have to suffer through sentences such as 'When an architect completes his or her education, he or she will be able to apply his or her skills to problems presented to him or her. . . .' " (JAMES TREFIL, *writer*)

gen•u•lit *n* [*genuine* + *genu* kneel to + *literature*]: Poetry and prose distinguished by acknowledged merit rather than gender, race, or any affiliation of the author. "Though she had been considered primarily a Virginia feminist, her work was beginning to appear in genulit courses in many universities." "Genulit 101–102: a two-semester survey of the best writing of women and men of the world." (ELIZABETH SEYDEL MORGAN, *poet*)

geor•gic *adj & n* [fr. Gk *georgios* farmer]: Being in or practicing agriculture or animal husbandry or both; the farming-herding, preurban stage of culture. "Getting horses led the Plains Indians to regress from georgic to theratic culture." See THERATIC. (L. SPRAGUE DE CAMP, *writer*)

glam•or•ose *n* [*glamour* + *morose*]: Self-pitying reclusiveness often used by the famous to appear more interesting than they actually are. "Greta Garbo and Ernest Hemingway epitomize the glamorose." (CAROLE SEBOROVSKI, *artist*)

glum•si•ness *n* [*glum* + *clumsiness*]: The tendency to drop or break things when one is in a depressed mood. By extension, the tendency to put one's foot in one's mouth when talking to others while in such a mood. "Susan looked from the broken dish to Howard's face, each so perfect a reflection of what her glumsiness had wrought that her depression deepened into thorough despair." (JANE HIRSHFIELD, *poet*)

gland•il•o•quent *adj* [*gland* + *grandiloquent*]: Being unusually articulate and graphic in describing sexual matters; a characteristic developed during the sexual revolution of the 1960s and 1970s when the euphemistic blather of earlier eras —about one's "dancing" ability, etc.—was replaced by strangely earnest discussions of the sex act itself, all, of course, in the name of clinical enlightenment— "Betty, I have always thought a woman should experience multiple orgasm; I realize that few other men embrace this position, but it's something I firmly believe"—but are, in their own paradoxical way, coy forms of

glandiloquent

flirtation. "Frank's glandiloquence was so polished that he could begin a conversation about the capital gains tax and move it seamlessly into a knowledgeable peroration on the creative uses of ben-wah balls." (MARK DOWIE, *journalist*)

goo•ber•mensch *n* [fr *goober* peanut + G *Ubermensch* superman]: One who is not seen as a leader by those whom he wishes to lead. "He thinks he's Charles Darwin, but he is just another goobermensch." (HIROSHI AKASHI, *scientist*)

gran•di•grose *adj* [*grandiose* + *gross*]: Of or pertaining to a person, place, or thing which is at once grand and grossly disgusting. "The Chateau Versailles is exquisitely grandigrose." (CAROLE SEBOROVSKI, *artist*)

green•speak *n* [*green marketing* + *Greenpeace* + *newspeak* from George Orwell's *1984*]: The peculiar proenvironmental language spoken by public relations staffs in oil, plastics, and chemical companies intended to give their industries a pro-Earth spin. "Example of greenspeak include: Cans of aerosolized deodorant boasting 'ozone friendly; no CFCs,' when chlorofluorocarbons have been illegal for thirteen years, and national ads touting Pampers and Luvs diapers as 'compostable,' even though there are only a dozen special facilities in the country to compost them." "Greenspeak pollutes the marketplace the way garbage pollutes the environment." "The term 'green collar' describes the expanding army of those who develop and talk greenspeak, used by New York City Consumer Affairs Commissioner Mark Green when he said, 'To advertise that these products are environmentally benign—and charge up to 15 percent more—is green-collar fraud.' " (MICHAEL ALCAMO, *consumer advocate*)

grin•ace *n* [*grin + grimace*]: A facial expression of an open and turned-up mouth that is reminiscent initially of a frozen grin and a gape; a response, invariably, to a certain limited social predicament in which one party expresses a sentiment utterly contrary to that held by a second party in the belief that the second party will be in complete accord; the second party, embarrassed for the first, and amused to be himself so misjudged, begins to grin, confirming in the unwitting mind of the first party the assumed congruence of sentiment, which perceived complicity freezes the second party in a painful, fixed, open smile; the second party at this point will shake his head slightly, partly to convey his incredulity at the gall of the first

goobermensch

party and partly to attempt to relax his face; which headshaking the first party will mistake for the second's incredulity at how right the first party is in his monstrous sentiment. "A provincial father asks his son, home from college his first Thanksgiving, 'You still dating that hebe?' Before his son can compose his freshman Ciceronian denouncement of anti-Semitism, the father says, 'Well?' The son begins the helpless smile that forms the grinace." "Steve, a young writer, says to Don, an established writer, that Ann, a middle-rung writer who is a favorite of Don's (a fact that should be known to Steve), 'can't write for shit.' In fact, of the three, Steve is the one who can't write for shit. Don, embarrassed for him and amused to be expected to concur with the absurd opinion, begins the incredulous grin that freezes with his mouth open and his head shaking ever so slightly, and Steve, confirmed by this as a sign of accord, reaffirms: 'Am I right or what?'" Invariably, if the grinacing party is capable of speech, the only word he can utter is the name of the offending party: " 'Well, you going with the hebe or what?' 'Dad . . . ?' " " 'Am I right? Ann can't write doodly squat!' 'Steve . . . ?' " (PADGETT POWELL, *novelist*)

grite *v* [*gripe* ɪ *to be right*]. To complain about something, and be proved right later on; the sentiment contained in the phrase, "I told you so" and often accompanied by a self-

grinace

satisfied smirk, and spoken in a rising, whining tone of voice. " 'I told Mike not to ride around in that damned tank! He looked like a squirrel chasing a nut,' the governor's ex-press secretary grited." (DON SHARE, *poet*)

grom • me • try *n* [*grommet* or *eyelet*]: To be staring at a speaker, pretending to listen, but in fact to be more concerned that one is giving the appearance of attentiveness. "Thomas dreaded these literary cocktail parties—the fawning and stroking of egos, the vacuous grommetry that precluded any serious conversation." (SVEN BIRKERTS, *writer*)

grub • ble *v* [*grub* + *grovel*]: To enjoy the largess of one's betters while harboring resentment against them. "Many who grubble in the governor's mansion will not turn a hand to see him reelected." (DANIEL MARK EPSTEIN, *writer*)

guff *n*—**guf • fy** *adj* [*onomatopoetic*]: 1: Vapid, high-flown, or homiletic filler; 2: Those passages commonly including clichés, jargon, and uplifting yet vague generalities that make long speeches out of short ones; 3: Sententious fluff. "The debate in Congress was padded with so much guff that even the reporters began to doze off." (DANIEL J. BOORSTIN, *Librarian of Congress emeritus*)

gup *n* [acronym for *grace under pressure*]: A quality of successful action noted for both bravery and subtlety. "The word gup can be used in the same way as the word 'guts,' with all its implications of boldness and audacity, but with the additional connotation of being aware of nuances and capable of smiling pleasantly while gritting one's teeth invisibly. Those who have gup in great abundance are sometimes known as guppies." (MARGARET ATWOOD, *novelist*)

H

handilingual

hand·i·lin·gual *adj* [*hand* + *lingual*]: Able to speak to others only while touching them with one or both hands. "I'm glad you warned me; I didn't know Bob was handilingual." (FRANK GANNON, *writer*)

hand·some *n* [fr. *handsome adj*, comely, well turned, pleasing and dignified in appearance; fr. ME *handsom*, easy to handle. This new meaning of handsome was inspired by an anecdote recited privately by American humorist Roy Blount, Jr.: A well-known television actress, having come in haste from her dressing room and seated herself, leisurely and spraddle-legged, among friends for a party backstage, looked down to discover she had forgotten her underpants. "Oh goodness," she said, half amused, "everybody can see my pretty."]: The deserving counterpart to the female "pretty"; the male organ of copulation, especially in higher vertebrates. "Hemingway was so gauche as to report, among other things, Scott's handsome was small." Or, "Reginald, age 14, who sat behind Monique in civics, realized, when Ms. Hatchet called on him for his end-of-the-term speech, that his handsome was out of control again.'' ''Handsome might be a replacement for the objectionable term 'penis envy,' as in 'Her handsome envy, according to her male analyst, had frustrated her attempts (thrusts is the word he actually used) at self-actualization,' although the expression 'Handsome is as handsome does' is left open for discussion.'' (JAMES SEAY, *poet*)

ha • thos *n* [*hate* + *happy* +*pathos* + *bathos* + *lachrymose*]: A pleasurable sense of loathing, or a loathing sense of pleasure, aroused by the schmaltzy, falsely sincere, maudlin, self-congratulatory, or politically outspoken performances and/or offstage statements and actions of certain celebrities. ''Hearing the audience applaud when Dr. Joyce Brothers told Merv Griffin that, aside from being a brilliant comedienne, Charo 'is a genius on the classical guitar' filled Ned with hathos.'' (ALEX HEARD, *journalist*)

ha • to • pi • a *n* [*hat* + Gk *topos* a place + -*ia* a suffix connoting ''region'']: 1: The experience of looking for one's hat without realizing it is on one's head. 2: By extension, any ludicrous failure to perceive the obvious. (RON PADGETT, *writer*)

heb • do • ma • ti • tism *n* [fr. Gk *hebdomas* week + -*itis* suffix indicating inflammation + -*ism*]: The disease of the week; a medical problem commanding headlines, soon to be displaced by the next. By extension, any currently hot problem to be forgotten rather than resolved. ''Last decade's hebdomatitism was herpes. Ever read about a cure for it? Do you suppose there's any less of it going around than there was a few years ago? What happened to the children born to parents who crippled their chromosomes with LSD? Does swordfish still contain mercury? Are you eating it again? Did we ever declare victory in the War on Poverty? Can Johnny read yet? Did anyone defuse the Population Bomb?'' (ALBERT SHANKER, *educator*)

hec • ti • city *n* [*hectic* + -*ity*]: A state of disarray, of high and frenetic demand, or of superheated activity. ''The hecticity of his daily routine in the trading room brought on a nervous collapse.'' (WILLIAM F. BUCKLEY, JR., *journalist*)

heir • head *n* [*heir* + *head*]: A political candidate who runs for public office not because of any constituency, record, or intelligence but largely because he can self-finance a campaign due to inherited wealth (or, for an expanded definition, wealth obtained by any source). "One still wonders why George Bush would pick an original heirhead such as J. Danforth Quayle as his running mate over more than qualified prospects such as Bob Dole." (MARK GREEN, *politician*)

hel·lu·cyo·na·tion *n* [*hell + halcyon + hallucination*]: The intoxicated delusion that an earlier era in one's lifetime—the 1940s (if that is when you were young) or the 1960s (if that is when you were young)—seems in retrospect to have been a paradise. "The old yuppie's eyes glazed over in a state of hellucyonation as he recollected the days of Michael Milken, when everyone was rich, any fool could make a profit, and the living was easy." (MICHAEL THOMAS, *writer*)

helm·sou·flage *n* [fr. eponymous hero *Senator Jesse Helms*, conservative U.S. Senator + *camouflage*]: The concealment of a weary old racist campaign behind the facade of legitimate issues. "The Republican National Committee took a poll to see if helmsouflage would succeed in the industrial Midwest." (KATHLEEN KENNEDY TOWNSEND, *politician*)

he·te·ro·duck *n* [*heterosexual + to duck*]: Apologies, preemptive self-criticisms, or other ritualized expressions of multicultural sensitivity offered by a straight, white, middle-class man. "By vetoing the Civil Rights Act of 1990, pursuing a restrictive policy on abortion, and taking no initiative against AIDS, President Bush showed his more mollifying statements to have been mere heteroducks." "After a few opening heteroducks, Professor Kimball regaled the Modern Languages Association convention with his paper, 'Writing Our Wrongs: Male Critics versus the Major Novels of Fannie Hurst.' " (STUART KLAWANS, *journalist*)

hig·gle·dy-pig·gle·dy·o·lo·gy *n* [*higgledy-piggledy + -ology*]: The serious study of muddle and the science of lawless events. "Scientific and journalistic interest in the study of chaos as a scientific discipline has led to the endowment of a new Institute of Higgledy-piggledyology here at the University of Slippery Rock." (JOHN D. BARROW, *cosmologist*)

hind·ser *n* [*hindsight + answer*]: The appropriate response or rejoinder, witty or argumentative, that comes too late; the precise phrase one should have used but did not under stress; the answer in hindsight that would have made sense. "In hindser he was eloquent but was tongue-tied in her presence." (NICHOLAS DELBANCO, *writer*)

hip·po·sy *n* [*hippopotamus + posy*]: A fallacious belief that the inability to draw precise lines of demarcation makes it impossible to distinguish between extremes. "Although it is impossible to distinguish between an animal and a vegetable in some infusoria, where does that leave the hippopotamus and the violet? For all practical purposes they're distinguishable enough. No one but a Barnum or a Bailey would send one a bunch of hippopotamuses as a token of regard." (IAN STEWART, *mathematician*)

His·lam *n* [*his + Islam*]: A religion based upon the teachings of men, any men, believing in one God (Him), and having a body of law derived from high school locker rooms, bars, country clubs, or anywhere else a guy can find it. "Christianity may be a powerful tonic, but Hislam remains the one true faith of the Republican party." (JOHN CALDERAZZO, *writer*)

his·to·ry·whore *n & v* [*history + whore*]: 1: A ruthless opportunist seeking timeless fame; a person with a fortunate proximity to someone or something famous, who unscrupulously schemes to attain unwarranted recognition for himself. 2: A person whose need to be recognized by history is far greater than his or her historic contributions; a person who will unashamedly exaggerate, distort, lie, and perform desperate but empty gestures in order to grab a counterfeit place in the "annals of time." "The 'bile pile' of kiss-and-tell books that came tumbling out of the Reagan White House—possibly the most abject display of orgiastic historywhoring in the two hundred years of the American presidency—only served to exemplify and prove the assertions of Reagan's critics who argued that the ebb and flow of his eight years in the presidency was nothing more than a peristalsis of raunchy and unredeemable self-interest. Even Reagan's own daughter, Maureen, in her monumental work of historywhoring, *First Daughter, First Father: A Memoir*, argues with a straight face that she is responsible for pushing her father into reviving U.S.–U.S.S.R. relations in the 1980s—possibly, but publishing it in a book is a clear case of historywhoring." (MICHAEL HOLMAN, *filmmaker*)

ho·las·tic *adj* [*holistic* + *elastic*]: All-encompassing, even if intellectually deficient. "Certainly the holastic curriculum must include more than a mere introduction to the Patsy Cline oeuvre." (WALLACE E. KNIGHT, *professor*)

hol·den pat·tern *n* [*Holden Caulfield* + *pattern*]: The impulse to compare all first novels, and all novels about adolescence, with J. D. Salinger's *Catcher in the Rye.* "Judging from his review of *A Boy's Tears,* Malcolm is still very much in a holden pattern." (STEVE MESSINA and LYDIA BUECHLER, *editors*)

hol·ly·per·bo·le *n* [*Hollywood* + *hyperbole*]: A dialect spoken by members of the film industry characterized by excessive use of superlatives and lack of any negative terms when addressing anyone capable of advancing the speaker's career. "The young producer spoke such fluent hollyperbole that he was able to tell the screenwriter that he remained a 'major, major fan' while keeping the screenwriter's replacement on hold on another line." (SARAH BIRD, *writer*)

Hol·ly·world *n & adj* [*Hollywood* + *world*]: The world yielded by images in accord with the visions of filmmakers, i.e., the world as seen by Ronald Reagan. "The quest for Hollyworld peace led President Reagan on many missions to Hollyworld capitals such as Bitburg, Germany, and Orlando, Florida." (BENJAMIN BARBER, *professor*)

ho·lo·man *n* [*hologram,* and perhaps influenced by T. S. Eliot]: An apparently real person, but without substance. "Examples of holomen abound: Max Headroom, Bob Forehead, Dan Quayle." (PAUL BICKART, *chemist*)

hom·in·i·lu·nacy *n* [fr. L *homo, hominis* man + L *luna* moon]: The fallacy of comparing difficult social tasks with difficult technological ones. "The phrase, 'Any country that can put a man on the moon surely ought to be able to . . .' begins many complaints about the urgent unsolved problems of life in America. The next sentence usually suggests that a few Stealth bombers could pay for it. But nobody can agree on what to do to achieve the desired good." (PAUL BICKART, *chemist*)

hope·fol·ly *n* [fr. eponymous hero *Bob Hope* + *folly*]: The practice of repeating in a louder voice a gag line that didn't get a laugh the first time. "Repeating a line that did get a laugh is the mark of an amateur. Repeating a line that got no laugh is the hopefolly of a person living in a world all his own and happy there." (WILL STANTON, writer)

hor•ri•cious adj [horrible + delicious]: An object or cultural artifact characterized by such ugliness or bad taste as to be entertaining or delectable for its excesses. "The movie last night threw in every melodramatic device invented since Theda Bara. It was so shameless, it was horricious." (EVA HOFFMAN, writer)

hor•ro•ne•ous adj [horror + erroneous]: Simultaneously shocking and wrong; applicable to negative critiques of one's own work as well as to speeches made by politicians trying to excuse their own illegal or immoral behavior. "No review, however horroneous, can keep me from starting to write volume two of my trilogy." Or: "The senator's testimony was so horroneous that it was the lead story on all the evening news broadcasts." (JANE AND MICHAEL STERN, writers)

hos•pi•ti•li•ty n [hospitality + hostility]: Sadistic entertaining; the inviting of guests with the intention, whether expressed or unconscious, of making them miserable. Crude public manifestations include the celebrity roast and the old Morton Downey, Jr., Show. More sophisticated and more private versions exist. Among the most subtle is that variation on competitive gourmet cooking in which the host makes it clear that he or she has been put to enormous and exhausting trouble to entertain people who are perhaps insufficiently appreciative of the effort involved; the crowning touch is provided by the food (served as unbearably late as possible, short of actual starvation) being truly awful. (ALBERT SHANKER, educator)

hous•in v [fr. house]: To engage in a contemporary form of urban pastime in which one or more people entertain themselves inside an apartment building sometimes for days at a time; the secular equivalent of monastic life. "Housin can be applied to days-long drugfests, but can also describe a more cheerful kind of technological slumber party, at which a host invites friends to stay for days and live among VCRs, computer games, cable programming, and other technodelights." (BAJON KAHLIL SIRON-EL, *lyricist*)

hu•me•di•a•tion *n* [*humiliation* + *media*]: A sudden, dreary, and quickly passing sense of ignorance brought on by the discovery that some quality piece of information—something important such as the overturning of *Roe v. Wade*, or something relevant such as a new essay declaring the End of Economics, or something gossipy and delicious such as Madonna punching Prince in the face at a club—has found outlets in any number of media organs without encountering your attention. "Despite reading two morning papers, monitoring C-Span and CNN during the day, listening to National Public Radio over coffee, watching the news after Willard Scott's spasm, and tuning in to the morning *Newsbreak*, Melvin was taken aback when he arrived at his office and learned that the United States had declared war on Tahiti." (JACK HITT, *journalist*)

hy•per•bite *n* [*hyperbole* + *sound bite*]: An exaggerated statement conveniently condensed for purposes of broadcasting. "The political neophyte must master the hyperbite." (DONALD RITCHIE, *historian*)

hy•per•bo•lie *n* [*hyperbole* + *lie*]: The art of modern American politicians to make a statement couched in cloying sincerity and righteous conviction that has no basis in fact but nonetheless is taken as gospel by the majority of Americans. "All Reagan had to do was use his skills of hyperbolie to say that Ollie North was a true American hero and most everybody believed him, even though common sense made it clear North was a criminal." "Bush really poured on the hyperbolie when he stood before the American people and said that we were not fighting Iraq to protect oil interests but were there to stop aggression. If that was our policy, I wondered where we'd been when there was aggression in China, South Africa, Ethiopia, Afghanistan, Cambodia . . ." (DAN LORBER, *book dealer*)

hy•po•crat *n* [*hypocrisy* + *autocrat*]: One in a position of authority who, by attempting to impose unrealistically high standards of conduct, forces people (often including the person doing the imposing) to become hypocrites. "These new laws against insider dealing are the work of hypocrats." (MICHAEL LOCKWOOD, *philosopher*)

I

i•a•coc•tion *n* [fr. eponymous hero *Lee Iacocca* of the
Chrysler Corporation]: An ar-
rangement by which, in the
name of free enterprise and private capitalism, a corporation is
sustained by a combination of
massive government loans,
arrogance, hype, and the
tolerance of competing companies. (EUGENE J. MCCARTHY,
politician)

ick•y•lex *n* [*icthyology* a
branch of zoology dealing with
fish + *lexis;* literally, "fishy language"]: A series of rhetorical
devices, stock phrases, and syn-
tactic structures that reveal to
trained observers the presence
of unsavory or suspect inten-
tions. "Like officialese, ickylex
features abstract nouns, the passive voice, and numbing repetition, but makes greater use of
emotive terms ('share,' 'concern,' 'deeply committed') as
well as emphatic fragments ('absolutely!') or specialized jargon
('point in time,' 'responsibles,'
'advice of counsel'). Many documents, such as environmental
impact reports, grand jury tran-
scripts, and the *Congressional
Record,* are written almost entirely in ickylex." (WILL BAKER,
writer)

i•con•o•clysm *n* [*iconoclasm* +
cataclysm]: A cataclysmic destruction of idols, a monstrous
act of iconoclasm. "Wallace Ste-
vens was describing an iconoclysm when he wrote the line,
'The death of Satan was a huge
tragedy for the imagination.' "
(RONALD SUKENICK, *novelist*)

i•di•o•lex•i•con *n* [*idio-* +
lexicon]: A dictionary of a single
person's language; a dictionary
of the words a single person invented. "An idiolexicon of
James Joyce's neologisms would
be a large reference work and
useful for neophytes to *Finnegans Wake.*" (GEOF HUTH, *writer*)

i•di•o•syn•tac•tics *n* [*idio-*
+ *syntactics*]: An individual's personal syntax, especially if it is
somehow different from the
norm. "The child's idiosyntacty,
centered as it was on the repetition of words, drove his father
to distraction." (GEOF HUTH,
writer)

i•di•o•wise *n* [*idiot* + *-wise*]:
Media personalities who use

nonexistent adverbs by adding -wise to nouns; usually sports broadcasters, weathermen, weatherwomen, and news presenters who mistakenly believe they are journalists. " 'Temperaturewise and atmosphericwise, East Nutley is now enjoying weather that is perfect footballwise,' said Channel 5's idiowise." (WALTER LAFEBER, *historian*)

ig•no•ra•mo•rus *n* [*ignoramus* + *amorous*]: 1: A person habitually inclined to love things of which he or she has no knowledge. 2: A person in love with being ignorant. 3: A person who is ignorant of the appropriate ways of showing love. "On their first date, Greg and Sheila (an art historian) went to the museum where Greg rushed through all the exhibits, stopping every once in a while to exclaim proudly, 'I don't know anything about art, but I sure know what I like!' Once outside, he stopped at a souvenir shop, bought a painting of the city's skyline on blue velvet, and gave it to Sheila as a present, all the while professing his profound love for her. 'What an ignoramorus! I'll never go out with him again,' Sheila thought, holding the velvet painting gingerly between her thumb and

forefinger." (MAYA SONENBERG, *writer*)

ig•no•rant *adj* [*ignorant* meaning lacking in knowledge]: 1: Pertaining to a work of art or any other form of human expression that appears amateurish, tacky, awkward, and/or wrong, but works brilliantly in spite of itself. 2: A way of describing a work of art so inappropriately good it is genius; a work of art so stupidly brilliant it is startling; art cleverly awkward, "so off it's on"; an oxymoron. "Examples of ignorant art are Jean Michel Basquiat's paintings and Jeff Koons's sculptures; ignorant films are David Lynch's *Eraserhead*, Rob Reiner's *Spinal Tap*, and Elio Petri's *The 10th Victim*; ignorant literary works are Stanislaw Lem's *A Futurological Congress* and any of Dr. Seuss's books; ignorant musical compositions are any of Nino Rota's scores for Federico Fellini films." (MICHAEL HOLMAN, *filmmaker*)

il•lit•er•a•ture *n* [fr. L *il-* not + *literature*, after *illiteracy, illiterate*]: Stories, proverbs, songs, and conversation—and all the other wisdom carried in the language but not written. Imperfect synonyms include the more restrictive *storytelling* and *folklore*, the cumbersome and pompous *oral literature* or its strained contraction *orature*. "Illiterature is to literature as jazz is to written music, or as Mozart's improvisations may have been to his written scores, and a language is clinically dead when its illiterature leaves it, though a literate tradition may sustain the semblance of life for many centuries." (ROBERT BRINGHURST, *poet*)

im • mo • ra *n, pl* **immorae** or **immoras,** whichever you classicists deem is proper [back-formation fr. *immoral*]: Immoral behavior; those acts deemed beyond the pale; the antonym to virtue, but lacking any of the criminal connotations of the word "vice" and any of the religious connotations of the word "sin." "In these secular times, one has to wonder just what would be the Seven Deadly Immorae and to contemplate the immorae of our time, the immorae of adolescence and the ubiquitous immorae of Western civilization." (WILLARD GAYLIN, *M.D.*)

im • mor • tat • tle *n* —**im • mor • tat • lize** *v* [*immortal* + *tattle*]: Posthumous gossip; the evil that men do lives after them, in the form of immortattle. "James Boswell's *Life of Samuel Johnson* was an inspired work of immortattle, one that

immortatlized its author as much as the peculiar lexicographer, a harmless drudge." (STEVEN G. KELLMAN, *professor*)

im • prave • ment *n* [*improve* + *deprave*]: The corruption of a feature meant to improve into something worthless, even harmful. "The invention of the flintlock rifle was a serious impravement in the history of weaponry. It was only after many calibrations that the armament could be kept from disfiguring the face of its user." See DEPROVEMENT. (MOLLY IVINS, *journalist*)

in • ce • ly *adv* [transposition of the letters of *nicely* to suggest *inchly*]: Perfectly, nicely, to the smallest unit of measurement. "The child played with the marbles quietly, incely lining up all the red ones in declining order of size." (GEOF HUTH, *writer*)

in • cerpt *n* [opposite of *excerpt*]: A passage or section placed within another document, transcript, etc.; a passage surreptitiously added to a document to change the document's meaning to later researchers. "Hauser maintained that Shamela should not have been incerpted into the corpus of Fielding's work." (GEOF HUTH, *writer*)

in • curse *v* [back-formation fr. *incursion*, as used by the Nixon administration to describe the invasion of Cambodia]: An incursion is more of a happening, an existential act, carrying no responsibility; without the verb, to incurse, responsibility is not fixed nor is there a way out, as there is in the case of an invasion. (EUGENE J. MCCARTHY, *politician*)

in • dig • ni • tary *n* [*indignity + dignitary*]: A high official treated with the respect ordinarily accorded a lower one. Indignitaries include the ambassadors who got the second-best seats on opening night at the Opéra during the French Revolution Bicentennial celebration, the defunct heads of state who didn't even get Dan Quayle at their funerals, or the U.S. Cabinet member who was addressed as "Mr. Mayor" by the then president. (ALBERT SHANKER, *educator*)

in • fa • tal • ity *n* [*fatality + infidelity*]: In the face of sexual temptation, the conviction that no ethical concern or fear of consequences can arrest it. "Wife, children, and reputation barely flickered at the edge of his consciousness as he gazed at her in a rising flood of infatality." (HARRY MATHEWS, *writer*)

in • fla • tu • late *v*
—in • fla • tu • lant *adj* [fr. L *inflatus* inflate + *art* + L *flatus* blowing, snorting]: To call nonart art in an attempt to elevate its status. "She inflatulated her perfumery by naming it 'The Aromatic Arts.' " Also, an exclamation: "Inflatulations!" Also a noun: "Among inflatulants, it is an expression of pleasure in another's good fortune." (DAVID SWANGER, *poet*)

in • ter • face • lift *n* [*interface + face-lift*]: Attendance at a seminar on interpersonal communication and human interaction. "Jack, you've gotten so involved in this software project that I don't think you've said hello to anyone in months. I'd say it's time you had an interfacelift." (RICHARD SELTZER, *writer*)

in • tern • i • fy *v* [*intern + -fy*]: To use prestige to elicit free or severely underpaid labor. "The producers at CBS's *60 Minutes* often internify ambitious young newspaper reporters, who wind up doing weeks of free legwork." (RICHARD ZACKS, *writer*)

in • ter • va • land *n* [*interval + land*]: A country that suddenly becomes worthy of passionate, albeit parenthetical, interest and even intervention, charitable or aggressive, on the part of a powerful country or person. " 'I'm sorry, honey. I'll be late for dinner again tonight. We've got another catastrophe in—another intervaland,' a quotation attributed to Dan Rather, who had called his wife after hearing that a devastating earthquake had killed one hundred thousand inhabitants of a country he had never mentioned once on the *CBS Evening News.*" See FARLAND. (ARIEL DORFMAN, *writer*)

in • to • lyte *n* [*interest + acolyte*]: A person who has a seemingly religious interest in things that almost everyone else considers furniture; first used in association with rock music but then transferred to unrelated objects. "He is a videodisc intolyte." "I am an intolyte about Tofutti." (EDWIN SCHLOSSBERG, *artist*)

in • tri • cate *v* [*interest + implicate*]: To interest, intrigue, involve, and thus to implicate; to draw another person into a situation to a point at which he or she is inextricably enmeshed. "To intricate is to enlist a skeptical recruit in a good cause, although Machiavelli might have found quite a different employ-

ment for it." (ELLIOT RICHARDSON, *lawyer*)

ip • so • nym *n* [fr. L *ipso* thing in itself + *nym;* a companion to *eponym,* meaning one for whom something is named, as in Kafkaesque or Elizabethan]: A name that describes or characterizes the person so named. "William Gass, a word-drunk literary theoretician whose detractors claim that he's full of hot air, could hardly possess a more appropriate ipsonym." "How fortunate we are to have a new novel by the ipsonymous Francine Prose." (JAMES ATLAS, *editor*)

ir • re • spond *v* [*irresponsible + respond*]: To respond as one must; to respond in an unexpected or even antisocial manner; in any case, to disappoint the hoped-for reply. "We try to elicit from the living the response we want because ours is a society devoted to that effort: a consumeristic, ad-prompting system of cheats and designs. The irresponse is not to our expectation and as a result we are left grieved, fretful, short of cash. Irresponding foils the patterns, designs, outlines, and blueprints that we seek to live by and are destroyed by our refusal." (GEORGE A. SCARBOROUGH, *writer*)

J

journalize

jane•fool•er•y *n* [by association with *tomfoolery*]: Ridiculous behavior or rhetoric in a feminist cause; *jennyrot*. "Although there seems to be only one authenticated public bra-burning on record, the event was branded on the national consciousness as the archetypal example of this noun." (PAUL BICKART, *chemist*)

jet•back *n* [*jet* + *wetback*]: A college-educated illegal immigrant to the United States. "She's dating a jetback. He's marrying her for a green card and a loft in SoHo." (EMILY PRAGER, *novelist*)

jizz *n* [*gestalt* + military slang *jizz,* meaning "general impression and shape"]: The sum of a person or object's physical properties; one's subtle but distinctive body structure and language, which separates one from others, often detectable from some distance away. "Jizz constitutes the collective characteristics by which a spouse can pick you out of a crowded room." "The hawk flashed low over the marsh, and as it hurtled closer, she could see that it had the bullet-sleek jizz of a falcon." (CHARLES HOOD, *poet*)

joe•bob *v* [fr. arch nickname common in the American South]: To use one's nickname as an official name for political advantage. "Jimmy (James Earl) Carter, Dan (J. Danforth) Quayle, Pete (Pierre S.) du Pont (IV), and Dick (Richard M.) Cheney all joebobbed their names to pass as just plain folks, as young people of unfashionable ethnicities bobbed their noses to pass as just plain Americans. George Herbert (Walker) Bush uses a modified joebob, eliminating one name. (PAUL BICKART, *chemist*)

jour•nal•ize *v* [*journal + ize*]: 1: To accidentally or deliberately misrepresent an argument or person; to miss the point of something. 2: To write what you always intended before you came into contact with the facts. "Did they tell the truth about you? No. I was journalized." (DAVID HARE, *playwright*)

K

keat *v* [*kite* + *cheat* + back-formation fr. eponymous hero *Charles Keating*, late-20th-century S&L robber baron]: To swindle, usually on an astronomical scale, in business transactions. "His political connections made it possible to obtain loans under false pretenses and to thereby keat the public." "He was such a small-time operator, it was impossible to accuse him of keating." (GLADYS SWAN, *novelist*)

kink•et *n* —**kink•ette** *n* [*kinky* + -et, diminutive, and applied to men; + -ette, diminutive, and applied to women]: A person who indulges in kinky behaviour and attitudes. "Look, I want to introduce you to this glorious woman who plays the harp, makes apple brown Betty, and is definitely no kinkette." Or, "I hear her years in China turned the Duchess of Windsor into a kinkette and made her attractive to the duke." (BARBARA PROBST SOLOMON, *writer*)

kin•ni•tus *n* [*kin* + *tinnitus*]: The internalized voices of relatives; that inescapable ancestral

keat

drone of commentary and judgment. "Joan fought in her head with her mother whenever she worked on her novel, but when she cooked, the kinnitus subsided to a buzz of pleasure and approval." (ELLEN GRUBER GARVEY, *writer*)

kin•tin•nab•u•la•tion *n* [*kin* + *tintinnabulation* a ringing of bells]: The sound of massed relatives, sometimes psychically painful. "Aunt Dora's persistent refrain, 'Where is it you said you're working?' pierced through the dining room kintinnabulation at Thanksgiving." (ELLEN GRUBER GARVEY, *writer*)

kiss•in•bull *n & v* [fr. eponymous hero *Henry Kissinger* + *bullshit*]: Rambling and empty statement or presentation by a ponderous so-called expert who is totally devoid of either feeling or substance. " 'These changes in the Soviet Union indicate that we are entering a difficult and potentially dangerous transition period in which several variables could ultimately affect the final outcome,' said the kissinbulling Kremlinologist on *Nightline*, and kissinbulling a bit more, added, 'naturally this

presents serious challenges for the United States which can only be met by vigilance and an enhanced defensive posture.' " "I kissinbulled my way through that essay exam and the teacher never noticed and gave me a B!" (HAROLD J. GOLDBERG, *historian*)

klutz fac•tor *n* [*klutz* + *factor*]: The degree to which a new technology will be misused, mistakenly used, or abused because the backers of said technology measured its efficacy by how well trained professionals were able to make use of the new tool rather than asking average human beings prone to klutziness to try to make it work. "The klutz factor accounts for all the bad prose posing as writing simply because it has been vomited into a word processor, and all the mangled messages on an answering machine." (WILLARD GAYLIN, *M.D.*)

kool•ish *adj* [*cool* + *foolish*]: Characteristic of someone who desperately needs to be cool, often to the point of self-parody. "David Byrne is a very koolish fellow." (BRIAN MCCORMICK, *writer*)

L

lab•lib *n* [*labor* + *ad lib* + *liberal*]: A knee-jerk prolabor liberal whose knowledge and conclusions with respect to important (and not so important) political events and personages are arrived at without recourse to facts and profound thought. " 'Of course Fidel Castro had to throw all those people into prison. They were traitors to the revolution,' said the lablib whose knowledge of events in Cuba had been picked up from other lablibs." (WILLIAM HERRICK, *novelist*)

la•chry•ma•po•ta•mi *n* [fr. L *lacrima* tear + Gk *potamos* stream]: Rivers created through excessive crying. "The most famous lachrymapotami are found in the opening chapters of Lewis Carroll's *Alice in Wonderland*. 'As she said these words her foot slipped, and in another moment, splash! she was up to her chin in salt water. Her first idea was that she had somehow fallen into the sea, "and in that case I can go back by railway," she said to herself. (Alice had been to the seaside once in her life, and had come to the general conclusion, that wherever you go to on the English coast you find a number of bathing machines in the sea, some children digging in the sand with wooden spades, then a row of lodging houses, and behind them a railway station.) However, she soon made out that she was in the pool of tears which she had wept when she was nine feet high. "I wish I hadn't cried so much!" said Alice, as she swam about, trying to find her way out. "I shall be punished for it now, I suppose, by being drowned in my own tears! That will be a queer thing, to be sure! However, everything is queer to-day." ' " (LOUIS PHILLIPS, *writer*)

lack•ti•tude *n & v* [*lack* + *attitude*]: That blankness, ennui, or glazed detachment lately seen to overtake millions of North American persons, especially on the job, especially in work viewed as demeaning, unworthy, boring, trivial; that is, most American work, especially that requiring the donning of unflattering and brightly colored uniforms and unisex paper hats. Also, a verb: To engage in the action via which said malais is visited upon clients/customers though they are often fellow sufferers. "The word lacktitude can be used in a variety of ways, such as the following: 'I got lacktituded crosseyed just now at City Hall'. More generally the widespread dazedness evinced by 'alienated labor' (Karl Marx, 1818–1883) in a declining empire where meritorious individual effort comes to seem a compromise of personal dignity, and when courtesy finally appears futile, weak, even ludicrous. Most often found in wealthy nations whose underclass's minimum wage still hovers below three dollars per hour (that is take-home pay for family support—twenty-three dollars per diem—before taxes). Early usage in popular journalism include *The Plain Dealer* (Cleveland) headline: 'Ohio Lacktitude Cited, "Seek Industry," Mayor Urges.' Or, *Parenthood* magazine, article, September issue: 'Lactation and Lacktitude: Even in Our Apathetic Age, the Breast-Feeding Debate Continues.' Or, *The New York Review of Books,* four-part Janet Malcolm series, August-November issues: 'Rilke, Lacktitudinal Crosscurrents in the Psychoanalytical Model, and the Recent Random House Shake-up.' Or, John Cheever's last, posthumously discovered story (rejected by *The New*

Yorker), 'Woodsmoke, Rectitude, Lacktitude and the Yelvertons' Dacquiris.' Or, the widely popular Rod Stewart recording hit, 'Full Arms but Them Lacktitude Eyes.' In some parts of the country, a variant has been heard in fast food restaurants, **Maclacktitude,** as in, 'The staff's all out smoking in the parking lot but there's still so much Maclacktitude in here, you could cut it with one of those plastic knives, if they'd left any out.' " (ALLAN GURGANUS, *novelist*)

lapsed • a • the • ist *n* [*lapsed* + *atheist*]: Any person, usually over the age of forty, who for most of his or her life has apparently been irreligious, but who then declares a belief in a God, usually quite suddenly. "One man's born-again Christian is another man's lapsedatheist." (HENRY S. F. COOPER, *writer*)

lard • ist *n* [*lard* + *artist*]: Any artist whose ego and wallet have been fattened to a degree disproportionate to his or her talent. "Julian Schnabel is a great lardist." (BRIAN McCORMICK, *writer*)

laud • ar • rass • ment *n* [*laud* + *embarrassment*]: Embarrassment stemming from excessive praise—either when the applause goes on too long, or, especially, when one knows the applause to be undeserved. "Was Ivan Boesky laudarrassed by his deification as a financial wizard when he knew his 'brilliance' stemmed largely from inside information and felonies?" (ANDREW TOBIAS, *writer*)

la•va *v* [fr. L *lavare* to wash, emphasizing the Latin sense of volcanic implications]: In reference to a city, a region, or a sport, suggestive of a sentiment, "Not only do I wash my hands of this place, I heap upon it great rivers and mounds of smoldering distaste." "On bumper stickers it is depicted as a jagged pattern of five orange streams resembling a hand, e.g. 'I (Lava) Racquetball,' or 'I (Lava) Anaheim.' The word does not always imply outright rejection, since flowing lava is at once fearful and wondrous, signifying both destruction and renewal. Thus the secret desire to bury a place or a pastime or an organization—'I (Lava) The NFL'—is joined with the idea that almost everyone deserves another chance. Use of this term can connote a muted and perhaps begrudging affection, suggesting that if there were a way for certain demeaning or disagreeable features to be re-moved, you would support such a cleansing one hundred percent." (JAMES D. HOUSTON, *writer*)

law•shit *n* [*law* + *shit*]: The author of expensive incomprehensible contracts written for the sole amusement of other lawshits. "Lawshits are often in the company of managers." (LOU REED, *musician*)

len•ti•di•gi•ta•tion *n* [fr. L *lentus* slow + *digitus* finger, and by association with *prestidigitation*]: An excruciatingly slow display of manual nondexterity, especially as practiced by ticket sellers, toll takers, and bank tellers. "The toll taker's lentidigitation caused a two-mile backup at the bridge, plus three accidents involving cars desperately trying to switch to other lanes at the toll plaza." See LOURDEMAIN. (MARK J. ESTREN, *writer*)

le•pi•do•pho•bia *n* [*lepidoptera* + *phobia*]: Morbid fear of butterflies, a novel affliction currently confined solely to meteorologists. "The plague lepidophobia can be traced to a quotation attributed to Edward Lorenz: 'The flapping of a butterfly's wings in Japan can cause a hurricane in Brazil a month later.' " (IAN STEWART, *mathematician*)

lessism

less • ism *n* [*less* + *-ism*]: The philosophy whereby one reconciles oneself with diminishing expectations of material wealth. "Now that I'm into lessism I don't care anymore about making a killing or playing big shot —I'd rather just find happiness and open up a little roadside cafe in Idaho." (DOUGLAS COUPLAND, *writer*)

le • thar • gist *n* [*lethargy* + *activist*]: One who is consciously, purposefully, and decidedly inactive in community affairs; one who endeavors to diffuse the activism of others. "A good lethargist has really only one ambition —to thwart political zealots at every turn." (GEORGE THRUSH, *architect*)

li • ber • nu • tri • phile *n* [fr. L *liber* free + L *nutrire* to feed + Gk *philos* loving]: One who disagrees with conservative economist Milton Friedman's assertion, "there's no free lunch"; e.g. liberal politicians who favor national health care and extended social spending, but who tactfully avoid the question of financing. "Democratic libernutriphiles resolved at their national convention to uphold the party's proud tradition of encouraging voters to expect gratuitous benefits from the government." (LOUIS LASAGNA, *dean*)

li•ber•teen•a•ger *n* [*libertine* + *teenager*]: A licentious adolescent bereft of both superego and taste. "2 Live Crew's liberteenager lyrics were as enticing to youth under twenty as they were offensive to people over forty." (BENJAMIN BARBER, *professor*)

li•te•rai *n* [fr. L *litera* letter(s) + Yid *chazzerai* pigmeat, unkosher, vulg., edible trash, belly burners, empty calories, stuff that will ruin your supper]: Word games, intellectual Tootsie Rolls, lists of neologisms. See CHAZZERATI. (DANIEL PINKWATER, *writer*)

loch•sam *adj & n* [portmanteau word fr. *flotsam* + *jetsam* + *flock* + *loch* Scottish lake]: 1: Of or pertaining to that quality in a natural scene in which birds are flying gently over a body of water, usually but not always a lake, that brings from the viewer, however hardened, a sense of "all's right with the world" this one second, often followed by a need to join an environmental group to protect such untrammeled wilderness from the noxious fouling by invisible pollutants and the encroachment of greedy developers. 2: An urban landscape that brings on a feeling of satiety and altruism is as fair a candidate for the description as the rural scene. 3: The feeling evoked by such a landscape; use of the word is related to the way in which "cross," meaning angry, came to signify the feeling of frustration one undergoes when one is crossed, stopped in one's tracks, thwarted in straightforward motion ahead. "After our visit to Dutchess County, where we picked apples in the warm, crisp October sun, the sky blue, and the leaves providing the music of endings and dry things that will return again soft green, we came home lochsam, lit our first fire of the season, drank warm cider, and fell into a deep sleep in each other's arms." Also used both more pointedly and as frequently as the current youth culture's "awesome." One says of any concert, holiday, outing, meal with friends, movie one has enjoyed thoroughly and felt both humbled and silenced by: "It was lochsam." (ELIZABETH ANNE SOCOLOW, *poet*)

log•i•cate *v* [*logic* + *-ate* as in elevate or extricate]: To elevate and refine a primal feeling or emotion into a more logical form of consciousness. "We logicate pain and exultation, building spider webs of law." (DAVID THORNBURGH, *musician*)

lo•go•bumf *n* [fr. Gk *logos* word + *bumf* bum fodder, British for excess paper]: Undesirable electronically generated messages of any kind, including but not limited to junk fax, prerecorded telephone solicitations, and electronic or paper junk mail; all varieties have roughly the same intent and suffer the same fate after causing varying degrees of annoyance. "Clean up the logobumf around the fax machine, will you?" "This must be important: (insert name of public relations firm here) has been bombarding us with logobumf for three days already." (PAUL WALLICH, *journalist*)

lo•lo•da•ci•ty *n* [*low, low, low, way low* + *perspicacity*]: Campaign strategy in which politicians hit far, far, far, very far below the belt. "His remarkable feats of lolodacity would have surprised even Nicolo Machiavelli, his mentor." "After one act of lolodacity, Richard Nixon is reputed to have said, 'It is a very, very, very low thing I have done. . . .'" (LEWIS BURKE FRUMKES, *writer*)

long•age *n* [*long* + *age*]: An excessive amount; antonym to shortage. "If a community requires 100 units of energy to live for one year (at a specified standard of living), but is able to secure only 99, it is automatically said that 'there is a shortage of energy.' Instead of speaking of a shortage of supply we could just as truly say that there is a longage of demand. Though every shortage of supply is equally a longage of demand, commercial agents always focus on shortages. Curing shortages produces profits. Manufacturers, transporters, and merchandisers all stand to gain by increasing supplies. Longages are another story. If, in our minds, we translate a shortage of energy into a longage of people—or a longage of demand per person—we then discover that it is not easy to find competent enterprising agents who stand to gain by reducing a longage. For many centuries philosophers, clergymen, and idealists of many sorts have harangued humanity about the importance of reducing demands, curbing extravagance, and living a simpler life; but no Fortune 500 business has ever been built on reducing demand. So why mention longage at all if there is no profit in it? When we come to population matters there are good reasons for at least considering the possibility of reducing demand. When population growth is involved we face this paradoxical truth: You can't cure a shortage by increasing the supply. Given the exponential nature of population growth, once the repressive effect of a felt shortage is removed, the multiplication of demanders soon nullifies any increase in supply. The increased supply is converted to a larger population. At that point the uncomfortable feeling of a shortage is reestablished, but this time at a higher level of population." (GARRETT HARDIN, *ecologist*)

lour•de•main *n* [Fr *lourd* heavy + *de* of + *main* hand]: Heavy-handedness as a form of concealment and trickery. "The toll taker's lourdemain was so egregious that I floored the accelerator to get away from the toll booth as quickly as possible after he finally changed my $20 bill. It was only after I had gone a half mile that I realized that he had shortchanged me $10." See LENTIDIGITATION. (MARK J. ESTREN, *writer*)

love•dice *v & n* [*love + dice*]: To gamble that one can, indeed, be in love with two people at once. "Boris Pasternak understood the concept of lovedice when he wrote (almost), 'And while the young man shuddered and helplessly dabbed his eyes and cheeks with a handkerchief, and crumpled and uncrumpled it, shaking his head and beating the air with his fists, like someone giggling, like someone who had choked and was surprised

lovomaniac

because, God forgive him, he was still whole and the experience of lovedicing had not shattered him.' '' (DON SHARE, *poet*)

lov•o•man•i•ac *n* —**lov•o•man•i•a•cal** *adj* [*love* + *maniac*]: A person who can attain ultimate love only through mass adulation and for whom one-on-one relationships provide no emotional or sexual gratification; one who knows that the ultimate orgasm comes from the love of the masses, i.e., 100,000 people giving a standing ovation. "Despite his devotion to Priscilla, Elvis displayed severe lovomaniacal tendencies." (RONA BARRETT, *journalist*)

M

mac•gy•ver *n* [fr. TV character *MacGyver*, known for his resourcefulness]: To make repairs in an emergency situation from whatever materials are at hand; to cobble together. "When the windshield wipers decided to fall apart during a sleet storm in the middle of a long road trip, he macgyvered them with a piece of wire from a spiral notebook and a straw left over from a fast-food trek." (DIANE CRISPELL, *editor*)

Mach•i•a•pub•li•can *adj* [fr. *Machiavelli* or *Machiavellian* + *Republican*]: A right-wing politician who cynically takes advantage of a perceived conservative shift in the body politic to institute trials of Americanism for no greater good but headlines and dubious personal glory. "Before the glare of cameras and the gullibility of reporters, the eager young Machiapublican senators from California and Wisconsin took turns shouting down the witness's futile attempts to defend himself against false accusations." (ELLEN ABRAMS, *writer*)

mal•cle•ment *n* [*malcontent* + *clement*]: One who cannot enjoy a balmy winter day because of fear that it signals the growth of the greenhouse effect. "As the other chlorofluorocarbon propellant manufacturers frolicked in the surf at our annual New Year's convention in Atlantic

City, I wondered: Was it just my cold that kept me out of the water, or was I becoming a malclement?" (ELLEN GRUBER GARVEY, *writer*)

mal·colm *n* [fr. eponymous hero *Malcolm Wilson*, governor of New York (for a few months in 1974), whose only enduring accomplishment was arming state toll collectors with weapons of deadly force]: A ratings system, akin to the Nielsens, that measures the banality of American politicians. "The malcolm can be used to gauge the lunatic behavior of any kind of politician but is especially efficacious as a measure of presidential competence since Americans prefer to elect presidents of utter banality and those few who possess actual ability are rarely permitted to survive the experience. For example, Millard Fillmore checks in with a malcolm rating of 100 because he opened trade to Japan, not the greatest idea in the world, and topped off his retirement years by repeatedly running for president as the candidate of the 'Know-Nothing party.' Franklin Pierce comfortably topped the 100 level through his support of the Fugitive Slave Act. And James Buchanan joins his brethren for having been elected to the presidency pre-

cisely because of his blandness and because he managed to take a position of 'no stand' on the issue of slavery. These three towering figures of vapidity—mocked even by their contemporaries as the 'doughfaces' for their excessive pointlessness—achieved the critical mass of this rating, 300 malcolms, which history has shown is more than enough to start a civil war." (L. J. DAVIS, *journalist*)

mal·colm·ize *v* [fr. eponymous hero *Janet Malcolm, New Yorker* writer]: To invent dialogue and attribute it to an interview subject in a work of nonfiction. "While readers have always accepted malcolmizing in the tabloids, they still maintain faith, perhaps naïvely, in the accuracy of quotations in more serious publications." (RICHARD RHODES, *writer*)

mal·e·dic·ta·pho·bia *n* [fr. L *mal-* bad + *dicta* words + Gk *phobos* fear]: The excessive, unreasonable, or childish fear of so-called bad words (insults, slurs, curses; vulgar, profane, or obscene words) afflicting most editors, publishers, journalists, book reviewers, popular-word gurus, professors, religious fundamentalists, and similar immature minds. "Even now, despite the retirement of the pure-minded Abe Rosenthal, the staff at *The New York Times* is still suffering from acute maledictaphobia." (REINHOLD AMAN, *editor*)

mall•i•day *n* [*mall + holiday*]: A minor federal holiday that once had meaning but is now marked primarily by a paid day off and an annual sale at the local mall. "Since next Monday is a malliday, I thought I'd go to check out the CD players at the Sears Presidents' Day sale." (KAREN KARBO, *writer*)

mal•lif•lu•ous *adj* [fr. L *mal*-evil + *mellifluous*]: Of or pertaining to melodious speech of ill intent. "The War Resolution followed upon the President's mallifluous entreaties." (TED KOOSER, *poet*)

man•a•cur *n* [*manager + cur*]: A particularly venal person—usually in charge of the finances of an artist in the music industry and allied fields. (LOU REED, *musician*)

mar•ling *adj* [*mawkish + darling;* coined by Lord Stanley of Alderley and his many siblings in the early 1900s]: Of or pertaining to the prickly embarrassment caused by, for example, a hearty, jolly-good-fellow brand of clergyman, or a person talking baby talk to a dog. "Isn't A. A. Milne's poem, 'Christopher Robin Is Saying His Prayers,' perfectly marling?" (JESSICA MITFORD, *journalist*)

mas•sa•fy *v* —**mas•sa•fi•ca•tion** *n* [fr. U.S. Southern and West Indian *massa* master; cf. former prime minister of Trinidad, Eric Williams, author of *Massas Day Done*]: To imitate the abuses of a master; as a victim, to replicate the deeds and/or sensibilities of one's victimizer. The inversion of empowerment between the haves and the have-nots of a place, culture, or nation in which the formerly oppressed and downtrodden behave in a manner indistinguishable from (or worse than) the behavior of their former oppressors. Massafication occurs in a society with few or no democratic traditions, or the absence of any pattern of power sharing (such as the racial groups in the United States). Regardless of the method of enfranchisement—violent upheaval, colonial retreat, attrition, dissipation, or the deliberate "gift" of office (as, say, in the case of Samuel Pierce, secretary of HUD in the Reagan administration)—the sociopolitical intention of the inversion is reform, but the actual outcome is a steady continuation or intensi-fication of abuse and exploita-tion. For the majority of subjects within the system, nothing ap-pears changed other than the face and tone of power—a weary, imperial self-conscious-ness replaced by a vigorous, in-digenous self-righteousness. In effect, when old masters acqui-esce, new masters rise from within the underclass, implying that power corrupts even those who have for generations been painfully sensitized to the con-sequences of injustice, arro-gance, inequality, and avarice. Massafication also implies that revolutionary ideology—the politics of reform—is not as po-tent as, or an antidote to, the shortcomings of human nature, and that a ruling class is a ruling class is a ruling class. "After the downfall of Somoza, massafica-tion among the Sandinista elite made North American liberals uneasy in their support of the new regime." "Within a short time, Joseph Albritton had mas-safied his appointment as minis-ter of labor of the new indepen-dent state by purchasing a Daimler limousine and a posh residence in the suburbs of the capital. His former comrades forgave him this display of privi-lege and luxury, telling them-selves that 'to the victor go the spoils.' " (BOB SHACOCHIS, *writer*)

mass • de • bate *v* [*mass* + *debate* + *masturbate*]: To engage in pub-lic discussion in which partici-pants, ostensibly addressing each other in solemn delibera-tions, in fact have no ambition of persuading their opponents, but rather, address another, sometimes absent, audience and from minds unreachable by any actual argument. "The Congress was massdebating all Monday on the war." (LEONARD NATHAN, *poet*)

mass • ess *v*—**mass • ess • ment** *n* [*mass* + *assess*]: The sometimes unknowing assessment of some-thing by a great mass of unre-lated people. "A typical mas-sessment is that of consumer products: Even if people don't consider what they are doing, when they buy or don't buy something, they are helping massess that product." (GEOF HUTH, *writer*)

mas • tur • piece *n* [*masturbation* + *masterpiece*] **mas • tur • ba • ture** *n* [*masturbation* + *literature*]: Any writing by a man that deals solely with men's issues, or is likely to appeal only to men; also applies to men's pornogra-phy. "Tom Clancy's novels are swollen works of masturba-ture." See CLITERATURE. (BRIAN MC-CORMICK, *writer*)

maul•ette *n* [corruption of *mallette*]: Female member of adolescent gang frequenting suburban shopping centers, who preys on the elderly, the weak, and the stores with lax security systems. "The arrival of the maulette seems to have coincided with the advent of inner-city malls and the concomitant rise in violence." (RON KOLM, *writer*)

maunch *n* [*mouth* + *munch* + *moan* + *raunchy* + *morning* + *yawn*]: The taste in one's mouth after waking from a long night's sleep and prior to rinsing; especially the aftertaste and residue of a celebratory excess. "Hattie said, 'My mouth feels like the bottom of a birdcage. Maunch. Can I borrow your tooth-brush?' " (NICHOLAS DELBANCO, *writer*)

mech•an•o•mor•phism *n* [fr. Gk *mechane* machine + Gk *morphosis* form]: 1: The pseudo-scientific attribution of mechanical characteristics to living organisms, especially humans; the inverse of the pathetic fallacy, wherein writers credit nature with human emotions. "The editors of *The New York Times* engaged in classic mechanomorphism on February 22, 1988, when they praised the Supreme Court ruling backing the patent-ing of certain forms of life and wrote, 'Life is special, and human even more so, but biological machines are still machines that now can be altered, cloned, and patented.' " 2: Generally, the bestowal of mechanical characteristics on human organs. "Everyday mechanomorphisms include 'My brain just short-circuited,' and 'The old pump (heart) just isn't working like it used to.' " (ANDREW KIMBRELL, *writer*)

me•di•a aut•o•ga•my *n* [*media* + *autogamy* self-fertilization]: An increasingly common practice in which the difficulties, peculiarities, and absurdities of reporting a particular news event are reported as news. "After endless accounts of air strikes against Iraq grew monotonous, ABC and the other networks soon began to engage in the inevitable bout of media autogamy, airing stories about the obstacles placed in the path of reporters by military censors." (GARY KRIST, *writer*)

me•dia•cra•cy *n* [*media* + *-cracy* rule by]: Government by the media, pandering to the vulgarism of public opinion. Antonym: *democracy*, government by informed, deliberate citizens. "The chastisement of Gary Hart was less an exercise in democracy than a tribute to mediacracy." (BENJAMIN BARBER, *professor*)

me•di•ate *v* [*media* + *ate*, past participle of verb *to eat*]: To be consumed by overexposure to the media; to be vacant and boring since everything and every part of your being has been said and discussed and analyzed on or through the media. "I saw Henry Kissinger on TV last night. The guy is completely mediated." (EDWIN SCHLOSSBERG, *artist*)

me•dia•tro•phic *adj* [*media* + Gk *tropos* turning]: Of or pertaining to a person who bends inexorably toward and persistently shows up on some form of media with little or no reason to be there. "Carl Sagan is totally mediatrophic." (EDWIN SCHLOSSBERG, *artist*)

med•i•cide *n* [*medi* medical + *cide* killing]: A form of euthanasia that began to be practiced in the late 20th century, in which the person who chooses to die is assisted by legitimate medical personnel, such as a physician, nurse, paramedic, medical technologist, or military corpsman. "Medicide is always euthanasia, but the reverse is not necessarily true." See OBITIATRY. (JACK KEVORKIAN, *M.D.*)

me•dio•phil•ia *n* [fr. L *medius* middle + Gk *philia* love]: The desire to be, or pleasure in being, less outstanding than another. "Vice-President Dan Quayle said he is proud of his mediophilia 'because I'm just a country boy, I mean, the country isn't the city, the country is out there on the other side of the city, you're really in it when you're out there in the country, I believe in this country.'" See PRIGNANT. (TODD GITLIN, *writer*)

mem•o•ra•bil•i•ous *adj* [*memorabilia* + *bilious*]: The quality of making a person feel bitter, irascible, and nauseous through memory of a related situation. "After her divorce from the gardener, even a rose seemed memorabilious to Eve." (ELTON GLASER, *poet*)

men•do•lo•gism *n* [*mendacity* + *neologism*]: A lying neologism, intended to conceal or confuse its own meaning. "'Spin control' is a classic Reagan era mendologism." (MADISON SMARTT BELL, *writer*)

met•a•pha•sia *n* [*metaphor* + *aphasia*]: The inability to perceive metaphor. "Said the teacher, 'As you can see, class, it is pure metaphasia to see *Moby-Dick* as nothing but a good yarn.' " (DOUGLAS COUPLAND, *writer*)

met•a•phorm *n & v* [*metaphor + form*]: 1: An object, image, idea, or process that is compared to something else. "When we say that the mind is a machine, the machine becomes a metaphorm representing the mechanical aspects of the mind. Similarly, the mind represents the organic aspects of machines in this comparison, and both are expanded by this new association." Also as a verb: To compare an object, image, idea, or process to something else. "One metaphorms the concept of society by relating it to a colony of organisms, insects, or machines." (TODD SILER, *artist/writer*) 2: The form metaphor gives to the thing described; that which metaphor changes things into. "The love of language is usually a love of how metaphorm changes reality." (GEOF HUTH, *writer*)

Met•so•po•ta•mia *n* [fr. *Mets* shorthand for a National League baseball team + *Mesopotamia* a rich riverland]: Originally, the baseball land between two rivers, probably the Delaware and Connecticut, but in wider cultural parlance, the narrow band in which New York sports teams and their followers are looked upon with warm, albeit critical, affection, as against the remainder of the continental United States, where they are viewed with xenophobic rage. (ROGER ANGELL, *writer*)

mi•cro•fu•ture *n* [*microtechnology + life in the future*]: A world in the future where advanced technologies, computer systems, electronics, robotics, and a few without names yet will have been so dramatically miniaturized—even to the point of virtual invisibility—that there will be little need to change our world to accommodate them. "In the microfuture, there will be no need to update the designs or materials used to manufacture most consumer goods, private and commercial dwellings, or mass transportation equipment and aerospace vehicles since microtechnology will be able to evolve existing designs or materials unseen from within. For example, in the microfuture, it will be possible to insert self-maintaining microcomputerized heating and cooling systems into a single fiber of wool or cotton, allowing for one layer of clothing, of modest design and natural fibers, to keep the wearer comfortable in any weather. In the microfuture, most people will choose to adopt a more agrarian lifestyle as microtechnology will be able to unobstrusively provide a higher level of comfort, security, and communication, while living a simpler lifestyle (reprogress), all without heavily taxing the planet's raw materials supply and environment. In the fall of 2098, Grandma will sit comfortably in her 17th-century-modeled English country cottage, handweaving enough microcomputerized wool fiber to make her grandson a suitable sweater to wear in the harsh winter to come. The white plaster walls of Grandma's cottage will have been integrated with microcomputerized heating and cooling spores as well as a micro-solar-panel system on the roof for Grandma's comfort, and the same microtechnology will keep the henhouse and the cow barn comfortable too. Late at night, Grandma will fall asleep before a giant television image, emitting from a microthin layer of visual screening material covering a nine-by-twelve-foot wall; and when turned off the television screen will seem to have disappeared completely. But with all the advanced microtechnology surrounding her in the microfuture, Grandma will continue to wake up to the crowing of her rooster, 'Pex.' " (MICHAEL HOLMAN, *filmmaker*)

mi•cro•mil•ken *n* [fr. Gk *mikros* small + *eponymous hero Michael Milken*]: Unit of income equal to $550, one millionth of a "milken." "The micromilken, a unit somewhat larger than the annual per capita income of most of the world's population, is one millionth of the salary that Michael Milken, late-twentieth-century American leveraged-buyout specialist, received in 1987 for his expert assistance in converting large amounts of equity into even larger amounts of debt. Used because the parent unit, the milken, is inconveniently gross for ordinary purposes. The milken has about the same absolute value as the STEALTHBOMBER. For purposes of comparison: The salary of the president of the United States is 364 micromilkens; in 1984, the budget of the Republic of Iceland (pop. 200,000) was just about one milken; the gross national product of Chad (pop. 4.9 million) was about 660,000 micromilkens." (PAUL BICKART, *chemist*)

mil•ium *n* [*milieu* + *medium*]: The contextual influence that enables information coded in data strings to become meaningful, analogous to the role of a VCR in transforming magnetic fields into pictures, the human ear and brain in transforming

misstery/mistery

sound waves into verbal communication, and the biological processes in cells that transform DNA code into a living creature. "With apologies to Marshall McLuhan, but 'The milium adds the meaning.'" (IAN STEWART, *mathematician*)

mi•mi•bok *n* [fr. Gk *mimesis* imitation + ON *bok* a root of book]: An object copying or imitating a book, with the physical appearance but none of the qualities of a true book; e.g. collections of self-help aphorisms, celebrity autobiographies, and film novelizations. Mimiboks are often larger and more expensive than books. "The publisher predicted huge sales for the fall list of mimiboks." (SALLIE TISDALE, *writer*)

min•u•etc *n* [*minuet* + *etcetera*]: Movement of a classical symphony, in three-four time, in which there is no way out of the repeats, once one has blundered into them. "The minuetcs in the tafelmusik by Telemann are not interminable, they just seem that way." (DAVID RAKSIN, *composer*)

mis•an•dro•ny *n* [fr. Gk *miso* hatred + Gk *andros* male + *drone* monotonous buzzing]: Hatred of men, especially by a woman. By extension, an irrational fixation on the idea that males are individually and collectively the source of all the world's ills. (ANDREW KIMBRELL, *writer*)

miss•tery *n* [*miss* + *mystery*]: Honorific used to describe a woman of indeterminate sexual inclination. "Misstery Madonna will show her fans what for tomorrow night." (BRIAN MCCORMICK, *writer*)

mis • tery *n* [*mister* + *mystery*]: Honorific used to describe a man of indeterminate sexual inclination. "Mistery David Bowie performed ambiguously last night." (BRIAN MCCORMICK, *writer*)

mo • no • math *n* [by association with and as an antonym to *polymath*]: A person with an exhaustive knowledge of a single, often utterly trivial, subject, and who knows absolutely nothing about anything else. "A typical monomath is a teenage girl who believes that all of human history is explained by the music of Jon Bon Jovi." (L. J. DAVIS, *journalist*)

moon • shoot • er *n* [derivative of the phrase *shoot the moon*, used in the card game of hearts]: One who takes a glorious gamble, knowing that he will fail spectacularly, but is unable to resist the attention that will be focused on him during the attempt; an expensive way to live out a fantasy. "The moonshooter is not to be confused with the hearts player who prudently 'shoots the moon' when his hand assures him good odds of success, or the crapshooter who will almost certainly fail but is motivated by a hoped-for gain, because the moonshooter cares only for the attention, touched up with a bit of masochism." (ANDREW TOBIAS, *writer*)

mo • to *adj*—**mo • to • li • ty** *n*—**mo • to • ism** *n* [acronym for *master of the obvious*]: Of or pertaining to a comment that makes great the painfully obvious, typically with the goal of filling an uncomfortable void. "Moto observations range from the clown standing before a Rembrandt at the Metropolitan Museum of Art who says, 'Rembrandt—what a great painter,' to the March 21, 1991, broadcast on *NBC News at Sunrise* during which the reporter said, '*The New England Journal of Medicine* today warned that American soldiers returning from the Persian Gulf could be carrying rare diseases such as plague, dysentery, and some with names right out of the medical books,' to the remark made by one of the great motoists of modern politics, George Bush, after the liberation of Kuwait, 'Kuwait is liberated.' The motolity of a motoism can be measured by the ease with which flows the rejoinder 'obviously.' " (MICHAEL ROSENBLUM, *journalist*)

mouse *v* [fr. *mouse* any of numerous small rodents]: To explore a town with the eager curiosity of a mouse nosing down alleyways and peeking into corners, always on the lookout for hidden marvels; may refer to shopping, but only if it's done with rodentlike verve, appetite, and joyous gusto for exploring. " 'Okay, you stay here and make the world safe for democracy; I'll mouse the shops.' Should not be used when referring to natural wonders. For example, it would be inappropriate to say at a cocktail party: 'Have you moused the Grand Canyon yet?' But it would be perfect form, on the same occasion, to observe: 'Napoleon—now there was a man who could mouse a whole country.' " (DIANE ACKERMAN, *writer*)

mrok *v* [fr. French eponymous hero *Jean-Pierre Mroque* (1870–1946), harelipped French shipbuilder, long a resident of Brest, who habitually, when entering a house or a room, emitted a sound most often heard as "mahk," which was his tender way of hailing or greeting either occupants or what they occupied]: To intone a certain sound, with a rising or falling inflection, and to denote in the intoner feelings of excruciating delicacy, as if to proclaim: "No one enters this room and house, greets these people with the highly evolved finesse that I

do." "Mrok has overtones of smugness or hubris in spite of the near-monumental refinement evinced in the actual call or cry. Sometimes heard as a bleat, a baby call, or the cry of certain monkeys. Typical use in society: 'Mrok as you would be mroked.' " (PAUL WEST, *writer*)

mu·chis·mo *n* [fr. Sp *mucho* much or plenty; and back-formation fr. *machismo* swaggering, assertive masculinity]: The bravura born of owning many trendy objects, often characterized by the obvious display and constant discussion of one's possessions. "As the lawyer described the Nautilus machines and Sharper Image massage center in front of his 46-inch high-resolution monitor with Bose speakers, she became increasingly enthralled by his muchismo." (LIA MATERA, *writer*)

mug·ger·nate *v*
—mug·ger·na·tor *n* [no known root or origin]: To mull over a problem for a long time without coming to a definite solution, but should not be considered a waste of time; the muggernator makes some progress. "Jenny muggernated over whether to charge her boss with sexual harassment, knowing that if she did it would probably

mean her job." (ANNE BERNAYS, *novelist*)

mule•stool *n & interj* [*mule + stool*]: Something just short of, and with all the implications and connotations of, horseshit; an indoor word for an outdoor concept. "As a rule, mulestool is nothing more than euphemism, a good way to say a good word in front of your mother. In a similar vein, those in the country are said to say 'cowcake' when near their mothers and 'cowturd' when with their fathers. Similarly one might say 'henshit,' although never 'roostershit,' perhaps because that great red-gold-black creature is far too magnificent to indulge in such doings. His business is crowing. To explode with 'horseshit' in the safety of a stall or a shed is proper, but indoors, 'mulestool' is the ordure of the day." (GEORGE A SCARBOROUGH, *writer*)

mul•rooned *adj* [fr. eponymous hero *Brian Mulroney*, prime minister of Canada, 1984–present, who instigated and guided the dismemberment of the Canadian union of provinces in the 1990s + *marooned*]: Of or pertaining to the state of nations that have been crippled and then abandoned by their leaders. "Once the dirty deed was done and the broken nation had been mulroned in the frozen north, Brian retired from politics and became the permanent houseguest of George and Barbara Bush." (TIMOTHY FINDLEY, *novelist*)

mul•ti•verse *n* [*multi + universe*]: The conception that outer space is made up of more than one universe. "Until astronomers have mapped our universe, they will not be able to understand the multiverse beyond." (VERA RUBIN, *astronomer*)

must•lunch *v* [contraction of "we must have lunch sometime"]: 1: To issue a casual, pro forma social invitation with the intention that it not be taken up. "Sure, I'd mustlunched George half a dozen times, but I never expected that he'd show up at my office at noon. What a boor!" 2: By extension, any invitation given in deference to social convention but not in earnest. "They've invited me to their summer house, but I can't tell whether they're just mustlunching or I should buy a new bathing suit." See PSEU-DINVITE. (ELLEN GRUBER GARVEY, *writer*)

mynd *n* [*my* + *mind*]: The solipsistic mind; the mind that can believe in the reality of only itself, believing the existence of all other minds to be impossible to prove. "The child's is always mynd, unable to accept the existence of other consciousness." (GEOF HUTH, *writer*)

N

name•slug *v* [*name* + *slug*]: To drop names, on paper; to write something filled with famous names without any other content or redeeming quality. "Page 6 of *The New York Post* is totally nameslugged." (EDWIN SCHLOSSBERG, *artist*)

nar•cis•so•path *n* [fr. the god *Narcissus*, who became transfixed with admiration of his own reflection in a pool + *pathology*, the unhealthy deviation from a sound condition]: One who is irritatingly, insensitively, bursting with self-confidence, self-esteem, and can-do optimism, especially in front of tired co-workers or housemates. See SISYPHOPATH. (LIA MATERA, *writer*)

near•al•gia *n* [*near* + *nostalgia*]: A deep sense of longing for the extremely recent past. "Clarice felt a deep pang of nearalgia for last week when everything in the world seemed so much better." (DOUGLAS COUPLAND, *writer*)

neg•en•trope *n* [*negative* + *entropy*]: Any propagating or reproducing system that tends towards self-organization in the direction of increasing complexity, in apparent violation of the second law of thermodynamics. "Living organisms, ideologies, and technology are all negentropes." (IAN STEWART, *mathematician*)

neur•ro•ti•ca *n* [*neurotic* wracked by anxiety, compulsions, phobias, or other mental functional disorders + *-otica* suggesting a collection or oeuvre]: That body of literary work devoted to psychological self-improvement. "Neurrotica includes such titles as *Codependent No More, Healing the Child Within,* and *The Cinderella Complex.* Also used in the broader context of literary and cinematic works celebrating an intensely urban, sometimes Jewish, sometimes academic outlook. *Annie Hall* is considered Woody Allen's finest piece of neurrotica." (LIA MATERA, *writer*)

nex *v* [*negative* + *hex*]: To manifest the character trait that causes a person to make the choice that causes him or her the worst possible outcome. "The word is perhaps best defined in a short poem by the early-20th-century Greek poet C. P. Cavafy, 'Che Fece . . . Il Gran Rifiuto': 'For some people the day comes/when they have to declare the great Yes/or the great No. It's clear at once who has the Yes/ready within him; and saying it, he goes from honor to honor, strong in his conviction./He who refuses does not repent. Asked again,/he'd still say no. Yet that no—the right no—drags him down all his life.' (tr. by Edmund Keeley & Philip Sherrard) Yet that no— the right no—nexes him all his life." (JANE HIRSHFIELD, *poet*)

Ni•co•de•mus *v* [fr. *Nicodemus* the Jewish ruler who came to Jesus by night]: To ballyhoo a person or thing so far in advance as to make it doomed to disappoint. "All the hype and attention in the week before the Super Bowl had Nicodemused the actual game into nothing." (FRANKLIN BURROUGHS, *writer*)

nil•an•thro•py *n* [*nil* + *philanthropy*]: A late, inverted form of philanthropy marked by an extreme, often sentimental love of nature and animalkind and a corresponding hatred of humans; any near-religious or messianic feeling of moral presumption and mission (seemingly to fill in the void left by religion and '60s radical politics) —especially to reverse or nullify the effects of civilization by degrading its human roots, as when People for the Ethical Treatment of Animals codirector Ingrid Newkirk observed, "I don't believe human beings have the 'right to life' . . . a rat is a pig is a dog is a boy"; any of the various cruelties and paradoxes revealed in the pursuit of painlessness. "Setting AIDS-infected lab rats loose is certainly one instance of nilanthropy, but fortunately a rival group, the Pied Pipers, returned the infected animals to their new rodent hospice." (BRUCE DUFFY, *novelist*)

nim•nut *n* —**nim•nut•ry** *n* [*natter* + *dim* + *nut*]: A person addicted to forms of garrulous proselytizing of no consequence, such as the past-life theories of Shirley MacLaine or the ethical views of Werner Erhardt; occasionally pernicious to others when one's jaws lock after waves of malignant yawning. Also **nimnutry** *n*: The unrelieved evangelizing of a nimnut. "Nimnutry, as a belief system, is sometimes associated with philosophic hit musicals." (HERBERT GOLD, *writer*)

Nin•ten•tion•al fal•la•cy *n* [*Nintendo + intentional   fallacy*]: The false insistence, by those who wage war, that high-tech weapons cause only clean, antiseptic damage to military targets and never endanger living beings or the inanimate objects (e.g. houses and water systems) necessary to living beings' survival. " 'I suppose I'm falling victim to the Nintentional fallacy,' he conceded, 'but that footage where the bomb goes down the elevator shaft? It's excellent!' " (STEVE MESSINA, *editor*)

Nix•on•er•ate *v* [*Nixon + exonerate*]: To devote oneself steadfastly to the public rehabilitation of a reputation. "After such a fall, will he have the stamina to Nixonerate himself?" (DONALD RITCHIE, *historian*)

no•men•dul•ger *n* [*nomenclator + indulgence*]: An individ-ual who habitually attempts to coin new words for popular trends and modern phenomenon not currently included in a desktop *Webster's* in the hopes of seeing the word put into everyday usage, and then being able to boast about it in a weekly column if it is. "The great triumvirate of nomendulgers is: Bob Greene, George Will, and William F. Buckley, Jr." (TOM BODETT, *writer & commentator*)

no•mo *n* [*no + mo*]: A person of no discernible sexual proclivity. "Unmarried? Lives alone in a New Hampshire farmhouse? Clearly, Judge Souter is a nomo." (JAMES ATLAS, *editor*)

no•no•log•isms *n* [*no-no +* L *nolo contendere* literally "no contest," a plea in a court of law that stands between "guilty" and "innocent" + *neologisms*]: Neologisms thrown out by zealous magazine copy editors because they may unduly trouble readers and invite nasty letters. "Grubstreet, the author, wanted to use the neologism 'snoosed,' as in 'he snoosed down into the mummy bag and went to sleep,' but Dr. No ruled it a nonologism and, much to everyone's relief, the more pedestrian 'snoozed' was used instead." (BRUCE DUFFY, *novelist*)

no•no•no *adv* [*no* + *no* + *no*]: Extreme form of the negative "no!" "Nonono is properly reserved for difficult situations from which you wish to extricate yourself, such as date rape ('Nonono, you son of a bitch, you'll have to kill me first!'), or for refusal to let someone in ('Nonono' followed by something clever like 'not by the hair of my chinny chin chin.'). Not to be employed by the faint of heart." (LEWIS BURKE FRUMKES, *writer*)

non•swer *n*—**non•swer•er** *n* [*non* + *answer*]: A nonresponsive response to a question, most frequently encountered in intergender conversations. "A typical nonswer exchange yielding a nonswer goes like this: 'Will you need the car this afternoon?' 'Today is Tuesday.' Nonswers also turn up regularly at press conferences, news interviews, oral exams, and indeed throughout our public and private culture. 'Will you be running for ratcatcher next fall?' 'The primary isn't till March.' A distinctive mark of the amateur nonswer is that the nonswerer lives under the delusion that she or he has in fact answered the question: 'Did you have a good lunch today?' 'Pauline came by.' The professional nonswerer, by contrast, intends the nonswer to be received as a genuine response: 'Did you know at the time that X was under indictment for jury tampering?' 'Senator, my practice throughout my career has been to give everyone the benefit of the doubt.' The nonswer should not be confused with the *subshift*, a much lower order of semantic evasion, in which the conversational topic is brutally changed: 'Why did you do that?' 'Oh, look, it's snowing,' or 'Has anyone seen my glasses?' Will the nonswer be recognized as a universal disjunctive procedure that threatens the future of coherent communication? Human nature is notoriously unpredictable." (GEORGE T. WRIGHT, *writer*)

non•ten•do *n* & *adj* [fr. Sp *no entiendo* I do not understand]: To be hopelessly out of step with contemporary trends; specifically, ignorance of the nuts and bolts of electronic culture; by extension, someone who appears smart or savvy but hasn't a clue to how things really work. "The term nontendo became necessary in the aftermath of the Persian Gulf War when the Republican faithful struggled to describe Democrats who voted for economic sanctions as opposed to war. 'He claims it was a vote of conscience, but it was really nontendo.' Among preadolescents and teenagers, nontendo is synonymous with wimp, especially anyone who repeatedly loses at computer games." (VICTOR PERERA, *writer*)

non • y • mous *adj* [back-formation fr. *anonymous*]: Having a name. "Because no medieval architects were nonymous, the Chartres telephone directory never went beyond the letter *A*." "Because readers prefer narrators to be nonymous and to the point, Melville begins *Moby-Dick:* 'Call me Ishmael.' " (STEVEN G. KELLMAN, *professor*)

No • o • scene *n* [fr. Gk *noos* mind + *cene* an epoch in the Cenozoic era]: The new geological epoch that we are now entering, marked by catastrophic changes in the atmosphere, biosphere, and hydrosphere, driven by the arrival on this planet of a new geological force, the human mind. "Ever since life entered the Nooscene, it's been one damn thing after another." (JONATHAN WEINER, *scientist*)

not • so *infix* [*not + so*]: An infix inserted into a word in order to weaken or reverse its meaning. "English has its share of intensives: the suffix '-eroo' and the family of infixes: '-goddam-' and '-bloody-' and '-blooming-' such as the phrase 'absobloom-

inglutely' uttered in the movie, *My Fair Lady*. This infix is the equivalent of a sniffy 'I don't think so' when inserted in a word, such as, 'She sure is beautinotsoful.' " (PAUL BICKART, *chemist*)

nu • di • ments *n* [*nude + rudiments + oddments*]: Rules of pornography. "The original nudiments were found in the cave of von Sacher-Masoch and Krafft-Ebing who then gave them over to Al Goldstein for refinement." (LEWIS BURKE FRUMKES, *writer*)

nu • mer • o • cre • du • lous *adj* [fr. L *numerus* number + *credulous*]: A superstitious reliance on numbers, especially ratings and polls, whether or not they correspond to reality. "The senator was too numerocredulous to vote without consulting the latest surveys of public opinion." (SCOTT RUSSELL SANDERS, *writer*)

nu • min • i • tion *n* [*numinous + intuition + premonition*]: The instinctive, extrasensory awareness of the presence or attention of another person or creature. "She must have felt the pressure of my infatuated gaze on the back of her head, even across the crowded ballroom, for what else but such a numinition would have caused her to turn so suddenly and catch me,

unrepentant." (LAWRENCE E. JO-
SEPH, *writer*)

nunch *n* [contraction of *none-such*]: A person whom one cannot give anything that he or she

does not already own. "My
brother, that infuriating nunch,
stopped by the mall to buy the
foot massager I had picked out
for his birthday present." (SCOTT
RUSSELL SANDERS, *writer*)

nudiments

O

o·bi·ti·a·try *n* [fr. L *obitum*
decease + *-iatry*]: The extraction
of medical benefit, such as re-
trieving organs for transplanta-
tion or conducting medical ex-
perimentation, from the bodies
that result from MEDICIDE, or doc-

tor-assisted euthanasia. "There
is little doubt that obitiatry will
increase the number of available
donor organs and will accelerate
progress in certain fields of medical research." See OBITORIUM.
(JACK KEVORKIAN, *M.D.*)

o•bi•to•ri•um *n* [fr. L *obitum* decease + *arium* room]: Clinic or other edifice built for the exclusive practice of the arts of MEDI-CIDE and OBITIATRY (see both words, above). "We were going to take Grandmother to the obitorium today for her appointment, but the protesters were such an annoyance that we returned home." (JACK KEVORKIAN, *M.D.*)

obit•phem•ism *n* [*obituary* + *euphemism*]: 1: A phrase used in obituaries to avoid referring to a surviving member of an unmarried couple as a lover. " 'Companion,' 'longtime companion,' and 'close associate' are currently the favorite obitphemisms among newspaper writers; 'secretary' and 'devoted friend' are earlier ones." "Did you see that obitphemism in the National Portrait Gallery—the picture label describing Alice B. Toklas as Gertrude Stein's 'devoted alter ego'?" 2: By extension, the range of phrases meant to conceal or to give prominence to certain aspects of one's life deemed worthy/unworthy of mention in a newspaper. "The most common obitphemism, universal to all newspapers, is the reference to the recently deceased rich as philanthropists." (ELLEN GRUBER GARVEY, *writer*)

ob•lee•go *n* [*oblique* + *ego*]: The pose of embarrassment and masked satisfaction that one adopts when one is praised to others while present. "The introduction was long and excessively celebratory; Max occupied himself by cultivating what he felt was the proper obleego." (SVEN BIRKERTS, *writer*)

ob•nox *v* [back-formation fr. *obnoxious*]: 1: To offend, to cause someone to feel disgust or revulsion. "I was completely obnoxed by Jim's behavior at the party last night." (DEBORAH SCHNEIDER, *literary agent*) 2: To persist in ideological argument. "People who are ideological antagonists and persist in arguing with the expectation of converting each other are obnoxed." (ANDREW FETLER, *writer*)

ob•so•lene *adj* [*obsolete* + *obscene*]: Characteristic of an obscenity that has been rendered obsolete, either from common usage or from its replacement by a new obscenity. "Karen Finley's yam-cramming has rendered John Waters's movies obsolene." (BRIAN McCORMICK, *writer*)

od•eur *n* [*odor* + *auteur*]: An auteur for whom the perfume of fawning critics has given way to the funk of serious criticism.

"Many once-adoring critics now treat Peter Sellars as opera's greatest odeur." (BRIAN McCORMICK, *writer*)

oe•di•fy *v* [fr. *OED* common abbreviation for *Oxford English Dictionary* + *edify*]: 1: To request further information on word usage. "Hip? Hep? Oedify me." 2: By extension, to express a certain skepticism with an interlocutor's formulations. "Is that oedifiable?" (JOSE YGLESIAS, *writer*)

ol•ly•ism *n* [fr. eponymous hero *Lt.-Col. Oliver L. North* + *euphemism*]: A statement that can be perceived as false but is wholeheartedly told as truth in order to protect another entity either real or unreal (oneself, a loved one, the Constitution of the United States, or the greater good of mankind). "The best ollyism is still the original: During the congressional testimony of Lt.-Col. Oliver North during the Iranscam hearings, he admitted to making statements not wholly true or necessarily false in order to protect a higher code of ethics, and said, 'That is a bald-faced lie I told to the Iranians, and I will tell you right now I'd have offered the Iranians a free trip to Disneyland if we could have gotten Americans home for it.'" (JOHN W. HART, III, *poet*)

one-down•man•ship *n* — [antonymous formation fr. *one-upmanship*]: 1: The technique of seeming to have, need, or want less than the next person. "In a disarming move of one-downmanship, the surgeon confessed to his guests that he could afford his thirty-room house only because it was built exclusively from stones he had gathered while living in a tiny beach house when he was in medical school." Also **one-down** *v*: "When Sally asked Susan where she bought her lovely sweater, Susan one-downed her by saying, 'Buy? I could never afford to buy a sweater like this —I knitted it, of course.' When Sally then said, 'But where did you buy the gorgeous yarn?' Susan one-downed her again: 'Buy? I could never afford to buy this yarn; I got it in trade for some firewood I cut for Eva, who raises sheep. I suppose you don't know poor Eva; I'm probably her only friend.'" (JIM HEYNEN, *writer*) 2: A competition between two or more people over who has the most depressing, melancholic, disgusting, or embarrassing self-revelatory stories or statements. "Phil Donahue and Oprah Winfrey engage in an almost daily game of one-downmanship." (BRIAN MC-CORMICK, *writer*)

oopsht *interj* [*oops* + OE *scitan* shit; indication of dismay, disapproval, or frustration, as in "Oh, shit"]: A narrative interjection, chronologically and sequentially mimetic, representing the two phases of an accident, first surprise and then dismay. "Oopsht! I accidentally dropped the egg and it fell onto the cat's head and now I've got to clean up the mess." (DAVID BAKER, *writer*)

op•por•tom•ist *n* [*opportunity* + *Uncle Tom*]: An African-American who has some antiblack sentiments and is obsequious toward whites in order to increase his or her personal advantage. "When white conservatives are in power, more opportomists surface in hopes of advancing their careers." (ALVIN F. POUSSAINT, *psychiatrist*)

or•i•fic•ial *adj* [*orifice* + *official*]: Characteristic of spoken comments from a member of a government body. "On the 4th of July, many politicians feel uncontrollably orificial." (ELTON GLASER, *poet*)

out•kvetch *v* [*out* + *kvetch*]: To top someone else's whining by delivering even more agonizing complaints of one's own. "He outkvetched Woody Allen by claiming to have lived most of his childhood in the packing room of an elephant fertilizer plant in the Bronx." (RICHARD ZACKS, *writer*)

o•vart *v* [*over* + *art*]: Any activity pursued with an unbalanced concept of beauty. "When time slows down in Wagner, or when one winds up counting the cupids in Raphael's *Galatea* or cataloging the architectural details of the arches in his *The School of Athens*, one is ovarting." (WYATT PRUNTY, *poet*)

o•ver•board *v* [fr. naut *man overboard!*]: To overcompensate for fears about the future by plunging headlong into a job or lifestyle seemingly unrelated to one's previous life interests, i.e., Amway sales, aerobics, the Republican party, a career in the law, or cults. "The summer after he graduated from Ball State, Dave really overboarded and grew obsessed with his job as grill crew chief in a Fort Wayne Wendy's burger franchise." (DOUGLAS COUPLAND, *writer*)

o•ver•ling *n* [*over* + *underling;* although the concept has been around forever, this word was first used in the hallways of *Time* magazine soon after Carl Bernstein was hired and made "special correspondent"]: 1: Someone in a position of authority whose abilities actually make him suitable for a position at a lower station in life. 2: A big-deal employee who has usually misled his bosses to get where

he is but hasn't fooled those beneath him. 3: Shit that has risen to the top. "My boss doesn't know what he's doing. How that overling got to where he is today is a mystery to all of us." (TOM PRINCE, *editor*)

P

Pab•lum•ize *v* [*Pablum* + *-ize*]: To reduce debate to soothing mush. "The senator excised all controversy from his report and gave a Pablumized version of the riot that reduced the issues to a bland mush of minor disagreements needing only a gentle moderator for swift and permanent resolution." (JUDITH MICHAEL, *writer*)

pa•le•o•lo•gism *n* [fr. Gk *palaios* ancient + *neologism*]: An old word whose root sense is worth reviving, or which has additional or newly meaningful senses. "Paleologisms worth considering are 'trumpery' and 'precinct.' The word 'claptrap'—lines inserted into a speech to catch applause—is a paleologism that deserves reviving with specific respect to political speech." (PAUL BICKART, *chemist*)

pal•in•drone *v* [*palindrome* a word, verse, or sentence that is the same when read backward or forward + *drone* to utter in a dull, monotonous tone]: To belabor an issue backward and forward until the directions are no longer recognizable. " 'If guns are outlawed, only outlaws will have guns,' palindroned one saloon patron to another." (GEORGE THRUSH, *architect*)

pan•dic•tic *adj* [*pan* + L *dicere* to say]: Aspiring to say everything that can be said, characteristic of bards, barflies, and blowhards. "Walt Whitman was pandictic, while Calvin Coolidge was not." And, "When the pandictic novelist submitted his manuscript over the transom, the doorpost collapsed." (STEVEN G. KELLMAN, *professor*)

panx • i • ety *n* [*panic* + *anxiety*]: Uneasy thoughts or fears over present and future misfortune, but heightened and uncontrollable; the panic engendered by worry; the condition of angst in a crowd; mass hysteria. "Panxiety became the order of the day; misrule was everywhere, and screaming in the streets." (NICHOLAS DELBANCO, *writer*)

par • an • noyed *n* [*paranoid* + *para-* prefix suggesting almost, as in paratrooper or paralegal + *annoyed*]: The anger, diminished by satisfaction, that one feels when an initial suspicion, first dismissed as paranoid, turns out to be true. "When the S&L bailout turned out to cost three times what the President said, my wife was livid, but I was only parannoyed." (ETHAN CANIN, *novelist*)

pa • ra • pa • ra • dox *n* [*para-* + *paradox*]: A seeming paradox; thus, since a paradox is a seeming contradiction, a paraparadox is an actual contradiction that seems to be a seeming contradiction. "The idea of peace through war is a paraparadox; an unsettled peace might occur after war, but war is never a means of peace." (GEOF HUTH, *writer*)

par • chox *n* [*parchment* + *orthodox*]: The has-been who finds himself or herself mummified by having sacrificed all creativity so as to achieve a passing moment of fame or power by conforming to dominant fashions. (LUCIO POZZI, *artist*)

par • ty • fin • esse *n* [*party* + *finesse*]: The strategy of introducing a third party to the bore with whom you are stuck at a cocktail gathering, thereby freeing yourself, if you take two backward steps quickly and gracefully enough, for immediate escape. "He had so mastered the art of partyfinesse, even the most sophisticated partygoers were taken unawares." See SLOPE. (JOYCE CAROL OATES, *writer*)

pas • mind • ed *adj* [*past* + *mind*]: Of or pertaining to a person who lives, acts, and believes he is still living in a foregone era. "Leon was so pasminded from his breakup with a girl twenty years ago that he still drove a 1971 Duster, wore flowered shirts, and listened to Grand Funk Railroad and Karen Carpenter on his eight-track tape player." (BAJON KAHLIL SIRON-EL, *lyricist*)

pas • tri • o • tism *n* [fr. late ME *paste*, fr. Gk *pastos* sprinkled, + L *patris* fatherland, fr. *pater* father;

a father sprinkled everywhere (his stature annihilated), then moistened and kneaded, made into smooth dough spread over the land, suggesting a fatherland as a gigantic baked tart exuding sweetness, the citizenry melded into one another to form a smooth, creamy mass without bones, sticky to the touch]: The character or passion of one who hurls himself at national ideas and imagery like an animal jumping at a lifelike rag waved in front of it. "Pastriotism was first uttered by the poet Yevgeny Yevtushenko in his dacha at Peredelkina, outside Moscow, at 1:35 P.M., June 27, 1987, after this chronicler, dishing semiotic dirt on Peter Ueberroth, accidentally spilled jam on his Armani pants. Chronicler: 'Ueberroth told me he raised the . . . Jesus Christ, look what I've done . . . he . . . fuck it, he raised all the money for the '84 Olympics privately, by volunteerism, a word from the '50s, trick-or-treating for Unicef, get it?—planting trees in Israel —Jesus, just one more nostalgia ploy.' Yevtushenko (observing the raspberry stain on the thigh): 'I invent a new word. Pastriotism. Your country in the Ueberroth years was delicious.' " (MARSHALL BLONSKY, *educator/author*)

pat•ri•ot•ize *v* [*patriot* + suffix -*ize* with its connotation of creating a cheap, faddish verb from a noun, although the neologist believes he has coined a word that sounds hip and technological, as in "Simonize" one's car or "Midasize" one's muffler]: The practice of showing or professing one's patriotism by buying and displaying consumer products instead of some more active and constructive way such as demonstration or writing letters to a newspaper or politician. "Yeah, I told Midge to patriotize the house: two nice-size American flags, twenty yards of yellow ribbon, and 'Semper Fi' T-shirts for the kids. We'll show those A-rabs!" (DAN LORBER, *book dealer*)

pax•o•pho•bia *n* [fr. L *pax* peace + Gk *phobos* fear]: Fear of peace. "Readers of *Conservative Digest* who heard the President declare the Cold War to be 'over' gnashed their teeth in a reflex action understood by prominent physicians to be a symptom of paxophobia." (TODD GITLIN, *writer*)

pet quality *adj* [from the cat breeder's distinction between show quality cats, which are suitable candidates for ribbons and trophies, and pet quality cats, which have minor flaws that render them unsuitable for showing]: Of or pertaining to an object or person possessing defects that are part and parcel of their charm. " 'Ever since these boils appeared along with the tic in my left nostril, I've felt substandard.' 'You're not substandard, lovedunk. You're pet quality.' " (ALICE FULTON, *poet*)

phar•i•sant *n* [*pharisee* + *ant*]: An insectlike person who is strangely convinced that his participation in a close-knit social unit gives him authority over modernity. "Pharisants insist on their right to swarm, and they never understand what they destroy." (GEORGE TROW, *writer*)

phil•e•col•ogy *n* [fr. Gk *philos* love + *ecology*]: The effort or desire to increase the well-being of ecology and the environment. "Where philanthropy espouses the love of man, who is the source of substantial, persistent, and often deleterious problems facing our biosphere today, philecology embraces the environment of the whole planet." (EDWARD P. BASS, *investor/rancher/entrepreneur*)

pho•clo *n* [contraction of *phone* + *close*]: The litany of words, often meaningless, used to signal the end of a telephone

conversation. "The typical phone chat ends with a stream of hurried words, such as 'right, fine, okay, yes, okay, I'll take care of it. Right. Talk to you soon. Right. Okay. Bye.' This logorrheic stream of words comprises the phoclo and prepares the listener for the termination of the conversation. Phoclos are easily identified by being short, crisp, paced differently than the rest of the conversation, and always in agreement, regardless of the subject or the topic. The phoclo 'No. No. I don't think so. No. I completely disagree. Forget it. Uh-uh. No. Bye' doesn't work at all." (MICHAEL ROSENBLUM, *journalist*)

phys•ics en•vy *n* [*physics* + *envy*]: The belief that employing the mathematical methodology of the physical sciences will enhance the repute of one's own field. "The technical term for using a Cray XMP Supercomputer to cast horoscopes to an accuracy of plus or minus five in 200 billion is still called 'astrology.' As Sam Spade said, 'The cheaper the crook, the gaudier the patter.' " (PAUL BICKART, *chemist*)

pi•a•nist en•vy *n* [by association with the Freudian concept, *penis envy*]: An unfulfilled desire to sit down while playing a musical instrument. "Pianist envy is a condition common to singers, guitarists, bassists, and other musicians who have to stand while they perform." (BILL FLANAGAN, *musician*)

pla • ce • bi • tude *n* [fr. L *placebo* I shall please + *platitude*]: A phrase that while giving the impression of being useful or comforting to the listener is in fact quite vacuous; a sentiment offered often though not always cynically as a substitute for useful or helpful discourse. "Political speechmaking since 1980 has consisted for the most part of mastering the art of placebitudes." " 'Well,' the consulting physician advised, 'I think it's time for a few hearty placebitudes.' " (JANE HIRSHFIELD, *poet*)

plan • et • saur • us *n* [*planet* sphere + *saurus* lizard]: A person whose wastefulness of environmental resources demonstrates a hidebound shortsightedness of the need to protect our earth and value life. "Our neighbor is a classic planetsaurus—he doesn't even recycle bottles!" (WILLIAM K. REILLY, *environmentalist*)

plast • o • cra • cy *n* [*plastic* + *credit* + *-ocracy*]: A charge-based society dominated by a ruling class distinguished not by its royalty, wealth, or power but by its capacity for shouldering unthinkable amounts of debt; unlike other forms of political rule —such as plutocracy, oligarchy, theocracy, ochlocracy, or stratocracy where leaders assume power by, respectively, their wealth, privilege, mysticism, brute force, or weapons—plastocracy is the first form of rule in which the leaders hold power based not on anything that they actually possess at the time but the promise—strangely believed by everyone else—that they will soon have a lot of money, any day now, no, really, there's this guy who owes me. "So many of the mysteries of America's foreign policy, which does seem to adhere to the principle of 'Act now! Pay later!,' become clear when you realize that in this century democracy in the United States had changed to plastocracy." (MICHAEL GLOBETTI, *journalist*)

ple • o • ging • liasm *n* [fr. Gk *pleion* more + *ginglumos* a hinged joint, whether of a body or a suit of armor + *-asm* suffix associated with unusually vigorous states]: The condition of being overendowed with hinges; hence, dynamic complexity, in human organizations and in machines, when this is interpreted as an index of their likelihood to disappoint or injure. "The correlation is captured in the melancholy adage, 'The more moving parts, more broken hearts,' and in the Neo-Luddite doggerel: 'Many wings make light the leap,/But what's that clatter in the deep?/What's snapping in the techno-chasm?/ The jaws of pleogingliasm.'" "A converse but equally unhappy condition, *hypergingliosis*, has also been identified, in which too much is made to hinge on too little." (RICHARD TRISTMAN, *professor*)

plot • to *adj* [*blotto* drunk + *plot*]: Enthralled by story; incapable of understanding life except as narrative. "Plotto from an adolescence devoted to soap operas, he read elaborate meanings into a raised eyebrow or a dropped pencil." (SCOTT RUSSELL SANDERS, *writer*)

plu • ri • pe • ta • sate *adj* [fr. L *plur-* more + L *petasus* a hat with a low, pate-skimming crown and broad, circular brim]: Wearing more than one hat; i.e., having more than one vocation or profession. "Beset by budgetary matters—expensive retakes demanded by his celebrated director, tedious delays caused by his petulant star—producer Warren Beatty strode from the set of *Dick Tracy*. 'Save the lights!' the key grip cried, as the pluripetasate Beatty stood, huddled, mumbling, in a corner of the stage. Moments later, he returned inspired, beaming, equanimous once more. 'Quiet!' 'Rolling.' 'Speed.' 'Marker.' 'Action.' Beatty adjusted his fedora, spoke his line, hit his mark, and then, inaudibly but to his most intimate associates, sighed, 'Okay for us.'" Synonyms: *polypetasate, multipetasate, hyphenate, jack-of-all-trades,* and *Renaissance man,* each suggesting varying connotations of competence and flair. "*Pluripetasate* implies the practice of plural professions concurrently or in sequence with the properties and purposes of each preserved. *Polypetasate* suggests the melding of vocations such that in their simultaneous pursuit their distinctiveness is lost. *Multipetasate* reeks of the dilettante, speaks of seeds too widely sown, of ambition outstripping achievement. *Hyphenate* emphasizes the linkage among callings, not the callings themselves. *Jack-of-all-trades* suggests the practitioner is the master of the none. *Renaissance man,* obsolete." (MITCH TUCHMAN, *editor*)

po • et • i • cian *n* [*poet + politician*]: 1: A poet whose craft and talent for writing poetry is inversely proportional to his or her greater craft and talent for opportunistic scheming within the hierarchy of the poetry business. "The poetician can be identified by an attitude of sycophancy toward the powerful and a stream of jokes and comments that evoke grimaces on all except the flattered. The terms 'poet,' 'poetry,' and 'poetic' have lost their original meanings (that involved writers, words, and the quality of words) and have come to describe creators, creations, or the qualities of creations that possess lyrical, mystical, or bewildering qualities, e.g. when a food critic declares, 'The combination of blue cornmeal and pasta with catfish and kiwi sauce was pure poetry.' " 2: By extension, any artist or writer whose art is surpassed by guile. "It's the rare/God who needs less stroking than a rock/Star or poetician . . ." (ALICE FULTON, *poet*)

po•li•tec•ton•ics *n* [fr. Gk *polis* city + *tekton* builder]: Geopolitical structuring; formation, drifting, and breakup of international power groups based on geographic, cultural, political, economic, and military associations. (RAY S. CLINE, *political strategist*)

po•li•ti•pho•bia *n* [*politics + phobia*]: A disdain for or repulsion toward politics, usually felt by voters in a corrupt representative democracy that has largely disempowered them. "Although Americans retain a personal affection for their own representatives, they view their governmental institutions with a veritable politiphobia." (BENJAMIN BARBER, *professor*)

po•mo•e•ro•tic *adj* [*postmodern + erotic*]: That peculiar blank sexiness exhibited by the best and hottest of poststructuralists and their ethos. "His new show of photographers being photographed shooting camera-clad models seems like a hybrid of *Sports Illustrated* shimmy and *Dissent*-esque pomoeroticism." (DAVID FOSTER WALLACE, *novelist*)

pool•u•tion *n* [fr. *poule* lit. hen, fr. OF fem of *poul* cock + ME *pollution* fr. L *pollutus* por + *luere* (akin to L *lutum* mud, Gk *lyma* dirt, defilement)]: News reporting under censorship or collusion by military and/or political personnel, especially akin to or apropos of the Persian Gulf War of 1991; sanitized reporting reflective of the cocky politico-military mind. "The poolution was so extensive that news from the battlefront was null and void of body counts and caused reporters forced to belong to the pool to choke on the words they could not say." (IMOGENE BOLLS, *poet*)

pon • ti • fi • ca • tion point *n* [fr. the poised index finger that signals a pronouncement]: A punctuation mark that has long been searching for typographical expression; often called for in critical and political contexts, though not rare in church and in the home. "When lengthy passages require it throughout, to avoid redundancy an appropriate typeface may be used, as Pontification Demi-bold." (ELIZABETH MACKLIN, *poet*)

pop • syn • op • sis *n* [*pop* + *synopsis*]: Exceedingly short summary conceived in the TV era for young pop-minds bred on MTV and eight-second sound bites; essentially *Cliff's Notes* for *Cliff's Notes*. (LEWIS BURKE FRUMKES, *writer*)

po • pu • lu • tion *n* [*population* + *pollution*]: The condition that pollution, on a local scale, depends on population density; on a global scale, on the total world population and its consumption of resources. "It is generally agreed that population constitutes the most intractable problem of the 21st century, giving rise to conflicts over resources like fresh water and ocean fisheries." (S. FRED SINGER, *environmentalist*)

port • her • man • teau • phro • di • tic *adj* [*portmanteau* + *hermaphroditic*]: Relating to the combination of two things into one, especially if the things are opposites and difficult to combine. "He was unbearably proud of his porthermanteauphroditic house, with its Gothic facade and the rustic charm of a log addition and backyard outhouse." (GEOF HUTH, *writer*)

pos • a • tion *n* [*positive* + *negation*]: 1: The assertion of a point of a view by stating the opposite. "The critic John Barton engaged in the most transparent kind of posation when he reviewed Harold Bloom's work, *The Book of J*, and concluded, 'It may be brilliant, or it may be wildly anachronistic—I suspect it is both—but it is not a book one can ignore,' when, of course, he is suggesting that readers ignore it." 2: A form of euphemism so extreme that one ends up lying. "Posation became a necessary word during the '80s and '90s, an era in which public discourse degenerated into a swamp of double and triple negatives, litotes, contradictions, antitheses, and oppositions. When President Bush announced the nomination of Clarence Thomas, a black judge, to sit on the United States Supreme Court, he told the American people that he did not take race into consideration. Since it is no longer possible to call this kind of talk a lie, especially when a majority of the American people told pollsters that they didn't believe a word of what the President had said but insisted as well that it was not a lie, perhaps such rhetoric in the future can be called, politely, a posation." (JACK HITT, *journalist*)

posh•thu•mous *adj* [*posh + posthumous*]: Referring to elaborately annotated and bound editions of a recently deceased author's unpublished, minor, and/or hitherto ignored works in an attempt to capitalize upon his or her death and make a fine profit; implicitly this work is of dubious literary merit. "It has been learned that Samuel Beckett's publishers will even offer a poshthumous edition of his laundry lists entitled *Waiting for the Spin Cycle*." (HOWARD RABINOWITZ, *writer*)

post•min•strel de•press•ion *n* [*post + minstrel + depression*]: The dejection felt when a musical event has concluded. "After the Madonna concert,

thousands of virgin wannabees were treated for postminstrel depression." (ELTON GLASER, *poet*)

post•pro•to•torp *n* [*post- + proto* + reversed spelling of proto]: An imagined event as it actually happens. "The postprototorp of the confrontation was not as terrifying as he had feared; after only a few words, his father simply sent him to bed." (GEOF HUTH, *writer*)

pow•er•dis•i•ac *n* [*power + aphrodisiac*]: To reveal one's own personal power or wealth as a means to gain sexual favors. "He refilled her champagne glass and slipped her the ultimate powerdisiac by describing the family compound at Hyannisport." (RICHARD ZACKS, *writer*)

prag•my•o•pia *n* —**prag•my•o•p•ic** *adj* [*pragmatism + myopia*]: Excessive pragmatism; pragmatism to the point of blindness; self-destructive pragmatism. "West Bank elections could bring power to a Palestinian leadership far more radical than the pragmyopic Arafat." (JOE KLEIN, *writer*)

preg•na•pho•bia *n* [*pregnant + phobia*]: 1: A condition of fear experienced primarily, although not exclusively, by females gen-

prickle

erally between the ages of twenty and forty-five who believe they either are or will be pregnant before they are ready to enter into such a condition. "Mary was so stricken with pregnaphobia that she broke up with her boyfriend Bill after a four-year relationship." 2: Also, a correlated condition of fear experienced primarily, although not exclusively, by females generally between the ages of twenty and forty-five who believe they will not be able to become pregnant if and when they decide they are ready to have a child. "Mary was so stricken with pregnaphobia that she married her new boyfriend Bill after a one-week court-ship." (ROBIN M. KOVAT, *journalist*)

pre • mier cri *n* [fr. Fr; opposite of Fr *dernier cri*]: The original fashion idea on which the latest fashions are based. "The premier cri of today's sack-shaped miniskirts is the paper grocery bag." (MARK J. ESTREN, *writer*)

prick • le *n* [fr. *prick,* and by association with the idiom, "to prick a balloon," to unexpectedly let the air out]: To deflate another's ego; to take someone down a peg. "Mr. Rockefeller was lecturing his staff on the importance of hard work in getting ahead when Mrs. Rockefeller prickled him by mentioning that he had inherited his money." Also, a noun: "She's a nice enough person, but her husband is a real prickler." (BILL FLANAGAN, *musician*)

prig • nant *adj* [*pride + ignorant*]: Taking false pride in an intellectual failing. "A prignant declaration is usually followed by a prignant silence when used as a defense mechanism at parties: 'I was never any good at math when I was in high school.' " See MEDIOPHILIA. (IAN STEWART, *mathematician*)

pro • bot *n* [*propaganda + PR* public relations *+ robot*]: A representative of an organization or institution, especially the Pentagon, State Department, or White House, whose assignment is to make prepared statements and answer prepared questions at news conferences, military briefings, and the like. A probot is a sort of human word processor, or mechanical device given a human face, that conveys programmed disinformation in computerized language. A probot disseminates lies, distortions, and convenient truths composed by a superior. "Marlin Fitzwater is the President's number one probot." (DONALD W. BAKER, *poet*)

pro • cess • morph *n* [*process +* Gk *morph* form]: An entity different in structure or appearance from another, but sharing the same process. "Computers, power reactors, and weapon systems are some processmorphs of the human brain." "We are processmorphs of volcanic eruptions, earthquakes, and windstorms. Even though we don't look like any of these things in our outward appearances, the processes of our thoughts, feelings, and actions resemble them." (TODD SILER, *artist/writer*)

proc • to • lo • gen • sti • a *n* [*proctodaeum* anus + *intelligentsia*]: The self-appointed elite of the intellectual class that fervently believes in class, elitism, and self-appointment; they often speak with French accents, though they need not be French. "I thought it was a pretty damn good novel until the proctologentsia got hold of it." (JOHN CALDERAZZO, *writer*)

prop • a • goose *n* [pseudo-derivative fr. *propaganda*, punningly misread as *propa-* (or *proper-*) *gander*]: One who submits, passively or willingly, to the propagandist. "When propaganda comes to propagoose, eggs are not golden but addled." (BERNARD LEWIS, *professor*)

pro•se•try *n* [*prose + poetry*]: A composition in prose arranged on a page to look like poetry, usually written in lines of varying length, sometimes employing stanza shapes or placing expanses of white space at intervals as though meaningful. "Is most American poetry today mere prosetry?" (X. J. KENNEDY, *poet*)

pseud•in•vite *v* [fr. Gk *pseudes* false + *invite*]: To extend a social invitation to a person one dislikes knowing full well that he or she will be unable to attend, thus avoiding unwanted company while giving the impression of graciousness. "We're all doomed! I pseudinvited Emily to the cookout and she accepted!" See MUSTLUNCH. (BILLY COLLINS, *poet*)

pseu•do•fau•na•phi•li•a *n* [fr. Gk *pseudes* false or spurious + *fauna* animals + Gk *philia* affinity]: The support of "animal rights" as a politically correct cause, without thinking through the phrase. "At first, I thought the picketers really had a cause against wearing fur, but I realized it was pseudofaunaphilia when I saw they were wearing leather shoes." (MARK J. ESTREN, *writer*)

pseu•do•lit•er•a•cy *n*— **pseu•do•lit•er•ate** *n & adj* [fr. Gk *pseudes* false + L *literatus* lettered]: The ability to correctly encode (write) and decode (read) the symbols of written language without comprehending their essential meaning. "Pseudoliteracy is easily detectable in children who are able to sound out words beyond their comprehension using phonetic methods and therefore pronounce them correctly. Pseudoliteracy is also common but not so detectable in politicians whose slight expertise is rendered invisible by apparently correct usage of terms denoting complicated issues. In a generalized sense, pseudoliteracy can be defined as an inability to detect the existence of a subtext; pseudoliterates, many of whom are social reformers, tend to see texts as devoid of irony, to assume, for example, that the speeches of a fictional character necessarily indicate the attitudes of the actual author. The Iranian reading of Salman Rushdie's *The Satanic Verses* as blasphemous is an example of pseudoliteracy. Pseudoliterate discourse in general and literary criticism in particular are often distinguished by the use of words such as 'offensive.' Pseudoliteracy can further be defined as an understanding of denotation coupled

psychologic

with an ignorance of connotation." (DAVID BRADLEY, *novelist*)

pseu•do-pseu•do-low•brow•ism *n* [fr. Gk *pseudes* false + Gk *pseudes* false + *lowbrow* + -*ism*]: The avid consumption of low-quality popular culture, ostensibly undertaken in a spirit of irony, but actually stemming from a deep and secret addiction to trash. "Helen suspected that Howard's exaggerated admiration for *Love Boat* reruns was actually an expression of pseudo-pseudo-lowbrowism, a condition that she thought might make an interesting topic for the next *Geraldo*." (GARY KRIST, *writer*)

psych•ad•dict *n & v* [fr. Gk *psychikos* of the soul + L *addictus* surrendered]: One who goes from therapist to therapist, and indeed from therapy to therapy, in a vain search for an approach that will really work, and in the self-delusional belief that such an approach will eventually be found. "She tried everything from Neo-Freudianism to gestalt therapy to est to primal screams; then she decided she was becoming a psychaddict, so she switched to channeling and body massage." Also, as a verb, with the connotation of being more concerned with process than results: "As a nation, we are so psychaddicted to finding someone else to blame for our economic malaise that we can't seem to muster the will to do anything about our underlying problems." (MARK J. ESTREN, *writer*)

psy•cho•lo•gic *n & adj* [*psychology* + *logic*]: The kind of logic people actually use, as opposed to that referred to by logicians. Psychologic thinking is found in the following examples: "I just saw John at the library; he must be trying to impress a woman." "Mary sneered at me. She must like me." "Bush ran as the 'education president.' He will most certainly do nothing about the subject." (ROGER C. SCHANK, *professor*)

pul•prize *v* [*Pulitzer* + *pull* + *prize*]: To ignore talented applicants and repeatedly give prestigious awards only to people from the same handful of organizations. "The Emmys pulprized cable television shows for years." (RICHARD ZACKS, *writer*)

pu•org•ni *n* [fr. *in group* spelled backward]: A loosely knit group of men who have come out of the closet and have admitted with a certain stubborn pride that they are dull. "Puorgni are held together by common distastes, hating anything considered fashionable, trendy, or 'in.' They are dedicated to the preservation of the Tom Collins, the sidestroke, and carpet slippers. Their club blazer is blue serge with matching trousers (blue serge is the sidestroke of the garment industry). No puorgni has ever ordered a Harvey Wallbanger or ever will." (WILL STANTON, *writer*)

pure•mouth *n* & *v* [*pure* + *mouth*]: One who perpetually urges you to shun red meat, sugar, butter, chocolate, soft drinks, coffee, alcohol, tea, whole milk, plastic bags, disposable diapers, aerosal cans, nonunion grapes and lettuce, electric blankets, microwave ovens, genuine fur and leather, polystyrene boxes, etc.; also one who badgers you to remove the skin from chicken before cooking; recycle your newspapers; drive below fifty miles per hour; lower your thermostat; flush the toilet infrequently; exercise vigorously, with the proper stretches before and afterward; contribute your used glossy magazines to state prisons; have the mercury drilled from your teeth. "I was cornered by a puremouth at the Whole Earth Grocery." Also, as a verb: To harass in this manner; in particular, to remind anyone with ears that food is death. (MARTHA MC-FERREN, *writer*)

putsch-crow *n* [*putsch* + *crow*]: One who gives lip service to the overthrow of a political system or ideology but who clings to the status quo because of pressure, expediency, or self-interest. "He would always be a putsch-crow, siding with the forces of change while protecting his interests." "After the Reagan administration he made a lot of noise about throwing the rascals out, but it was the usual putsch-crow." (GLADYS SWAN, *novelist*)

pwoermd *n* [*poem + word*]: A one-word poem, such as Aram Saroyan's famous "lighght" or "eyeye." "The pwoermd is the most minimalist of texts, attempting to say what it means with a single word; because of this it is the least known of genres and when recognized is often rejected out of hand." (GEOF HUTH, *writer*)

Q

Q/A ratio *n* [fr. common abreviation for *question and answer + ratio* and by association with the common phrase *IQ ratio*]: A standard measure, not for intelligence, but for wisdom. "The Q/A ratio is determined by dividing the number of questions residing in a person's mind by the number of answers that reside there, and then by multiplying it by the age of, say, the 32-year-old smart ass who knows the answers to everything—in fact, he has nothing but answers—or by the age of the 70-year-old who might have been thought of as someone with more entitlement to answers yet finds at that age of his life that his mind is occupied almost entirely by questions." (WILLARD GAYLIN, *M.D.*)

qua•si•cag•lia *n* [*quasi + passacaglia*]: A musical procedure utilizing repetition of a motif or phrase. "In my score for the film *Forever Amber* there is a quasicaglia, so named by me because it combines the worst characteristics of the chaconne and the passacaglia, without any of their best features." (DAVID RAKSIN, *composer*)

quer-Schnitt•ke *n* [fr. G *querschnitte* pieces cut, usually at oblique angles, and joined together to make a collage + eponymous hero, composer *Alfred Schnittke*]: A musical collage combining diverse elements and styles. "The Fourth Symphony of composer Alfred Schnittke is an example of the quer-Schnittke." (DAVID RAKSIN, *composer*)

ques•chew *n* & *v* [*question* + *chew*, possibly *eschew*]: A feigned interrogation usually presented to guest experts on a news show in such a way as to elicit stylized chat; that is, an extended symbolic mastication of old chestnuts. "A queschew is followed by an enhancer, an assertion containing new beltway buzzwords requiring further ques- chewing, etc., ad infinitum." (WILL BAKER, *writer*)

quin•de•ci•mal•ite *n* [fr. L *quindecim* fifteen + *-ite*]: One who has already achieved his fifteen minutes of fame. "Warhol's prediction is proving correct: almost everyone in America is now a quindecimal-ite." (ROBIN FOX, *professor*)

R

rec•ti•pho•bia *n* [fr. L *rectus* straight + *phobia*]: 1: The inability of a person (usually male) to bring himself or herself to stop and ask directions when he or she is lost and/or is searching for a particular street address. "Rec- tiphobia is one of the unsolved mysteries of the human race be- cause no one can explain why a person (usually male) cannot rouse himself or herself to ask for help when it is definitely needed, though it has been pos- tulated by numerous social sci- entists that certain humans (usually male) are too proud to admit that they are incapable of reading a map or following sim- ple directions. On the other hand, there are those persons who actually enjoy being lost and who take delight in wan- dering through strange neigh- borhoods." 2: Fear of being right. "Rectiphobia, it should be noted, is one of the leading causes of divorce in the United States and Canada." (LOUIS PHIL- LIPS, *writer*)

re•de•con•struct *v* [*re-* + *deconstruct*]: To subject to novel and withering relativistic Amer- ican criticism objects already subjected to novel and wither- ing relativistic criticism quite some time ago by Heidegger, Nietzsche, and other German scholars; to take play a little too seriously the second time around. Synonym: *deconstruct*.

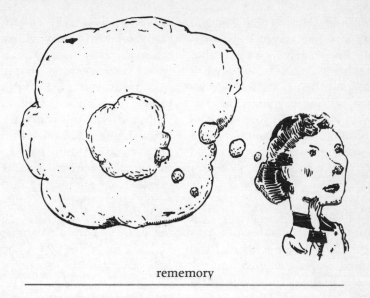

rememory

"With a formidable display of playful earnestness, he redeconstructed the obstinate deity with the simple phrase, 'Well, He *is* dead. Isn't he?' " (BENJAMIN BARBER, *professor*)

re · ject · a · late *v* [*reject + elate*]: To reject a proposal or a person in so flattering and subtle a manner the recipient has the impression he is being given encouragement; applicable in the context of personal relations, business, or the arts; to let one down easy. "The grunt hasn't got the talent for a bit part in a flea circus. Rejectalate him." Also, **rejectalatory** *adj* "She had become a master of the rejectalatory letter to soothe the egos of would-be authors." (GLADYS SWAN, *novelist*)

re · mem · ory *n* [*re- + memory*]: A memory of a memory; remembering remembering. "She realized that all she had of her childhood was rememory; her memories had disappeared but she still knew how her parents had remembered those years." (GEOF HUTH, *writer*)

re · par · so · lip *v* [*repartee + solipsism*]: To respond to any comment from speakers on their accomplishments not with acknowledgment but with self-congratulatory comments about one's own acomplishments, however incommensurate. "After I told Johnson that *Scientific American* had accepted my article, he reparsolipped, 'Really, I've been doing a lot of work lately on the newsletter for parents of fourth-graders in Mr. Tau's class. Did you see the piece I did on the paper drive? I thought it was a pretty solid job.' " (ANNE EISENBERG, *professor*)

re·pub·lo·crat *n* [fr. L *res* thing + *publica* public + Gk *krates* ruler or member of a ruling body]: Any member of the United States Congress and associated with either political party. "The republocrats are responsible for the budget deficit, trade imbalance, recession, and savings-and-loan debacle, so of course the voters keep re-electing them." (MARK J. ESTREN, *writer*)

ret·ro·jea·lou·sy *n* [fr. L *retro* backward + *jealousy*]: An irrational state usually experienced by males and characterized by unwarranted and inappropriate jealousy of a spouse or girlfriend and any romantic relationship she had prior to him. "My husband Bill has a retrojealous fit every time I so much as mention Harold's name, even though I went out with the guy only three times ten years ago and I haven't spoken to him since." (DAN LORBER, *book dealer*)

ret·ro·tort *n* [*retrospect* + *retort*]: An ideal remark that comes to mind hours, days, or weeks too late. "That afternoon, a retrotort occurred to Jim; when Natalie had asked him what he wanted for breakfast,

republocrat

he should have said, 'You, on toast.' " See STAIRWIT. (BERNARD COOPER, *writer*)

re • vers • a • cunt *n* [*reversal* + *cunt* + suffix -*ant* suggesting the achievement of an action taken, as an "applicant" is one who has succeeded in applying]: The redemption of a derogatory term by embracing it to signify approval rather than disgust. "Reversacunts are typically initiated by members of an outcast group who fling a word back into the faces of users and force an acceptance of a positive meaning. The most successful reversacunt is the word *black*, as in *black power* and *black pride*. The word *queer* is achieving a positive meaning through such usages as *queer nation*. In a land of politesse, reversacunts are few and far between, but keep your eyes open for that 'New York Jew' baseball jacket." (ANNE EISENBERG, *professor*)

rhy • thm • po • li • tics *n* [*rhythm* + *politics*]: Social interaction based upon or influenced by primal, instinctive perceptions of the correctness of rhythm; the disposition, attitude, or behavior that a person or a group of people displays toward another person or group of people based upon the way each dances, moves in repeti-

tion, or keeps rhythmic time. "The right wing of the South African government complained that even if they were to abolish apartheid, the rhythmpolitics involved in interracial sociocultural events would be intolerable; think of whites sitting through primal, funky tribal jukes or blacks enduring arrhythmic Boer folk dances." "The chief of police of Jerusalem was surprised and bemused by the minor scuffle between Palestinians and Hasidic worshipers at the Wailing Wall caused by the violent reaction of a young Palestinian who said he was annoyed to the state of delirium by the constant 'head bobbing' that accompanies Hasidic praying. While police, politicians, and sociologists always seem perplexed by such events, they are pure rhythmpolitics." "Most of the underprivileged, inner-city youth in New York choose to express their anger and frustration not through organized protest but with the rhythmpolitics of a gangster stride." (MICHAEL HOLMAN, *filmmaker*)

ric • tory *n* [origin obscure]: The feeling when doing a favor for someone, along with the reflected glory of being a provider, of the admiration owed you by its recipient; smugness at the heart of rectitude. "Oh, rictory! Virtue and vice alike!" (ALEXANDER THEROUX, *novelist*)

rock • u • lism *n* [*rock,* fr. eponymous hero Nelson Rockefeller, known for his campaign greeting, "Hiya, fellas" + L *populus* people + *-ism*]: The adoption of popular speech for purposes of increasing one's political popularity. "President Bush, accused of rockulism, said, 'Gee, sticks and stones, guys.' " (TODD GITLIN, *writer*)

roid *n* [fr. Fr *roi* king + suffix *-oid;* see etymology of FACTOID]: A king whose function has become contrived and mechanical. "I can't wait till Charles becomes roid, and his irrelevancy is made official." (JACK COLLOM, *poet*)

ru • mint *n* [*rumor* + *humint* U.S. Army Intelligence argot for human intelligence; entered common usage from U.S. military forces stationed in the Persian Gulf where little news reached the desert encampments]: Information gained by rumor; anything anyone finds out regardless of its truth or falsity. "What's the rumint, soldier? According to my rumint, we're moving out of here in two days." (LESLIE COCKBURN, *journalist,* and THE U.S. TROOPS)

S

Sad • dam • ize *v* [fr. eponymous hero *Saddam Hussein* + *-ize*]: To engage in aggression that takes the form of betrayal of a former ally, a shift in alliance, or a stab in the back. "Tired of Japan's resistance to a new trade agreement, the United States decided to Saddamize Japan, cut off negotiations, and ban all Japanese imports." (HAROLD J. GOLDBERG, *historian*)

safe • slide *v* [*safe* + baseball term *to slide*]: To keep a low profile, especially in business. "Those numbers look too good. Do you really want to draw that much attention to this project? Wouldn't you rather be safesliding?" (RICHARD SELTZER, *writer*)

Saf•ir•ize *v* [fr. eponymous hero *William Safire*, political columnist, popular novelist, and amateur linguist]: To attribute, often as an involuntary reaction, all the world's ills to international communism. "A State Department spokesman, commenting on an outbreak of amoebic dysentery in the Bolivian Army, Safirized the event, noting that a troupe of Soviet acrobats had recently performed in La Paz." (GILBERT SORRENTINO, *writer*)

Saint-paul *v* [fr. *St. Paul de Vence* town in southern France, where this neologist saw this action verb practiced from the *boule* fields to the open-air markets; and by association with the magic typically connected to the actions of saints]: To attempt, by means of various bodily contortions, gestures, sounds, or deep-image kharma, to project will of self into the trajectory, roll, spin, or drift of an object or image that is beyond the sphere of human influence. " '*A droite, à droite,*' begged the old *boules* player, as his *boule* began assuming a direction with full-strike potential, if only, *eh oui*, it would curve in to the right a bit more. Simultaneously his entire body mass was transforming itself with rightward-pulling dynamics as he went all out to Saint-paul his *boule* into his opponent's heartland. But just as victory seemed certain, his *boule* bounced slightly, lolled left, and went its own way. '*Mon Dieu!*' he moaned, wearily releasing his body from its tight parenthesis. '*Chier de merde!*' '' By extension the word may be used, say, in the stock market and other games of chance: "She knew she had Saint-pauled the fourth cherry cluster into alignment with the other three as the rain of tokens began and fellow believers looked up from their slot machines with admiration." Or. "After years of separation, Sluggo spied the sultry Nancy in an opera box below and tried with all his might to Saint-paul her gaze away from Pavarotti." (JAMES SEAY, *poet*)

Sam•beck•etted *adj* [fr. eponymous hero *Samuel Beckett*, Irish playwright, novelist, and poet (1906–1989)]: To remain abandoned, seemingly without hope. "Sambecketted in Parma, Ohio, our son's promise to bring the other car was now nearly a week old." (MARK IRWIN, *poet*)

Saw•yer•ism *n* [fr. eponymous hero *Diane Sawyer* + *voyeurism*]: The popular desire to see television anchorwomen in their underwear, especially in, but not limited to, *Vanity Fair* or

Esquire. "Hoping to cash in on what they perceive as rampant sawyerism, HBO executives have offered Connie Chung $1.4 million to moderate a panel on the homeless while wearing a 'modest Danskin leotard.' " (TOM DRURY, *writer*)

scha • den • droid *n* [fr. G *schadenfreude* joy in other's suffering + *android*]: Robotic lack of emotion, typically of a government official in the face of the suffering of others. "The State Department spokeswoman's response was a study in schadendroid: 'The value of an individual human life? I have been instructed not to comment on that at this time.' " (STEVE MESSINA and LYDIA BUECHLER, *editors*)

scha • den • scha • den *n* [by analogy with *schadenfreude* joy in other's suffering]: A feeling of helplessness, despair, or panic inspired by suffering in someone else. "I watched her crying and saw she needed help, but schadenschaden got the better of me and I just stood there waiting and feeling miserable." (HARRY MATHEWS, *writer*)

schlaumpfkth, schlompfkt *n* [coined to be the longest single-syllable word possible, until an *s* is added to the end of it to make it plural]: Filler language; any piece of language added to any other piece of language for no purpose other than to expand the latter's length. "The general's speech was all schlaumpfkth attempting to hide his lack of substance. After half an hour of 'in the current state of affairs' and 'at this juncture of historicity,' even the senators began to tire." (GEOF HUTH, *writer*)

Schrod • ing *adj* [fr. eponymous hero *Erwin Schrödinger*, German physicist, known for his famous thought experiment that employed a cat sealed in a box containing a lethal Rube Goldberg device: a flask of poison gas, a hammer to smash the flask when triggered by a Geiger counter, and a single radioactive atom with a 50 percent chance of disintegrating and activating the trigger in the course of the experiment. Quantum-mechanically speaking, the cat is neither alive nor dead; it exists as a superposition of two states—alive AND dead—whose relative probability is a time-dependent variable, until a "measurement" —opening the box and looking in—is performed]: in an indeterminate state; half-alive, half-dead. "During the last two years of his term, the President was Schroding." "The Congress of the United States has been

Schroding for well over a decade." (PAUL BICKART, *chemist*)

scoosh *prep* [fr. Early Modern F *s'accouche* to give birth to yourself]: And a fig for the farfetched fulminations of; though I do not doubt the reverse will be maintained with a baldfaced insistence by. Synonyms: *Pace, despite, regardless of, notwithstanding, maugre,* and *scoosh* are all used, in debate or argumentation, to assert or acknowledge divergence or disagreement with a specific adversary or opposed authority, with different degrees of politeness, of respect, of vehemence, of contempt. *Pace* (note the disyllabic pseudo-Latin pronunciation) is the most courtly and concessive. *Despite* is curt but not incourteous. *Regardless of* may be a shade more dismissive. *Notwithstanding* expresses no animus but a firm conviction and no concession to the opponent's claims. *Maugre* suggests even greater adamancy, but the very antiqueness of the word softens the aura, bespeaking merely the shared exuberance of sharp badinage among peers. *Scoosh,* however, disdains politeness and looks daggers, as in "Let my opponent rant; let him have a pup." "There is an American way, and it works. We spend ourselves silly and get rich on the wreckage, scoosh Galbraith and Friedman and all their panicky ilk." "Nobody doesn't love babies, scoosh Henry Hyde." (GEORGE STARBUCK, *poet*)

scrip • to • phile *n* [*script* + *phile*]: A lover of the physical act of writing by hand, especially with a high-tech or antique pen of quality; one whose hobby is guiding a writing instrument across a sheet of paper or other receptive surface; a desk athlete who likes to perform minuscule exercises with a stylus; a doodler or amateur calligrapher; a person who enjoys the dynamics of scrivening; a mano-kinetic scriptorial aficionado. "Devotees of word processing tend to sneer at scriptophiles." (WILLIAM WALDEN, *playwright*)

scud *v* [*SCUD* missile, one of Saddam Hussein's favorite weapons]: To cause only a minor explosion, when a larger, more showy one is expected. "After all the hype during David Lynch's two seasons of prime-time television, the final resolution of the mystery of who killed Laura Palmer scudded." (EMILY PRAGER, *novelist*)

scut • tle • butt • head *n* [*scuttlebutt* + *butthead*]: A person who delights in being the first to inform friends and office mates of breaking world news. "I found out that Whoopi Goldberg was nominated for an Academy Award the same way I found out that the Sandinistas lost the Nicaraguan elections—Scott, the office scuttlebutthead, poked his annoying face in my door and asked 'D'ja hear?' " (PAUL TOUGH, *journalist*)

se • crate *v* [back-formation fr. *desecrate*]: To cleanse a formerly holy place, object, or person; to de-defile; to practice, say, file-ment. "In 1990, Saddam Hussein suggested that one reason for his invasion of Kuwait was the secration of Mecca and Medina, polluted by the presence of infidel troops brought there to defend against him." "Pete Rose cannot be secrated until his lifetime ban from baseball is lifted." (PAUL BICKART, *chemist*)

seem • ius *n* [*seems* + *genius*]: Anyone who is good at pretending to be or at seeming to be like a genius. "Spalding Gray's preciousness and his sense that every word he says is important make him the world's leading seemius today." (BRIAN McCOR-MICK, *writer*)

self-ag • glan • dize *v* [*self-aggrandize* + *gland*]: To become more physically compelling through artificial means,

whether hormone treatment, steroids, or silicone implants. "Ellen tearfully told the amazed judges how she'd self-ag-glandized in order to improve her chances of winning the pageant." (MICHAEL GLOBETTI, *journalist*)

self-un • em • ployed *adj* [*self-employed* + *unemployed*]: The state of the eternal entrepreneur still waiting for his first deal. "We had no idea what Paul did for a living—he seemed never to work but spent an inordinate amount of time at home in front of his Macintosh—until April explained that he was self-un-employed." (EDWARD SILVER, *editor*)

se • mi • ob • ject *n* [*semi-* + *semiotic* + *object*]: Any semiotic object; an item with so much apparent or obvious semiotic value that the meaning of the thing begins to overcome the object it is. "He hoped Andy Warhol had understood Campbell's soup cans more as semiobjects than as mere commercial containers." (GEOF HUTH, *writer*)

se • mot *n* [fr. *sine emotiones*, as "snob" from *sine nobilitate*]: A person affecting a complete lack of emotions and sentiment in order to hide his or her fragile vulnerability in the realm of feelings. (LUCIO POZZI, *artist*)

sep•ul•chri•tude *n* [*sepulcher* + *pulchritude*]: The beauty of dead things. "The undertaker in Hartville was renowned for the sepulchritude of his clients." (ELTON GLASER, *poet*)

sex•amp *n* [*self* + *example*]: A word or phrase that defines and renders itself superfluous. "Take the sexamp 'unnecessary clutter.' The word 'unnecessary' makes the word 'clutter' unnecessary. The word 'clutter' turns the word 'unnecessary' into clutter. A person using the term 'cutesy-poo' is *being* cutesy-poo. The remark, needless to say, if true, is needless to say. Clichés are a dime a dozen." (WILL STANTON, *writer*)

sex•is•tence *n* [*sex* + *existence*]: The struggle to meet one's sexual desires in the face of increased peril from communicable disease and sexual misunderstanding, characterized by either diminished sexual activity or by the contemplation of imponderables such as how much sex is required for living and how much for the propagation of the species. "As a single man who'd found his libido debilitated by the times, Enrico knew that he'd continually have to grapple with sexistence." "Often used in the phrase 'sexistential despair.' " (MICHAEL GLOBETTI, *journalist*)

sham•di•date *n* [*sham* + *candidate*]: Person summoned for a job interview by people who have already decided to hire someone else. "The panel interviewed seven shamdidates even though the committee understood the job would go to Sinclair." (ANNE EISENBERG, *professor*)

sham-faced *adj* [*sham* + *shamefaced*]: Characteristic of an expression of apparent distress occurring when someone has ignored your repeated warnings and the thing you warned against has come to pass and you pretend to be sorry. "The following speakers are shamfaced: 'Damn it, Ronnie, I can't believe that your trickle-down theory hasn't erased the deficit.' 'Shoot, George, I was sure once you had Noriega out of the way the drug problem would disappear.' " (WILL STANTON, *writer*)

Sha•mir *v* [fr. eponymous hero *Yitzhak Shamir*, prime minister of Israel, 1983–present]: To visit someone, usually for political reasons, importunately to get him to be your friend so he can't be your enemy; an act always informed by guile, never grace. (ALEXANDER THEROUX, *writer*)

shee • it   *pron*   [*she + he + it*]: Third-person singular nonsexist pronoun, replacing he/she, him/her, his/her in contexts intended to be gender neutral. "I appeal to the reader to use sheeit's imagination." "Everyone has sheeit's place." "Ecce sheeit!" (ROBIN FOX, *professor*)

sheep • sta • sis   *n*   [*sheep + stasis*]: 1: A state of lethargy—found to exist throughout the range of jobs in America's technological economy—brought about by endless repetition of a boring task, such as counting sheep. "I was asleep at the desk because adding those columns of numbers had led me into a sheepstasis." 2: Most often associated with computational activity, but by extension refers to highly monotonous (possibly mindless) situations. "Together, the essays collected in this volume represent quintessential deconstructionist thought. However, let the reader beware: sheepstasis lurks at the turn of every page!" (DEBBIE CYMBALISTA, *writer*)

she • ro   *n*   [*she + hero*]: A valiant woman, overreaching, death dealing, and capable of multiple transformations. "The shero makes choices in order to define herself; she forms her world and lives at its center." See FACHO. (SALLIE BINGHAM, *journalist*)

shill • dren   *n*   [*shill + children*]: Children who are born from rented wombs. "Adopted children have nothing on shilldren when it comes to contemplating the issue of who their 'real' parents are. Two shilldren were recently born under these circumstances: The mother who wanted the shilldren couldn't have her own children so she purchased the eggs of one woman, had them fertilized, not by her husband (he was sterile) but by a sperm donor, and then had the fertilized eggs implanted in a surrogate mother. These shilldren have, by my count, five parents." (BRIAN McCORMICK, *writer*)

sim • pli • cist   *n*
sim • pli • cism   *n*   [*simplify + -ist*, denoting one who practices a craft]: A person, often in the fields of politics or journalism, sometimes science, who cooks, boils, and renders the beautiful, the interesting, and the complex into the tawdry simplicism of good and evil. "The work of simplicists abounds: In Iran, a religious sect with a tradition of struggle for the last 1,000 years finally succeeds in overthrowing the CIA-supported Western-ori-

ented government that the United States has been propping up with massive military aid, and the American public is told by three presidents and their water boys that the situation can be explained easily: 'Madman Khomeini.' Or, millions demonstrate in the streets on his behalf. Explanation: population insane. Or, an Iraqi military dictator whom the United States has been underwriting with money and military support suddenly invades a feudal theocratic oligarchy that has been stealing his oil and undercutting his only source of income for years. Explanation: 'Madman Saddam.' Across the Islamic world, millions take to the streets in his support. Explanation: population insane. Simplicists often find employment at television stations where they cleanse scripts of ideas and multisyllabic words and perform the modern alchemy of transforming the gold of human conflict into the lead of good and evil. By the simplicist's reasoning, the entire history of U.S.–U.S.S.R. relations in this century can be summarized as 'good empire at the turn of year 1900, evil empire under Lenin, good empire during World War II, evil empire during the Cold War, good empire again, so far.'' (MICHAEL ROSENBLUM, *journalist*)

Shir • ley *n* [fr. eponymous hero *Shirley MacLaine*, U.S. film actress]: To enthusiastically pursue New Age ideas in a flighty or undiscriminating way. ''He Shirlied his way through channeling, UFO studies, and Uri Geller's autobiography.'' (RICHARD MORRIS, *writer*)

Sil • ber • blus • ter *n & v* [fr. eponymous hero *John Silber + bluster*]: Crude, bullying, simplistic, but media-attracting political discourse, with an emphasis upon attacking powerless groups, i.e., ''welfare mothers,'' ''black drug addicts,'' ''the moribund elderly.'' ''His Silberbluster caught the attention of the media and brought him instant political success.'' Also, a verb. ''He Silberblustered his way to the top!'' (JOYCE CAROL OATES, *writer*)

si • lu • ta • tion *n* [*silence + salutation*]: A facial expression consisting of tightly clenched lips and downcast eyes. The silutation is a reaction to seeing someone, such as a fellow employee, whom you have very recently greeted; to greet this person again would be awkward, redundant, even ludicrous, but to ignore him or her would be rude; the clenched lips indicate a forced suppression of the natural desire to say hello, while the downcast eyes are a polite way to avoid seeing your silutation being returned. "Passing the new sales manager once again in the hallway, I had no choice but to give him another silutation." (BILLY COLLINS, *poet*)

sim·pho·bia *n* [*simple + phobia*]: The fear among radio and TV newscasters of saying anything in a straightforward, unequivocal manner. "Simphobia explains the fondness of broadcasters for such ambivalent expressions as 'governance,' which can mean government or the act of governing or the state of being governed, or 'adumbrate,' which means foreshadow, outline, or disclose partially, or the much-favored 'parameter,' which can be either a variable or an arbitrary constant." (WILL STANTON, *writer*)

si·syph·o·path *n* [fr. the god *Sisyphus*, condemned forever to roll a heavy stone up a mountain]: One who is certain no ap-

simphobia

parent improvement will last and no amount of effort will make a difference. Synonym: *former leftist.* See NARCISSOPATH. (LIA MATERA, *writer*)

skif-skaf *n* [onomatopoeia]: The sound of paper money being mechanically sorted by a financial institution's automated-teller machine, which usually heralds that the machine will deign to dispense currency at the request of a depositor; the sense of euphoria that accompanies the discovery that one has been found creditworthy by a computer chip; the emotional lift that comes at the conclusion of any successful business transaction with a computer located outside one's home or office. "We call skif-skaf and Christmas sleigh bells the sweetest sounds in the world, according to a telephone survey of seventeen adult Americans." " 'Like Bolivian marching powder, frequently indulging in the narcotic highs of pure skif-skaf demands an ample bank account,' said Jay McInerney." (WALTER SHAPIRO, *journalist*)

slard *n* [Am colloquial fr. an elision of *slower than molasses;* also fr. *slow + lard-ass*]: A comically overfed, indolent young urban professional. "Though they were not yet middle-aged, it was all the two slards could do to walk from the splendid restaurant, up the short hill to their apartment and, once within, fall heavily onto their bed." (TOM JENKS and CAROL EDGARIAN, *writers*)

slong *v* [*slow + sloppy + longing*]: To indulge oneself in overwrought public grief. "Ophelia slonged around Elsinore for weeks, sighing and refusing to eat." (BILL FLANAGAN, *musician*)

slonk *n* [*savings & loan + bunk*]. A hybrid chameleonlike monster that can simultaneously walk upright and crawl on its belly toward a nearby exit, talk from both sides of its mouth while simultaneously and incessantly eating, and spread spore colonies with great rapidity in dank places, that die quickly in sunlight. Also, **slonk** *v:* To gorge, especially on green matter; to bloat; to absorb and digest great quantities without leaving a trace. (WILL BAKER, *writer*)

slope *v* [origin obscure] To slip out of a room while keeping a low profile, used especially in uncomfortable social situations. "I pretended to go for another drink, then sloped." See PARTY FINESSE. (ALEXANDER THEROUX, *writer*)

smad *v* [*smeared* + *advertisement*]: To be attacked, smeared, and maligned through negative advertisement; generally used in the passive voice. "I was smad repeatedly during that campaign." (DONALD RITCHIE, *historian*)

smerg • dorf *interj* [*smorgasbord* + G *Das sind mir bohmischer Dorfe,* that is, "It's all Greek (literally, villages in Bohemia) to me"]: A host of incomprehensible, boring, and irrelevant reasons compel us to act in a certain fashion, to which the proper response is "smergdorf!" Please don't make me explain. The expression is equally suitable for explicating why kids put beans in their ears and how the Internal Revenue Service decides whom to audit. It is related by free association to the hacker terms *automagically* and *phase of the moon.* "So you file the pink insurance form in the morning by interoffice mail and the yellow one by U.S. mail that afternoon? 'Smergdorf!' " (PAUL WALLICH, *journalist,* and MARIA-CHRISTINA KELLER, *journalist*)

smersh [acronym fr. *Science, Medicine, Education, Religion,* and all that *Shit,* originally used by the late Howard Simons, former managing editor of *The Washington Post*]: That section of newspapers and magazines known in journalistic jargon as the "back of the book"; any story published in such a section characterized by an absence of news and an abundance of what fourth-rate, adjunct journalism professors call "color writing." (BEN BRADLEE, *editor*)

sminge *n* [*smile* + *twinge*]: An expression that forms on the faces of those who have just received bad news; particularly descriptive of the mouth. "When Sam was told his uncle had cut him out of his will, a sminge began to form at the corners of his lips." "A sminge, which initially signals disbelief, will often precede the act of cursing." (TIMOTHY FINDLEY, *novelist*)

snartyr *n* [*snarl* + *martyr*]: A person who takes on a martyr-like role but whose manner betrays a certain hostility to others deemed incapable of recognizing extreme personal sacrifice. " 'Well, yes, it was hand-blown crystal that has been in the family for years . . . but don't you stop drinking for a second and concern yourself with such a trifle! I'll just get you another more durable glass . . .' " she cried, pursing her thin lips, rolling her eyes, and looking every inch the snartyr. (CAROL MUSKE, *writer*)

snit • i • cal *adj* [*snit + snide + critical*]: A disparaging remark aimed at you but ostensibly about something else, made by someone afraid of appearing unhip by admitting irrational feelings of anger or jealousy. "When I told Chad I couldn't see him this week because I was going to Cancun, he waxed snitical, saying, 'Oh, that tourist trap.' " (KAREN KARBO, *writer*)

snoot • fest *n* [fr. *snooty* the 1920s slang for snout + L *festivus* merry]: A dull event that one feels obliged to attend in order to impress a boss or maintain a certain social standing; a room full of people who wish they were somewhere else, balancing finger foods on cocktail napkins as they drift in and out of conversations, wearing brave smiles, and watching the clock. (TOM ABATE, *writer*)

snow • bird *n* [fr. *snowbird* any of several birds, including the junco, seen under snowy winter conditions]: 1: Something that's really there but you just can't see it (i.e., because it perfectly matches its background). 2: Something that was really there, but has now flown away. 3: Something that will be there

but, in any event, will not be visible once it is there. "A snowbird can be used in medicine to describe X rays, pathology, or physical examination findings that are extremely difficult to perceive but later show themselves to have been present. An example of a snowbird is a very early tumor of the colon that was not visible to anybody by any method until the colon was removed for some other reason, and there it was." (FRANCIS D. MOORE, *M.D.*)

snurm *v & n* [*sneak + worm*]: To penetrate sneakily; to get through, over, or under surreptitiously; to worm one's way. Also, **snurmy** *adj*: as in "that snurmy bastard." (ELLIOT RICHARDSON, *lawyer*)

so • ra • cious *adj* [fr. OE *sorh* anxiety, sorrow + Gk *a*- not + L *audacia* bold]: A desolate wit; intellectual humor fueled by desperation. "Dr. Johnson was a soracious lexicographer." (EDWARD HIRSCH, *poet*)

sound • bite *v* [fr. the noun of television jargon *soundbite* a brief, pithy statement from a talking head]: To make a purposeful attempt to be pithy, clever, succinct, and manipulative. " 'Mr. President, read our lips,' Governor Cuomo soundbited. 'We need your help and we're entitled to it.' "(Joe Klein, *writer*)

sour·caus·tic *adj* [*sour* + *caustic* + *sarcasm*, the latter from the Gk *sarkazein* "to tear at flesh," "to bite one's lip in rage," as in Aristophanes, "scrabbling away like ravenous puppy dogs"]: Characteristic of "a sharp, bitter, or cutting expression or remark; a bitter gibe or taunt," which is the definition supplied by the *Oxford English Dictionary* for the word, now watered down, *sarcasm*, and even supported by George Eliot's delicious epigram, "Blows are sarcasms turned stupid." "Perhaps it is a part of a general decline in civility, but such pejorative connotations of *sarcastic* seem to have declined or vanished, in political discourse and also in the republic of letters. Of course it was always present, but somehow it has recently been regarded as bad form. Yet the English language has the charming habit of being able to indicate degrees of some quality not only by the comparative and superlative modes (or, in the vernacular by one or more interpositions of the word *really*), but by the discrimination of synonyms, such as the adjectives: crude, vulgar, obscene. Sourcaustic, by combining two of the senses, taste and touch, can perhaps serve as a comparative or superlative to restore some of the lost force of *sarcastic*. It also connotes, to the cognoscenti, that when someone is being sourcaustic to you, the deeper problem lies within the speaker and not in you, and therefore you do not have to be sourcaustic in return. As someone perhaps once said, 'a sour stomach maketh for a caustic tongue.' And it is still true, as King Solomon did say, that 'a soft answer turneth away wrath'—although sometimes it also compoundeth it." (Jaroslav Pelikan, *professor*)

space-poor *adj* [by association with the late-19th-century English term *land-poor*, owning vast amounts of land, but lacking the funds to develop it or pay the taxes]: The condition resulting from spending an excessive percentage of a country's or business's assets on research and hardware for space exploration, leaving insufficient funds for other necessary expenditures. "The American vision is becoming increasingly clouded by dreams of spacial glory and the resulting inevitability of becoming space-poor." (E. Ward Herlands, *writer*)

spack·le·bod·y *n* [*spackle* the stuff you use to fill in the cracks in the wall + *body* signifying human beings]: A person who is just in your life to fill time and/or space. "Betty cringed when she introduced her best friend to the spacklebody next door and said, 'Meet Dave,' and the spacklebody said, 'Betty, my name is Don.' " (MARGO KAUFMAN, *journalist*)

spe • çoid *n* [*species* + *-oid* resembling, like]: One of the millions of unnamed species supposedly inhabiting tropical rain forests. "Certain ecologists working with a fancy computer program can 'prove' that a single speçoid is worth more than the entire Great Smokies National Park." (DANIEL B. BOTKIN, *environmentalist*)

spec • tac • u • lar • ist *n* [*spectacle* + *ocular*]: A person fascinated with extreme situations. " 'No wait—' mulled Brian, a middle-aged spectacularist hopping on a commuter flight to Bozeman where he planned to bid on a property where he could wait out the millennium, 'should bodybuilder terrorists armed with AK-47s and ghetto blasters shrieking Guns 'n' Roses overtake this flight during a storm, the whole scenario would be more compelling if all passengers on the plane were, for some reason, naked.' " (DOUGLAS COUPLAND, *writer*)

spec • to • clo • a • ca • pho • bia *n* [*spectacles* + L *cloaca* sewer + Gk *phobos* fear]: The irrational fear, physiologically specific to males, that one's eyeglasses are in danger of falling down the hole of a Portosan while one is attending an outdoor festival, house tour, or rustic concert. (L. J. DAVIS, *journalist*)

spill • eng *n* [intentional misspelling of *spelling*]: Outré spelling; intentionally spelling a word differently than it is usually spelled to gain a certain effect. "He loved the spilleng of the American landscape: the Krispy Kremes, the Luvs, the shoppes, and the Krystals." (GEOF HUTH, *writer*)

spon • ta • ne • ous com • bus • ti • er *n* [*spontaneous* + *combustion* + *bustier*]: 1: The act or process by which prepubescent females transform themselves into approximate imitations of some person or object that they admire. 2: Any act performed by a person under the age of eighteen, without parental approval. "Spontaneous combustier can be understood or *felt* during certain precious life moments: With an explosion of hair reminiscent of Farrah

Fawcett circa 1975 but touched up the side with a good buzz à la Sinéad O'Connor and sporting a temporary tattoo of a skull bearing the slogan 'Can't Stop, Won't Stop' stenciled on the small of her back and wearing the kind of bra typically associated with Madonna and the black lacy leggings of Cher, my daughter said, 'Hey, Mom, chill, I'll be fine,' as she threw herself onto the back end of a 750-horsepower hog owned by her new boyfriend, Slaughter." (LEON BING, *journalist*)

spooks • per • son *n* [*spokesperson* + *spook*]: An unnamed but official source, increasingly the only source of information about the government. "Typically the spooksperson is the person one would expect it to be but for political reasons is not nameable. The essence of the spooksperson was captured in a transcript reported in *The Washington Post* when Chief of Staff John Sununu, who had accused the press of preferring 'background' interviews to 'on-the-record' ones, trapped himself in this eerie conversation with the media: Press Secretary Marlin Fitzwater: 'This afternoon's briefing is on background. It's attributable to senior administration officials. Not for publication or use. Governor Sununu will make some opening remarks to give you an overview of the State of the Union address. . . . So I'd like to introduce, first of all, Governor Sununu.' Question: 'Is this on the record, Mr. Sununu?' Fitzwater: 'It's on background, because the President's giving his address this evening. This is attributable to senior administration officials. That's the correct way to do it.' Question: 'What's correct about it? There's nothing here they can't say on the record, is there?' Fitzwater: 'The purpose is to give you information, to flesh out the facts. The President's words tonight will speak for themselves.' Question: 'Well, the governor's accused us of wanting it on background.' 'Yes, we're not the ones who want this in secret.' Sununu: 'I don't mind not briefing.' Question: 'Come on.' 'Wait a minute.' 'Don't be temperamental.' Sununu: 'I'm not being temperamental. I just don't want to cause a problem.' Question: 'You accused us of wanting to do everything in secret, Governor. Let's do it in the open.' Fitzwater: 'The briefing is on background. The record is as we stated.' Question: 'We don't want you to be a faceless—' Sununu: 'I don't mind giving you an on-the-record interview whenever you ask for one—'

Question: 'When?' 'Now?' Sununu: '—but the fact is that you wanted some background for tonight's speech, and that's what we're here to give you. If you want to talk on the record on other subjects, I'll be very happy to do so.' Question: 'Who said we wanted background?' Sununu: 'How are we going to do this?' Fitzwater: 'It's on background.' Sununu: 'It's on background.' " (PAUL BICKART, *chemist*)

sporch *n* [*sports* + *speech*]: The special language employed by athletes in brief, postgame "jockerviews"; characterized by lack of originality, fragmentary structure, frequent pauses, rapid lateral eye movement, and extensive repetition of certain mantric syllables such as "uh," "yeah," "huh?", "na," "daguys," "dateam," "dadeefense." (WILL BAKER, *writer*)

spous•o•nym *n* [fr. *spouse* + -*nym* name]: A name conferred as the result of marriage, generally by credit card companies, phone solicitors, or blind convention. "After George Jones marries Sharon Trinidad, a George Trinidad materializes, receiving offers of credit cards and books by the month. At the same time, a Sharon Jones also materializes, often at the insistence of the Social Security Administration and the IRS. George Trinidad and Sharon Jones are spousonyms." (RODGER KAMENETZ, *poet*)

sprag *v* [Pennsylvania mining term; while riding on a coal car, to drag one's heavy boots along the rough floor of a mine in order to slow and eventually to stop the car's movement; later, while lying prone on a sled on a downhill run, in snow, to use one's boots to slow down or to turn the sled, as before sliding out into an intersection at the bottom of the hill]: To perform any foot-dragging maneuver to delay a swiftly moving process, or to set up a countermovement, in case a course of action already begun needs suddenly to be aborted or to be turned sharply in a variant direction. (MICHAEL NOVAK, *philosopher*)

stair•wit *n* [translation of the Fr *esprit d'escalier*]: The act of suddenly thinking of a brilliant remark or riposte only after the occasion, ascending the stairs as you come home. Example: "When Koch said, 'Did you read my last book?' I should have said, 'I hope so.' " See RETROTORT. (KIRKPATRICK SALE, *writer*)

stat•fus•ca•tion *n* [*statistics* + *obfuscation*]: A kind of statistical analysis that initially renders information mildly confusing, then furiously baffling, and finally utterly meaningless by bringing to bear the enormous machinery of statistical analysis on increasingly small, arcane, and ultimately useless collections of information. "During the game, the announcers annoyed the viewers with endless bits of statfuscation: 'During the month of August, Pete Incavaglia hit .378 against left-handers with runners in scoring position.' " (BOB COSTAS, *journalist*)

stealthbomber *n* [*Stealth bomber* late-20th-century aircraft putatively invisible to radar]: Unit of government expenditure equal to $550 million. "In 1990, 'stealthbomber' replaced the older, smaller and less topical 'destroyer' as the basic cost unit of political discourse, as in the phrase, 'one stealthbomber would pay for (some suitably large number of socially worthwhile things).' " (PAUL BICKART, *chemist*)

stel•loid *n* [fr. L *stella* star + *-oid* having the form of usually implying an incomplete or imperfect resemblance; see etymology of FACTOID]: A person who is famous primarily for being famous. "Samantha often wondered what Zsa Zsa Gabor, Ed McMahon, and other stelloids did with themselves after telethon season was over." (GARY KRIST, *writer*)

story-eyed *adj* [variant of *starry-eyed*]: Feigning a look of innocence while attempting to deceive. " 'I know I'm late, boss,' Jess began, fixing his employer with a story-eyed gaze, 'but somebody in the next car saw this UFO and traffic backed up for miles.' " (X. J. KENNEDY, *poet*)

sub•laud•a•tion *n* [*sub* below + *laud* praise]: Covert hostility expressed as admiration; the act of subverting praise even as one is seemingly lavish with it, e.g. "strong," intending "insensitive"; "independent," intending "forward" or "presumptuous"; "scholarly," intending "without imagination." " 'Grace is so energetic that she knows what you need almost before you do.' Sublaudation: Grace actively manipulates people. 'Harry is always generous to those less impressive than himself.' Sublaudation: Harry is habitually condescending." Also, **sublaudator** *n:* One who hides spite in commendation. Also, **sublaud** *v:* To approve for the sole purpose of condemning. (CYNTHIA OZICK, *writer*)

sub•sid•i•ar•i•ty *n* [*subsidize* + *subsidiary* + *solidarity*]: The expanded community of nations that results from the subsidizing of poor nations by rich ones. "The subsidiarity of the European Economic Community is now contending with the possible admission of Turkey." (JEFFREY ARCHER, *writer*)

su•per•flu•nyms *n* [*superfluous* + *synonyms*]: Words of neither beauty nor force that seemingly exist only to fill thesauruses, dictionaries, or the mouths of aesthetes; any vainglorious, prissy, or pretentious word used as ornament or obfuscation; particularly disfigured or attenuated forms of otherwise useful words—words surely destined, in that slow but cleansing triage operation of language, for the term archaic. "William F. Buckley, perhaps the greatest master of the superflunym, was given to words like cacophrenic (pertaining to an inferior intellect) or purpuraceous (purple)." (BRUCE DUFFY, *novelist*)

su•per•globs•lap•cious *n* [*super* + *globs* + *lap* + *delicious*]: An unbelievably delicious, ec-statically, and delightfully tasty treat. "Superglobslapcious describes what never before in human history was possible, such as, say, chocolate sauce poured on chocolate chocolate chip ice cream dolloped on top of chocolate cake, arguably with whipped cream and a heavy sprinkling of raspberries." See GALUBCIOUS. (ANDREW M. GREELEY, *novelist*)

sur•feit•igo *n* [*surfeit* + *vertigo*]: A sudden sense of being stuffed to the gills by food, drink, friends, parties, invitations, fund-raising events, black-tie occasions, most commonly diagnosed in the season beginning with Thanksgiving and ending with Twelfth Night. "Her condition was misdiagnosed as Epstein-Barr syndrome, but was really an extreme case of surfeitigo, resulting in nausea, vomiting, migraine, dizziness, and diminished libido." (JOYCE CAROL OATES, *writer*)

sur•viv•u•lous *adj* [*survival* + *fabulous*]: Describes the pleasure felt when imagining what it would be like to be the last remaining person on earth. "What would be particularly survivulous would be to go up in a helicopter and throw microwave ovens down on the Taco Bell.'' (DOUGLAS COUPLAND, *writer*)

Swag•gart *n* —**Swag•gar** *v* [vulgar, fr. voyeur/evangelist *Jimmy Swaggart*]: A vulgarity for an erect born-again penis with an urgeful curiosity. ''Peeping through the hole, he grabbed his Swaggart.'' (Also, used in place of ''Johnson'' in the still cruder form, ''Well, boy, did I ever bend my Swaggart.'') Also, **Swaggar** *v:* ''Here I was, Swaggaring away, trying to purge myself, but it was like the l'il devil had a mind all his own.'' (BRUCE DUFFY, *novelist*)

swet•hert *n* [*sweetheart* + *sweat* + *hurt*]: Tender endearment exchanged by compulsive, athletic lovers side by side on their *stairmasters* or *lifecycles* in the health club. (HAROLD JAFFE, *editor*)

swoop•head *n* [*swoop* or *sweep* + *head*]: A balding man who chooses to grow the hair on one side of his head to a ludicrous length—long enough to comb or swoop it all the way over the balding spot to the other side of the head—apparently without the slightest intention of fooling anyone. ''Mr. Jones felt much better about swooping his hair after it was pointed out to him by a close friend that some of the greatest men in history were swoopheads, namely, Julius Caesar, Napoleon, General Douglas MacArthur, Zero Mostel, and, of course, Dick Van Patten.'' (MICHAEL HOLMAN, *filmmaker*)

swoophead

syn•tho *n* [fr. Gk *synthetikos* to put together]: Any artificial portion of the body, such as a valve, organ, limb, or joint. "At the rate he was undergoing opera- tions, Herman would soon be made up of more synthos than original equipment." (SCOTT RUSSELL SANDERS, *writer*)

T

Ta•ba•sic *adj* [back-formation fr. *Tabasco*]: Peppery spiciness in food. English currently has only one word, "hot," to denote both the temperature of food and its degree of spiciness. "Tabasic avoids unwieldy expressions such as 'Are you wincing because the enchilada is "temperature-hot" or because it is "spicy-hot"?' " (BILLY COLLINS, *poet*)

ta•ble *v & n* [fr. *table* the piece of furniture + *table* the motion in parliaments to delay]: 1: To argue in a group about which restaurant to patronize that evening especially in large cities, especially when part of that group is made up of out-of-town guests. "Maggie had wanted to go to the Hors Doeuvrey and wasn't in the mood for Thai food. So we stood on the platform and tabled for a while longer." 2: To quarrel over who will pay the check after dinner. "Before I knew it, Franz had tabled the check and was already asking what 15 percent of $73.95 came to." As a noun: The gesture that often accompanies the action of tabling. "When a person continues to converse while sliding the check facedown, slaloming it around the dirty dishes and into his or her own lap, he or she is said to have performed a table. The companions at dinner, when they notice the check is missing, revert to the stabbing lunges for the check from the guest who tabled it. This maneuver is called *table turning* and can be an expression of a sincere desire to pay the bill or not. *To split the table* is not the compromise that is often suggested, that of splitting the tab; it is the argument that leads to the compromise. Those from the city usually suggest an even division of the tab while the out-of-town guests who have frugally ordered the cheapest menu item in anticipation of paying for just what was ordered demurely swallow the subsidization of their hosts' meals." (MICHAEL MARTONE, *writer*)

tac・to・tum *n*—**tac・to** *n* & *v* [*tacky* + *tactic* + L *totem* everything + *factotum*]: An employee charged with various damage control errands of a low order; synonym for *spindweeb*. Usually shortened to **tacto.** "Better get some tactos on this after we deny it." Also as a verb: To engage in a protracted campaign of small evasions, misspeaks, disinfos, and micromanagement in order to infuriate. (WILL BAKER, *writer*)

taut・o・bar *n* [*tautology* + *barometer*]: The compulsive capacity for redundancy found especially among weather forecasters, spawned by the conviction that such terms as heat, cold, wind, and rain are meaningless to viewers without embellishment. "The most common tautobars are 'blizzard conditions,' 'thunderstorm activity,' 'a warming trend so far as the temperature side of things is concerned,' 'considerable sunshine during the daylight hours,' and 'seasonal weather

for this time of the year.' " (WILL STANTON, *writer*)

tech・no・gloat *n* [fr. Gk *techne* art or skill + *gloat*]: In general, profound satisfaction in technique, at the expense of purpose; particularly, intense joy at a weapon's effectiveness, without regard to its human cost. "Technogloat filled the general's face as he replayed the video of the smart bomb invading the bunker." (RODGER KAMENETZ, *poet*)

tech・no・peas・ant *n* [*technological* + *peasant*]: A person who is seriously backward in certain kinds of technical knowledge necessary for upward mobility in our society. "I don't know if I can work with such a technopeasant. I mean, he's never used a fax or a computer." (EVA HOFFMAN, *writer*)

tech・no・pho・ria *n* [*technology* + *euphoria*]: The feeling of exhilaration experienced by milquetoast columnists when they watch high-priced munitions blow up a third-world country. "A wave of technophoria came over Fred Barnes as he began typing his salute to the Tomahawk cruise missile." (SCOTT SHUGER, *editor*)

tech・nyo・kel *n* [*technology* + *yokel*]: One whose purview is defined by high technology and computers; an absorption into the realm of circuitry, software, and anything else electronic that diminishes social skills. "The woman threw herself wildly across the keyboard, but technyokel that he was, Garland worried only about the harm to his hard disk." (MICHAEL GLOBETTI, *writer*)

tech•toid *n* [*technology* + *-oid;* see etymology of FACTOID]: False technology, as in the plastic gadget you bought yesterday that broke today. "The most distinctive feature of a techtoid is that it has surpassed older technology that suffered from artificial obsolescence. For techtoids, the obsolescence is quite real and immediate." See ARTIFRACT. (DANIEL B. BOTKIN, *environmentalist*)

tel•e•ce•leb•u•al *n* [*television* + *celebrity* + *ritual*]: 1: The highly predictable give-and-take between television talk show host and celebrity guest, first developed by Jack Paar and formalized by Johnny Carson in the '60s, '70s, and '80s. 2: The ritual pattern that typically includes questions and answers about recent appearances, performances, products, endorsements, and upcoming events; comparisons between acting in film and on stage; birth, marriage, divorce, and affair announcements or denials; comments on recent tabloid defamation, and inquiries concerning major ethical issues answered in inane manner and followed by prompted applause. "I watched a half hour of *The Arsenio Hall Show.* That was enough to catch the whooping and wailing intros, the monologue, and two telecelebuals." (ERIC BRETTSCHNEIDER, *attorney*)

tele•crat•ic *adj* [*television* + *autocratic*]: 1. The authoritative voice of anything that appears on television, especially the voice of announcers, anchors, and other celebrities. "Charlton Heston is the telecratic spokesman for the Ten Commandments and the *National Review*, with equal impact for each." 2. A form of government that takes its authority from television. "Ronald Reagan was more telecratic than presidential, as is Dan Quayle." (JOAN KONNER, *journalist*)

te•le•fo•nade *n* [*telephone* + *-ade*]: A telephone conversation of extended duration and significance between two or more parties. "At three yesterday morning, Uncle Willy gave me a telefonade to explain why our family tree, which he said dated back to pirates, needs to be discontinued. I was up until dawn." Or, "Believe it or not, it was in a telefonade that Rusty and I decided we should get married." (Barbara Probst Solomon, *writer*)

te•le•mi•nate *v* [*television* + *ruminate*]: 1: To think about a television program after it is over. 2: To worry about the fate or future of a television character, especially a character that occurs in a situation comedy or in a soap opera. "Agnes teleminated over the fate of Agent Cooper in *Twin Peaks* so excessively that she included him in her prayers." (Louis Phillips, *writer*)

te•le•pa•the•tic *adj* [*telepathy* + *pathetic*]: A specious claim of mystical contact with another being. "When members of the studio audience failed to pick up her mental messages, Madame Rose looked telepathetic to TV viewers around the nation." (Marvin Bell, *poet*)

tem•press *v* [*temper* + *suppress* + *impress*]: To withhold natural anger and channel it into a solution to rid one of that which has angered one. "John was furious when his boss unfairly insulted him before his friends but tempressed his desire to shout back or worse; he only chuckled, sur-

prising his boss and thrilling his peers." (Bajon Kahlil Siron-El, *lyricist*)

ten•ta•ta•tion *n* [*tentative* + *temptation*]: A feeble temptation easily resisted. "Staring down from the observation platform to the pavement ninety stories below, Marge felt a fleeting tentatation to jump." (X. J. Kennedy, *poet*)

tes•ti•fe•rous *adj* [*testicle* + *testy* + *testosterone* + *-ferous*, bearing or producing]: Uppity, agitated, irritable, and ugly; the male counterpart to the word "hysterical." "Yosemite Sam is one of those hyperaggressive sado-macho types who have hair-trigger tempers, chips on their shoulders, and epinephrine-driven endocrine systems. What a testiferous little creature! Coyotes beware." (Lewis Burke Frumkes, *writer*)

tha•na•fac•tion *n* [*thanatopsis* + *satisfaction*]: The feeling of satisfaction, however fleeting, that comes upon the news of another's death. "Although it was sad to hear of President Nixon's death, many people had feelings of thanafaction." (Brian McCormick, *writer*)

the•or•i•ous *adj* [*theory* + *serious*]: Total devotion to theoretical concerns in any intellectual endeavor. "Immersed in examining the theories of such literary scholars as Harold Bloom and Northrop Frye, she was so theorious that she had little time or patience to read the literary texts to which they referred." (LEONARD NATHAN, *poet*)

ther • a • tic *adj & n* [fr. Gk *therates* hunter]: Being in or practicing the hunting-gathering stage of culture. "Neanderthal man was undoubtedly a theratic." See ASTIC. (L. SPRAGUE DE CAMP, *writer*)

thift *n* [*theft + thrift*]: Banking, often offshore, of the laundered proceeds of crime. "Well-known practitioners of thift include Robert Vesco, Manuel Noriega (at least, according to the U.S. Department of Justice), and, presumably, the late Ferdinand Marcos." (PAUL BICKART, *chemist*)

thin • u • ous *adj* [*thin + fatuous*]: Of or pertaining to a person provocatively lacking in presumption and chronic self-assertion. "Yes, George was the president, yes, George had gone to Yale, yes, George had struck oil, yes, George handled a golf cart like Juan Fangio, but throughout he maintained an air of thinuous bafflement that caused even close friends and large contributors to wonder why he seemed to lack the hormone supposed to urge him to grow into office." (LIONEL TIGER, *professor*)

thorsyndrome

thor•syn•drome *n* [fr. *Thor* Norse god of thunder, who was known for his hammer, Mjolnir, and his quick temper but not for his intellectual capacity +*syndrome*]: Overenchantment with a single tool; fixation on a single approach to a spectrum of problems. "Thorsyndrome is evident in the following sentences: When your only tool is a hammer, everything looks like a nail. You can use your spreadsheet program as a word processor, but a penciled note taped to the refrigerator may be more effective. You can send the army to Bolivia to solve the drug epidemic because the military approach worked in Grenada, didn't it? You can amend the Constitution to ban abortion, balance the budget, stop flag burning, and forbid dial-a-porn because Prohibition made liquor illegal, didn't it? You can kill a fly with a hammer, but you had better not care about what the fly is sitting on." (PAUL BICKART, *chemist*)

thought•let *n* [*thought* + *droplet*]: A first stirring of a thought or an embarrassed advance of an incomplete or risky inchoate idea. "I had this thoughtlet about our plans . . . my book . . . your work." (FRITZ STERN, *historian*)

threft *n* [*thrift* + *theft*]: Savings-and-loan malfeasance. "Well-known suspected practitioners include Charles Keating and Neil Bush." (PAUL BICKART, *chemist*)

tip•gore *n* [fr. eponymous hero *Tipper Gore,* late-20th-century record-labeler]: 1: A member of a hysterical band of promoters, entertainers, and hero-worshipers, roughly equivalent to the bacchantes of ancient Greece. 2: Initiator of great public spectacles, signifying nothing. "When things got slow, the tipgore ran amok, slapping stickers on records, hitting the children with hairbrushes, and drinking rubbing alcohol." (KEVIN BAKER, *writer*)

tor•ti•cul•ture *n* [*tort* + *culture*]: A society whose chief characteristic is derived from legal action; a culture in which the elements of life are less celebrated than their legal ramifications. "During the last half of the twentieth century, America became a blatant torticulture—and the legal aspects of art, film, sport, architecture, real estate, finance, engineering, and science became more prominent than the disciplines themselves. Jaded Americans ask themselves: 'Why read the book or see the film when I already

know the terms of the deal?' "
(RON CARLSON, *writer*)

tou•jours vu *n* [fr. Fr *already
seen*, in the sense of "seen everywhere one looks" and by association with *déjà vu*]: That
state of affairs where, once one
has been made aware of a condition or an object, one suddenly sees it with alarming frequency; e.g. a newly pregnant
woman will, for the first time,
see legions of other pregnant
women; anyone acquiring a certain breed of dog or type of
product or change of hairstyle
will see others like it daily, even
hourly. "It is unknown whether
toujours vu is a matter of enhanced pattern recognition or of
outside   conspiracy."   (LIA
MATERA, *writer*)

tour-worn *adj* [*tour* + *worn*]: Of
or pertaining to a crowded place
you think you deserve all to
yourself, that is, free of pizza
bones and bozo tour groups,
usually German or American,
waving gaudy time-to-board-
the-bus flags, but of course you
are one of the ones flocking
there to wear the place out. "He
went to the Piazza del Signoria
with high hopes and a copy of
Elizabeth Spencer's wonderfully
nuanced *Light in the Piazza* but
found the place so tour-worn as
to be almost tragic. Like flying
to the moon in a couple of centuries, he had gotten there too
late." "The word can suggest,
though seasoned travelers need
no reminder, the sort of extreme behavior that the condition is capable of precipitating,
especially in relationships that
are stormy to start with, as in
the following poem: 'In an earlier town by the tour-worn sea/
we had argued in a fury over
nothing/ more important than
where to spend the night/ or
who would drive or when./ I
wanted to stay and watch holiday fireworks—/ feu d'artifice—
and the arrival of a beauty
queen/ named Stephanie
Gomez, so I gave her the keys to
leave.' " (JAMES SEAY, *poet*)

traith *n* [*wraith* + *truth*]: That
which is lost in translation.
"Traith refers to the ghostly nuances that surround words in
another language and that no
English word begins to approximate. It can be used extensively
in scholarly studies where the
translator now can meet any
queries with 'Well, the truth is
that the traith of this line is
loosely connected to the traith
of the title, which, while seemingly inconsequential, offers us
even more possibilities for inter-
pretation—if we could find a
word to cover the distance be-

tween one traith and another.' " (JUDITH KITCHEN, *writer*)

tran•sci•ence *n*
tran•sci•en•tist *n* [*transient* + *science*]: The study of the transitory nature of science. "The transcientist recognizes that the scientific truths of today are destined to be revised or overturned by future generations of scientists." (TODD SILER, *artist/ writer*)

tran•si•fy *v* [*transitive* a characteristic of a class of verbs with implications of taking charge and pursuing action + -*ify* suffix suggesting "to make so"]: To change an intransitive verb into a transitive one, often performed by presidents, their sycophants, and their speechwriters and thereby to take responsibility for an action that would have happened otherwise. "All of our recent presidents have transified in an attempt to spread their tailfeathers: President Bush recently asserted that he would not 'screech' something 'to a halt' and that he would not 'vent a spleen' somewhere. President Carter once said he would 'evolve a foreign policy.' " (EUGENE J. MCCARTHY, *politician*)

trans•ish *v* [fr. L *trans* across, beyond, through, so as to change + -*ish* related to -*ition* as in transition or position]: To cross smoothly from one point to another, physical or ideological; to connect easily a great number of seemingly disparate ideas without their seeming disparate; in oral or written discourse to *swish* from one idea or paragraph to another with great facility; to link ideas smoothly with clear transitions. "In presenting her lecture, she transished from one point to another with great ease and clarity." "His schedule allowed him to transish from one plane to another without having to wait for interminable hours in crowded terminals." (IMOGENE BOLLS, *poet*)

trend•vane *n* [*trend* + *vane*, as in weathervane]: One who turns quickly and easily, to point in whichever direction the literary and intellectual winds of fashion are blowing. "I always read X's column before going to a party. It was a most reliable trendvane, and helps me to appear well informed and above all up-to-date." (BERNARD LEWIS, *professor*)

trip•i•da•tion *n* [*trepidation* + *trip*]: Travel anxiety. "He had such a bad case of tripidation that he reached the station three hours before departure time." (HARRY MATHEWS, *writer*)

tris • kai • de • ka • pho • bi • a • pho • bi • a *n* [fr. Gk *triskaideka* thirteen + *phobos* fear + *phobia*]: Fear of the dozens of cutesy-pie fear-of-the-number-13 stories invariably trotted out by the media every Friday the 13th. "After seeing two newspaper articles, three magazine pieces, and eleven television reports about the fact that tomorrow is Friday the 13th, I came down with triskaidekaphobiaphobia and decided to stay in bed all day, with the covers pulled over my head." (MARK J. ESTREN, *writer*)

tromp *n* [onomatopoeiac]: The sound and vibration of heavy earth-moving or agricultural machinery, derived from the lesser sound of marching feet. "The yearly tromp of vast and heavy machines and the generous spraying of herbicides and pesticides ensured that all but a few resistant plant and insect species were eliminated." (JAMES E. LOVELOCK, *scientist*)

trum • pery *n* [existing word meaning something without use or value, and by association with eponymous hero *Donald Trump*]: Self-advertising; the blazoning of one's name on hotels, casinos, and airliners; commercial graffiti. Examples of trumpery abound: Dr. Armand Hammer, the Occidental Petroleum billionaire and self-described friend of V. I. Lenin, tried without success to purchase the Church & Dwight Company, makers of Arm & Hammer baking soda. Amos wasn't famous until Famous Amos cookies made him famous. John De Lorean might have been better off if he hadn't named the car after himself. Nothing could have saved the Edsel. In a display of unrelieved trumpery, Donald Trump sued a credit card company for using Trump Card as a trademark. (ALBERT SHANKER, *educator*)

tump [*tumble* + *jump* + *dump*]: 1: To move clumsily over an obstructing object, thereby knocking over the object and falling oneself. 2: By extension, any action that combines the notions and motions of tumbling, jumping, and dumping at once. "Humpty-Dumpty tumped over a wall; Presidents Nixon and Carter tumped over public opinion." (JOHN STONE, *M.D.*) 3: To knock over accidentally, particularly some vessel full of something so that whatever it is in it spills out. "One spills a glass of water and tumps a can of coffee beans." (KENT NELSON, *writer*)

twick *n & v* [*twitch* + *tick*, the latter containing a reference to the passage of time]: The grimace that passes over the face when one suddenly recalls an embarrassing moment from long ago. Also as a verb: To make an utterance of acute embarrassment that escapes before one can stop it often causing another embarrassing event in the present moment that will be remembered suddenly years from now when it is least desired or expected. (MICHAEL MARTONE, *writer*)

ty•po•mort *n* [*typewriter* + Fr *morte* death]: The idea that companies will force a consumer to purchase the next higher level of technology by knowingly ceasing to produce replacement parts for his or her current machine. "I didn't want this laser-powered computer entertainment center, but it was typomort: I couldn't find anyone who could repair my record player." (ALBERT GOLDBARTH, *writer*)

tys•ter•i•a *n* [*testicle* + *hysteria*]: Male reaction to any stimuli, whether mild or extreme, as judged by observers of the female sex. "His case was severely undercut by the tysteria of his testimony." (JOYCE CAROL OATES, *writer*)

U

un•an•i•mal *n & adj* [fr. G *Untier* unanimal or nonanimal, which means *monster*, violation of nature]: A being who does great damage because of an inability to respond, understand, or resonate to the chastity and reason given in animal nature. Those forces and behaviors that we so often mistakenly call animal, as when we say that bureaucrats or brokers or mobs are behaving like animals. "No one ever saw an animal manipulate the stock market, run a scam on widows and orphans, or make the world safe for democracy (or for communism), and no one ever will. Crooked, sleazy behavior in the political, economic, demagogical, and academic worlds is unanimal." (VICKI HEARNE, *writer*)

un•der•par•a•noia *n* [*under* + *paranoia*]: An unhealthy level of trust, optimism, and faith; the condition of someone whose defense mechanisms are weak, inadequate, lacking a minimum level of suspicion; and unaware that a significant number of people are out to get you a significant percent of the time; does not connote the innocence of "unsuspecting" or "naïve." "George was underparanoid not to have suspected that those meetings his staff were holding without him were a threat to his leadership." (ERIC BRETTSCHNEIDER, *attorney*)

un•face *v* [*un-* + *face*]: To experience memory loss in which a name becomes unmoored from its corresponding face; more generally, the forgetting of meaningful details. "When I saw Mary I tried to recall how I planned to explain my absence the previous night, but the alibi had been unfaced." (LUC SANTE, *journalist*)

uni•sapi•en *n* [fr. L *unus* one and only one + L *sapiens* thinking, and by association with Homo sapiens, *thinking man*]: The human race seen as a single, living organism united by a simultaneous common thought; with needs, abilities, and a disposition entirely different from the human race conventionally defined as a collection of individual human beings. "As the human body is composed of a myriad of individual molecules bound together electromagnetically, the unisapien is composed of all living human beings bound together by a common thought or sentiment. Like a human amoeba whose protoplasm is the collective 'one thought,' the unisapien exists to usher humankind upward toward a more metaphysical state. Science fiction writer Arthur C. Clarke must have had the unisapien in mind when he wrote his masterpiece, *Childhood's End*." (MICHAEL HOLMAN, *filmmaker*)

up•data *v* [*update* | *date* | *data*]: The process of introducing new information about something, unrelated to time as in "update" or to social climbing as in ". . . crushed because he failed in his call to bag an update with the princess of Murmansk-Fiori." "Sadly Swofty had to updata Sonny on the number of sex pages in *Cross*

Those Lubricious when Prixie had second thoughts about the number of first experiences of the class of '96 she could recount in Chapter 2 and found that when they were set in Chapter 3 they flew by needingless description, less authorial involvement—simply, less is more." (LIONEL TIGER, *professor*)

V

va • ca • noia *n* [*vacation* + *paranoia*]: The mental state created when one is in one's vehicle headed for vacation and someone else in the car asks whether anyone turned off the stove or oven. "I'm overwhelmed with vacanoia, Marge. I'm going to have to go back and check." (FRANK GANNON, *writer*)

vague • nost • i • cism *n* [*vague* + *agnosticism;* pronounced *fognosticism*]: 1: A condition of being haunted by religious feeling with typically only the most meager or childlike understanding of religious questions and thinking; sentimental religious illiteracy, as with notions of Jesus as a "good dude," etc. 2: A desire for the authority, tradition, and moral comfort of religion accompanied by a resentment of the first two as requiring effort, and the third as something achievable with neither real commitment nor inward change. 3: The driftings, lame rationalizations, and postponements of parents in "shopping" for a religion for their children. "Finally, after a long period of vaguenostism, David's inner questions grew dim, then dimmer, and then it was pretty okay." (BRUCE DUFFY, *novelist*)

va • nish • ing hitch • hik • er *n* [from Jan Harold Brunvand's book, *The Vanishing Hitchhiker: American Urban Legends and Their Meaning*. The legend of the vanishing hitchhiker tells of a wayside traveler who, when picked up, climbs into the backseat, preaches, prophesies, and finally falls silent. The motorists turn to check on their voluble companion and find that he has disappeared. The story is always told as having happened to "a friend of a friend."]: A person who enjoys a reputation based largely upon hearsay. The term *vanishing hitchhiker* may describe, for instance, those writers or painters whom everyone seems to agree are wonderful writers or painters, but whose work no one seems to have actually read or viewed. "The career of a vanishing hitchhiker tends to enact the triumph of gossip over substance. The term connotes a high-profile presence who is along for the ride and who many people hope will have disappeared the next time they turn to look." (ALICE FULTON, *poet*)

ver•al•gia *n* [fr. L *veritas* truth + Gk *algos* pain]: 1: The pain associated with seeing things as they truly are. 2: The chronic condition of such pain, especially pronounced among young adults when they realize they have heretofore been living by myths, vain hopes, and blind adherence to social fashions. "A wave of veralgia swept over Todd as he regarded his First Boston pay stub and realized his annual income had plummeted." "Her strength sapped by veralgia, Nancy tiptoed past the baby's room, hoping to dodge for a few more minutes the squalid demands of motherhood." (LAWRENCE SHAMES, *writer*)

ver•i•lude *n*—**ver•i•lud•ic** *adj* [fr. L *veritas* truth + *ludens* play; and by association with *'lude* a colloquial abridgement of Quaalude, a prescription drug frequently, albeit illegally, purchased and consumed for its sensually stupefactive effects]: 1: A form of entertainment emergent in the United States in the last quarter of the 20th century, in which the distinction between straightforward and parodic representation is deliberately elided or erased, as in the now-classic "Blues Brothers" routines of comedians Dan Aykroyd and John Belushi on *Saturday Night Live* in the mid-to-late 1970s. 2: By extension, a form of political language or address arising during the same era in which what is officially asserted is, simultaneously, what is hidden or denied, and vice versa, as in the Reagan-Bush administration's overt, frequently reasserted support for the "covert" war against the internationally recognized, legal government of Nicaragua, 1981–1990. "By asserting both that 'the footage released by the Iraqi government today of dead and wounded civilians is pure propaganda,' and that 'in a war situation like this one, some collateral damage is inevitable,' the Pentagon spokesman veriludically proclaimed our country's innocence at the same time as he shrugged off its guilt." "Both the wacky whimsy evident in the most ostensibly sinister or violent episodes of *Wild at Heart* and the stilted affirmations of romantic and familial middle-class normality in *Blue Velvet* invite us into that characteristic state of languor in which assent, fascination, and a weary self-loathing coincide, known as the zone of the verilude, where Ronald Reagan is king-for-half-life, and film director David Lynch his jester on the nod." (FRED PFEIL, *writer*)

ve‧ri‧nym *n* [fr. L *veritas* truth + Gk *onoma* name]: A true name; a person's actual name, especially when it is an acceptable form or part of a name (like "Madonna" or "Prince") used by a person essentially as a pseudonym or as replacement for a full name. "Whatever his verinym, D. B. Cooper will remain famous under his adopted name, because the audacity of his crime and his subsequent disappearance continue to fascinate us." (GEOF HUTH, *writer*)

ve‧ri‧ty *n*—**ve‧ri‧tist** *n* [fr. ME *verite* fr. OF fr. L *veritas* truth]: Factual writing; nonfiction as opposed to fiction. "Verity is a necessary replacement for the now vacuous word *nonfiction* and can be used as in the following: 'Fiction and verity.' 'Fictions and verities.' 'Poet, novelist, veritist.' 'The Future of Poetry; The Future of Verity.' 'What do you do?' 'I'm a writer.' 'What do you write?' 'I write poetry/fiction/verity.' 'Are you working on a new verity?' 'Yes, my latest verity is ___.' 'Is this book fictional?' 'No, it's factual; it's a work of verity.' 'Is there truth in fiction?' 'Yes.' 'Is there truth in verity?' 'Yes.' 'Are they different truths?' 'Sometimes.' 'How often do fiction and verity differ?' 'Fiction is self-referential, whereas verity by custom is linked to external documentation.' 'Do you prefer the term *verity* to the term *nonfiction*?' 'Very much.' 'Then please share it around.' " (RICHARD RHODES, *writer*)

ves‧tite *n* [back-formation fr. *transvestite*]: A double cross dresser; a female female-impersonator. "Famous vestites are Julie Andrews's character in *Victor/Victoria*, Mae West, Marlene Dietrich, and Bette Midler." (PAUL BICKART, *chemist*)

vex‧il‧lol‧a‧try *n* [fr. L *vexillum* flag + Gk *latreia* worship that may be offered only to God]: Flag worship. "Vexillolatry is a religion publicly adhered

videolatry

to by many but privately practiced by even fewer than is Christianity." (PAUL BICKART, *chemist*)

vid·dy *adj* [*video* + *giddy*]: Compulsively interpreting one's life in terms of characters, plots, and images derived from television and film; possession by visual images. "Phillip was so viddy by the end of the film festival that he kept looking for the credits beneath his face in the mirror." (SCOTT RUSSELL SANDERS, *writer*)

vi·de·o·la·li·a *n* [*video* + *echolalia*]: Automatic, trancelike viewing of home videotapes depicting social or recreational activities that just took place. "Sociologists at the University of Alabama at Birmingham have conclusively linked the advent of the three- and four-day holiday weekend to the phenomenon of videolalia. 'Picnics, softball games, and even the simple preparation of meals now require twice as much time as they used to, due to the participants' apparently hypnotic urge to watch themselves doing what they in fact did only minutes before,' says the professor 'And that doesn't take into account the time consumed by people dancing around and cavorting in a way that would be regarded as very peculiar indeed if not for the presence of the camera.'" (TOM DRURY, *writer*)

vi·de·o·la·try *n* [*video* + *idolatry*]: Worship of televised images, especially to the point that the flow of television icons solidifies, becoming a motionless residue of reference. "A genetic basis for the religious impulse seems more credible after one observes the ease with which infants slip in to videolatry." (JACK COLLOM, *poet*)

ves • tite

vin • di • noi • a *n* [*vindicate* + *paranoia*]: The revelation that one's paranoia was grounded in a REAL menace. "Upon the release of secret police documents in 1990, the East Germans experienced a national surge of vindinoia, confirming that for years someone really had been watching them." (RICHARD ZACKS, *writer*)

vi • nyl • i • ty *n* [*vinyl* + *futility* + (maybe) *senility*]: A futile clinging to the purchase of goods for which the prevalent technology has become outmoded. "He stooped over the LP record bin searching for a copy of Madonna's latest single, a sign of his ever-increasing vinylity." (HOWARD RABINOWITZ, *writer*)

vo • lump • tu • ous *adj* [*voluptuous* + *lump*]: 1: The unfortunate and often disfiguring qual-

ity of extreme weight gain in formerly beautiful and buxom women; may be attended by obsessive overuse of cosmetics, heightening a florid and piglike demeanor, especially among the well-to-do. "It's a shame she's become so volumptuous; I'm surprised her husband hasn't found a mistress or filed for divorce." 2: The quality of pleasurableness or sensuousness now become obscene or fraudulent. Also, **volumptuary** *n* [*volumptuous* + *luminary*]: Volumptuous women who are well known to the public. "The Academy Awards celebration was attended by Liz Taylor, among other volumptuaries." (COLIN HARRISON, *writer*)

vorce *v* [back-formation fr. *divorce*]: To remarry one's former spouse. "Famous vorces are Elizabeth Taylor and Richard Burton, Melanie Griffith and Don Johnson, and the Federal and Democratic Republics of Germany." (PAUL BICKART, *chemist*)

vul • gar • ithm *n* [*vulgar* + Gk *arithmos* number]: 1: A unit measuring the velocity of popular culture toward the lowest common denominator. 2: The speed at which popular culture descends toward the lowest common denominator. "Every body-function joke on television is a vulgarithm." (RON CARLSON, *writer*)

W

walk • ie *n* [fr. *walkie-talkie;* first used in the early 1950s in association with people who would buy one walkie-talkie]: Someone who buys equipment without having a use for it. "That guy is a total walkie." (EDWIN SCHLOSSBERG, *artist*)

wall • poo • dle *n* [origin obscure]: A person inordinately—but secretly—fascinated with the interior decoration of other people's houses. "That bidet was a wallpoodle's delight." (ALEXANDER THEROUX, *writer*)

wan • na • BBC *n* [*wannabee* + *BBC*]: 1: The tendency displayed by the American upper class and haute bourgeoisie to speak and act as if they are living in the last days of a British colony; this tendency, as found in the young at prep schools who model their fashion and accents after the British lower classes while their parents ape the British upper classes. 2: The Public Broadcasting Service (PBS). "We had been viewing *The Simpsons* upon the Fox channel, but when the Queen's cousin stopped by for tea, we found it prudent to switch to wannaBBC." (BRIAN McCORMICK, *writer*)

war • gasm *n* [*war* + *orgasm*]: An ecstatic convulsion that periodically strikes nations, usually proceeding from the top down. "Telltale signs of a wargasm are renewed vigor in aging leaders with poll-anemia, press conferences featuring gestures of the hand as blade or cudgel, frequent use of the words 'peace,' 'reasonable,' 'more than halfway,' and 'massive troop deployments.'" (WILL BAKER, *writer*)

weenge *n & v* [*wee* + *twinge*]: In males, a brief, mild spasm of sexual pleasure without ejaculation, voluntarily produced by a constriction of the muscles in legs or thighs. "Cramped from long occupying his bus seat, without even having a love object in mind, Max crossed his legs and caused weenge after weenge to course over him." Also, as a verb: To induce such a spasm. "On the park benches lolled adolescent boys, weenging and gritting their teeth as girls walked by." (X. J. KENNEDY, *poet*)

wil・lie pep *n* [fr. eponymous hero *Willie Pep* (1922–present), professional prizefighter]: The act of two people attempting to go in opposite directions who wind up blocking each other's path by spontaneously moving back and forth rapidly, but always remaining directly in front of the other person. "I'm sorry I'm late. I had a willie pep with a guy in the hall." (FRANK GANNON, *writer*)

white el・e・phan・ti・a・sis *n* [*white elephant* + *-iasis*]: The apparently uncontrollable construction of large office towers in economically depressed areas with a high commercial vacancy rate. "A spokesman for Bloatcorp denied that last Monday's groundbreaking for its new headquarters, which coincided with the firm's filing for Chapter 11 bankruptcy protection and also with the city's bond default, is a symptom of white elephantiasis." (STEVE MESSINA, *editor*)

whuf・fle *v*—**whuf・fler** *n* [*whine* + *wheeze* + *snuff* + *sniffle*]: The annoying, scratchy sound made by weepy feminists as they lament the sufferings of women and, houndlike, sniff out evidence of male oppression in literature, art, and the media. "Some compare the sound of whuffling to the rustle of Victorian crinoline skirts. Others speak of a badmintonlike spank and whoosh. Still others think of a jumbled feathery flapping, as in the attic-torture of Tippi Hedren in *The Birds*. Of a femi-

willie pep

nist theorist: She whuffled her way to the top. Of a feminist conference: The room overflowed with whufflers. Of a feminist lecture: The whuffling was unbearable." (CAMILLE PAGLIA, *writer*)

wilkes *n* [fr. eponymous hero *John Wilkes Booth*, presidential assassin]: A primitive but demonstrably effective measurement of the compassionate genius possessed by American presidents. The standard of the wilkes system is seriously flawed because so few American presidents have possessed any genius, to say nothing of compassion, that precise quantification is impossible. James Madison probably rates three-quarters of a wilkes, and he was fortunate to have been born at a time when the martyring of chief executives was unfashionable. Jefferson, who was brilliant but not compassionate, is tentatively pegged at one-tenth of a wilkes, while Franklin Roosevelt, who was not compassionate but merely cunning, gets honors points and comes in one quarter of a wilkes. The all-time champ, Abraham Lincoln, is unlikely to be challenged in the foreseeable future. (L. J. DAVIS, *journalist*)

wom•an•ist *n* [by association with *womanish;* opp. of girlish; i.e., frivolous, irresponsible, not serious]: A black feminist of color, from the black folk expression of mothers to female children, "You acting womanish"; i.e., like a woman. "Usually refers to outrageous, audacious, courageous, or willful behavior; wanting to know more and in greater depth than is considered good for one; interested in grown-up doings; acting grown-up; being grown-up. Interchangeable with another black folk expression: 'You trying to be grown.' Responsible. In charge. Serious." See SHERO. (ALICE WALKER, *novelist*)

won *enclitic pl* **wen** [fr. *one,* but spelled *won* for aesthetic reasons and by association and contraction of the words *woman* and *man*]: A neutral suffix that can be appended to any appropriate noun to signal a desire for gender neutrality but indicating that a human being occupies the office. Also, in the plural, **wen.** "Certainly it is more melodious to the ear to refer to a chairwon or a policewon than a chairperson or policeperson." (WILLARD GAYLIN, *M.D.*)

wooped *adj* [*woo + pooped*]: Fatigue associated with vigorous but unsuccessful courtship. "Alphonse: Yo, Homes, what's the haps? Gastone: Babette, my man. A: You mean that full-sprung work of nature in ICU? G: The same, dude. I did everything. Flowers, candy, the midnight serenade, Wayne Newton imitations, fine corinthian leather, bonbons and bon mots. Geez, am I wooped!" (LEE K. ABBOTT, *writer*)

wores *n* [*mores + worry + wrong + worn*]: The customs regarded by a social group as being detrimental to its preservation and welfare; customs accepted as deviant by a group or community. "The wores of the underclass bothered the members of the garden club more than the debilitating effects of the elements on their automobiles." (GEOF HUTH, *writer*)

world•or•der•beat *n* [*new world order + worldbeat* term describing pop music from outside the first world]: Hymnlike pop music, usually originating in America, that celebrates the established world order and a belief in self-actualization as the solution to large-scale social problems. "Prime examples of worldorderbeat are Whitney Houston's anthem for the 1988 Los Angeles Olympics, 'One Moment in Time,' and Quincy Jones's 'We Are the World' and

'Voices That Care.' " (STEVE MESSINA, *editor*)

world-tears *n* [*world + tears;* neologism finding its roots in L *lacrimae rerum* (Virgil) and G *Weltschmertz*]: A feeling of vague sadness and nostalgia for who-knows-what, based not on personal fate but on reflection of life. "World-tears is a creative sadness, and it is also a bit of a luxury. You need a room of your own, to quote Virginia Woolf, and you need to know where your next meal is coming from, in order to experience it properly. The German *Weltschmertz* is more painful and quickly turns into aggressiveness. Virgil's *lacrimae rerum* is more matter-of-fact. World-tears is a more gentle feeling, close to the Portuguese *saudade* of their songs." (HANS KONING, *writer*)

wow•ful *adj* [*wow + -ful*]: Full of wow; a modifier expressive of strong, nonspecific disapproval or approval, intended to salvage the few remaining words of strong specific approval or disapproval such as awful, dreadful, terrible, horrible, frightful, etc., from further erosion. "Don't talk to me, I've got a wowful headache." Or, "I can't talk to you because I'm wowfully late." (LORE SEGAL, writer)

writer's ramp *n* [*writer's cramp* + *ramp*]: A too-quickly traveled path to literary renown, often followed by years of silence. "J. D. Salinger suffered most of his life from one of the worst cases of writer's ramp on record." (JOHN CALDERAZZO, *writer*)

wyllth *n* [fr. ME *wel*, fr. AS *wel*; akin to OS, OFris. & D. wel; Goth. *wail* + ME *welthe*, fr. *wel* + OS *velo*. cf. *well*, adv., *will*, *gallop*, *wealth* + ME *helthe*, fr. AS *haelth*, fr. *hol hale*, sound]: The state or condition of being intensely well, and all that it evokes, as after recovery from an accident in a beautiful place and wanting time to stop. The reverse of agony. Synonym: *Well-being*. Antonym: *Pain*. "To study the structure of a leaf in bright sunlight is evidence of wyllth." (GRACE SCHULMAN, *poet*)

X

xer·lu·sion *n* [*Xerox* + *delusion*]: The seductive, lulling belief that you've read an article because you've photocopied it. "Nona woke in a cold sweat: Was her preparation for her exams as thorough as she thought, or was it all xerlusion?" (ELLEN GRUBER GARVEY, *writer*)

xltn *n* or *v* [origin obscure, but also spelled *sgfs*, *qwlk*, *gdjp*, or *yttz*; several additional regional spelling variations also exist]: The last four-letter word needed to complete a crossword puzzle. "Three-letter and five-letter variants of xltn have also been reported." (MARK J. ESTREN, *writer*)

Y

yan•kee•phi•lia *n* [*yankee* +
Gk *philia* love]: Excessive admiration for all things American. "The Frenchman's crav-
ing for jazz, Coca-Cola, and
Jerry Lewis movies was suffi-
cient indication of his
yankeephilia. He didn't have to
buy a '78 Pinto to prove it."
(ROBIN FOX, *professor*)

y•clep•to•man•i•a *n* [*yclept*
+ *mania*]: A compulsion of some
novelists to appropriate names
of real persons for their fictions.
"Writer E. L. Doctorow is often
guilty of ycleptomania in his
books." (DAVID RAKSIN, *composer*)

yen•ta en•vy *n* [Yid *yenta*
blabber mouth + *envy*]: A condition found exclusively in men,
characterized by the masculine
desire to imitate the traditionally feminine propensity for dis-
cussing ad nauseum one's own
and other's psychological moti-
vations, particularly in the area
of romance. "Yenta envy is typically accompanied by a bit of
guilt and fear for loss of one's
own masculinity, as can be seen
in the work of filmmakers
Woody Allen and Henry Ja-
glom." (LAURIE WINER, *journalist*)

yoel *interj* [*yo!* colloq. + Heb. *El-
ohim* God]: A Jewish way of
greeting the Lord when one en-
counters Him on the street.
"One lively celebration of the
Jewish holiday of Purim at a
Harlem synagogue was punc-
tuated by the laughter of children in costumes and masks,
and by cries of 'Yoel!' resound-
ing through the neighborhood."
(DEBORAH MARGOLIN, *artist*)

yoel

Z

zeit•gei•sty *adj* [fr. G *Zeitgeist;* typically used in its superlative form, *Zeitgeistiest*]: Particularly successful at capturing and carrying the spirit of the age; trendy, hip, now. " 'Man,' shouted River Phoenix, straining to be heard over the house version of 10,000 Maniacs' 'Peace Train' as he downed his gluten-free milk, 'this place is the zeitgeistiest!' " (PAUL TOUGH, *writer*)

zoo *v* [fr. the noun *zoo*]: To confine for purposes of exhibition. "He had zooed two wives before he fell for the indomitable Dana." "Management zoos young women in the front office." (ELIZABETH SEYDEL MORGAN, *poet*)

Biographical Descriptions of Lexicographers

Tom Abate is a journalist and short story writer whose work has appeared in the *San Francisco Examiner* and the *California Journal.* **(snootfest)**

Lee K. Abbott has published his short stories in many magazines, among them *Harper's Magazine,* the *Georgia Review,* and *The Atlantic.* He is the author of *Living After Midnight* and is a professor of English at Ohio State University. **(wooped)**

Ellen Abrams is a writer living in New York City. **(frustulate, Machiapublican)**

Diane Ackerman is the author of ten books, including *The Moon by Whale Light, Jaguar of Sweet Laughter: New & Selected Poems,* and *A Natural History of the Senses,* and is a staff writer for *The New Yorker.* **(mouse)**

Joel Agee is the author of *Twelve Years: An American Boyhood in East Germany.* His work has appeared in *The New Yorker* and *Harper's Magazine.* **(ernesty, Eurojive)**

Hiroshi Akashi is a molecular biologist studying and working in the field of molecular evolution at Princeton University. **(goobermensch)**

Michael C. Alcamo is a special assistant in the office of the Commissioner of Consumer Affairs in New York City. **(greenspeak)**

Woody Allen is a film director. **(appucious)**

Jonathan Alter is a senior writer for *Newsweek* magazine. **(club-hearted, elefeign)**

Robert Alter is professor of comparative literature at the University of California, Berkeley. He is the author of *Necessary Angels: Tradition and Modernity in Kafka, Benjamin, and Scholem.* **(correctnik)**

Reinhold Aman is the editor and publisher of *Maledicta Journal* and is the author of *How Do They Do It? A Collection of Wordplays Revealing the Sexual Proclivities of Man and Beast.* **(cacademoid, maledictaphobia)**

Roger Angell is a fiction editor and writer for *The New Yorker*. He is the author of *The Summer Game, Late Innings, Season Ticket*, and *Once More Around the Park*. **(Metsopotamia)**

Jeffrey Archer is the author of the novels *Kane & Abel* and *As the Crow Flies*. **(subsidiarity)**

James Atlas is an editor of *The New York Times Magazine* and is the author of *The Book Wars*. **(ipsonym, nomo)**

Margaret Atwood is a novelist and poet whose work includes *Cat's Eye* and *The Handmaid's Tale*. **(gup)**

David Baker is the author of three books of poems, including *Sweet Home, Saturday Night* and *Haunts*. His work has appeared in *The New Yorker* and *The Nation*. He is the poetry editor of *The Kenyon Review*. **(amortal, ascudify, oopsht)**

Donald W. Baker is the author of *Unposted Letters* and *Formal Application*. His work has appeared in *Poetry* and *The Atlantic*. **(probot)**

Kevin Baker is a writer of fiction living in New York City. His first novel, *The Great Game*, will be published by Crown this year. He contributed research to Harold Evans's political history of the United States since 1889, *The American Century*. **(algore, cynaïveté, tipgore)**

Will Baker is the author of *Backward: An Essay on Indians, Time and Photography, Mountain Blood*, and *Track of the Giant*. **(dandaid, ethoplegic, ferrolunk, fictory, gacho, ickylex, queschew, slonk, sporch, tactotum, wargasm)**

Benjamin Barber is Whitman professor of political science at Rutgers University and the director of the Walt Whitman Center at Rutgers. His books include *Strong Democracy* and *The Conquest of Politics*. **(Hollyworld, liberteenager, mediacracy, politiphobia, redeconstruct)**

John Perry Barlow is a retired cattle rancher, a former Republican county chairman, and a lyricist for the Grateful Dead. He is writing a book titled *Everything We Know Is Wrong*. **(datacloud)**

Rona Barrett is a television journalist and commentator working the Hollywood beat. **(lovomaniac)**

John D. Barrow is professor of astronomy at the University of Sussex. He is the author of *The Anthropic Cosmological Principle*, *The World Within the World*, and *Theories of Everything: The Quest for Ultimate Explanation*. **(higgledy-piggledyology)**

Edward P. Bass is the catalyst behind many international ecological ventures, including Biosphere 2, a research and development project in closed-system ecology. He is also the founding trustee of the Philecology Trust, which funds nonprofit ecological projects. **(ecopreneur, philecology)**

Charles Baxter is the author of *A Relative Stranger* and *First Light*. **(fatuate)**

Madison Smartt Bell is the author of *Soldiers Joy* and *The Year of Silence*. His work has appeared in *Harper's Magazine* and *The Hudson Review*. **(mendologism)**

Marvin Bell is the author of *Iris of Creation* and *New and Selected Poems*. **(aftergraph, airfulness, telepathetic)**

Anne Bernays is the author of eight novels, among them *Professor Romeo* and *Growing Up Rich*. **(digabah, muggernate)**

Paul Bickart is an environmental chemist in the Office of Pesticides and Toxic Substances at the U.S. Environmental Protection Agency. **(bork, cacoscopy, dicate, ecoporn, erdmensch, fe, fector, holoman, hominilunacy, janefoolery, joebob, micromilken, notso, paleologism, physics envy, schroding, secrate, spooksperson, stealthbomber, thift, thorsyndrome, threft, vestite, vexillolatry, vorce)**

Leon Bing is a journalist living in Pasadena, California, and is the author of *Do or Die*. **(spontaneous combustier)**

Sallie Bingham is an author whose most recent book is *Passion and Prejudice*. **(shero)**

Sarah Bird is the author of *Alamo House: Women Without Men, Men Without Brains,* and *The Boyfriend School,* and of the screenplay for the film based on the latter titled "Don't Tell Her It's Me." Her most recent novel is *The Mommy Club.* **(hollyperbole)**

Sven Birkerts is the author, most recently, of *The Electric Life: Essays on Modern Poetry* and is a frequent reviewer for *Mirabella.* **(duraws, grommetry, obleego)**

Marshall Blonsky teaches semiotics at the New School for Social Research and Queens College. He is the author of *American Mythologies* and *On Signs.* **(demockeracy, pastriotism)**

Tom Bodett is a former commentator for National Public Radio's program *All Things Considered.* He is the author of several books, among them *The End of the Road* and *The Big Garage on Clear Shot.* He is currently the host of *Everyday People,* a nationally syndicated radio program. **(faxraff, nomendulger)**

Imogene Bolls is the author of *Earthbound* and *Glass Walker.* **(concrastinate, poolution, transish)**

Daniel J. Boorstin is the Librarian of Congress emeritus and the author of many books, among them *Image: A Guide to Pseudo-Events in America, The Discoverers: A History of Man's Search to Know His World and Himself,* and the three-volume study *The Americans.* **(guff)**

Ken Bosee is the former president of *The New Yorker.* **(beezle)**

Daniel B. Botkin is professor of biology and environmental studies at the University of California at Santa Barbara and author of *Discordant Harmonies: A New Ecology for the Twenty-first Century.* **(arsinine, athdive, dustbelt, ecophist, gaied, speçoid, techtoid)**

Ben Bradlee is the former executive editor of *The Washington Post.* **(smersh)**

David Bradley is the author of *South Street* and *The Chaneysville Incident* and is a professor of English at Temple University. **(pseudoliteracy)**

Eric Brettschneider is an attorney who teaches social welfare at New York University and is coordinator for Agenda for Children Tomorrow, a child-welfare collaboration project between charities and the mayor's office in New York City. **(telecelebual, underparanoia)**

Robert Bringhurst is a poet whose work includes *The Black Canoe* and *Pieces of Map, Pieces of Music.* **(illiterature)**

William F. Buckley, Jr., is editor-at-large of the *National Review* and the host of the weekly television program *Firing Line.* **(hecticity)**

Lydia Buechler is a copy editor at Simon & Schuster. **(fawnetics, holden pattern, schadendroid)**

Michael J. Bugeja is the author of *What We Do for Music, The Visionary,* and *Platonic Love.* **(bardbash)**

Franklin Burroughs is the author of *Billy Watson's Croker Sack* and is a professor of English at Bowdoin College. **(Nicodemus)**

John Calderazzo teaches in the MFA creative writing program at Colorado State University and is the author of *Writing from Scratch: Freelancing.* **(bamboid, endowager, environnui, gangst, Hislam, proctologenstia, writer's ramp)**

SueEllen Campbell is a writer and English professor at Colorado State University. **(ecologue)**

Ethan Canin is the author of a short-story collection, *Emperor of the Air,* and a novel, *Blue River.* **(parannoyed)**

Ron Carlson is a writer of fiction who lives in Arizona and is the author of *The News of the World* and *Plan B.* **(torticulture, vulgarithm)**

Ray S. Cline is an adjunct professor of international relations at Georgetown University and chairman of the U.S. Global Strategy Council. He is the author of *Metastrategy: National Security Memorandum for the President* and *Chiang Ching-Kuo Remembered: The Man and His Political Legacy.* **(politectonics)**

Leslie Cockburn is the author of *Out of the Control* and coauthor of *Dangerous Liaison*. She is a correspondent for the public television program *Frontline* and produces programs for ABC News. **(rumint)**

Billy Collins is the author of *Questions About Angels, The Apple That Astonished Paris,* and *Video Poems,* and his work has appeared in *The New Yorker, The Paris Review,* and *Poetry.* **(pseudinvite, silutation, Tabasic)**

Jack Collom is a poet whose works include *Arguing with Something Plato Said* and *The Fox.* **(assoholistic, roid, videolatry)**

Frank Conroy is the author of *Midair* and *Stop-Time.* He is the director of the Iowa Writers Workshop. **(brownspeak)**

Bernard Cooper is the author of *Maps to Anywhere.* His work has appeared in *Harper's Magazine* and *The Georgia Review.* **(digredote, retrotort)**

Henry S. F. Cooper writes about science for *The New Yorker.* **(contraschadenfreude, lapsedatheist)**

Christopher Corbett is the author of *Vacationland.* His work appears in *The Washington Post, The New York Times,* and the *Philadelphia Inquirer.* **(autotonsorialist)**

Bob Costas is the host of the NBC program *Later with Bob Costas.* **(statfuscation)**

Doug Coupland is the author of the novel *Generation X: Tales for an Accelerated Culture.* **(bambify, berumptotfreude, doriangray, emallgrate, lessism, metaphasia, nearalgia, overboard, spectacularist, survivulous)**

Norman Cousins was editor emeritus of *Saturday Review* and the author of many books, among them *Anatomy of an Illness as Perceived by the Patient: Reflections on Healing and Regeneration.* **(exasperats)**

Diane Crispell is an editor of *American Demographics.* **(macgyver)**

Debbie Cymbalista is the author of a collection of short stories titled *Danger.* **(sheepstasis)**

L. J. Davis is a contributing editor of *Harper's Magazine* and is currently at work on a new book about the American economy. **(gaulle, malcolm, monomath, spectocloacaphobia, wilkes)**

L. Sprague de Camp is the author of many works, among them *Lest Darkness Fall* and *The Ancient Engineers.* **(astic, dynatic, georgic, theratic)**

Nicholas Delbanco is the author, most recently, of *The Writers' Trade and Other Stories* and *Running in Place: Scenes from the South of France.* **(hindser, maunch, panxiety)**

Vine Deloria, Jr., is a professor of law, history, religious studies, and political science at the University of Colorado at Boulder and is the author of *Custer Died for Your Sins* and *The Nations Within.* **(bureaucraniac)**

Ariel Dorfman, a Chilean, is the author of *Last Waltz in Santiago: And Other Poems of Exile and Disappearance, Mascara,* and *Death and the Maiden.* **(farland, intervaland)**

Mark Dowie is editor-at-large of InterNation, a transnational feature syndicate based in New York. **(corporado, dexaggerate, glandiloquent)**

Tom Drury is a writer of fiction whose work has appeared in *Harper's Magazine* and *The New Yorker.* **(crewcify, easturbinversion, fondanoia, Sawyorism, videolalia)**

Bruce Duffy is the author of *The World as I Found It,* and his work has appeared in *Harper's Magazine.* **(anxnicity, nilanthropy, nonologisms, superflunyms, Swaggart, vaguenosticism)**

Carol Edgarian is author of the forthcoming novel *Rise, the Euphrates.* **(slard)**

Anne Eisenberg is a professor of humanities at Polytechnic University. Her most recent book is *Technical Editing.* **(consumassault, corpeye, deprelder, reparsolip, reversacunt, shamdidate)**

Sheldon Ekland-Olson is a professor and special assistant to the chancellor at the University of Texas, and is author (with Steve J. Martin) of *Texas Prisons: The Wall Came Tumbling Down*. **(bureaucrademia)**

Daniel Mark Epstein is a poet and essayist and is the author of *Love's Compass* and *Spirits*. His work has appeared in *The New Yorker* and *The Atlantic*. **(cankertone, grubble)**

Mark J. Estren is the author of *A History of Underground Comics*, and was general manager of Financial News Network, president of UPI Television, executive vice president of Infotechnology, and editor of *High Technology Business*. **(chairperdaughter, cong, connounce, conpose, corvo, ectotheism, endotheism, fug up, lentidigitation, lourdemain, premier cri, pseudofaunaphilia, psychaddict, republocrat, triskaidekaphobiaphobia, xltn)**

Donald Fagen is a member of Steely Dan, whose recordings include *Countdown to Ecstasy, Gaucho*, and the solo album *The Nightfly*. **(ethalpian, ethicoterratropism)**

Andrew Fetler is the author of *To Byzantium* and *The Travelers*. **(obnox)**

Timothy Findley is the author of *The Telling of Lies, Not Wanted on the Voyage, Famous Last Words*, and *Dinner Along the Amazon*. **(copolyte, flustrate, mulrooned, sminge)**

Bill Flanagan is the editor of *Musician Magazine* and the author of *Written in My Soul* and *Last of the Moe Haircuts*. **(pianist envy, prickle, slong)**

Robin Fox is university professor of social theory at Rutgers University. His latest books are *The Violent Imagination* and *The Search for Society*. **(engynocize, quindecimalite, sheeit, yankeephilia)**

Lewis Burke Frumkes is the author of *How to Raise Your IQ by Eating Gifted Children, Name Crazy*, and *Manhattan Cocktail*. **(copulescence, floit, lolodacity, nonono, nudiments, popsynopsis, testiferous)**

Alice Fulton is the author of *Powers of Congress, Palladium*, and *Dance Script with Electric Ballerina*. In 1991 she received a MacArthur

Foundation fellowship. **(bloaf, estrogen poisoning, pet quality, poetician, vanishing hitchhiker)**

John Kenneth Galbraith is professor emeritus of economics at Harvard University and author of many books, among them *The Affluent Society* and *Economics in Perspective: A Critical History.* **(ecofraud, econtrivance)**

Janet Gallagher is an attorney with the office of the New York City Corporation Counsel. **(dissix)**

Frank Gannon is the author of *Vanna Karenina* and *Yo, Poe.* **(handilingual, vacanoia, willie pep)**

Ellen Gruber Garvey is completing a dissertation on advertising and fiction in turn-of-the-century American magazines. Her short stories have appeared in a dozen anthologies. **(acquisit, closethanger, confloat, dissix, foetish, kinnitus, kintinnabulation, malclement, mustlunch, obitphemism, xerlusion)**

Roy Gary is an art critic living in San Antonio, Texas. **(arssurdity, ferversion)**

Willard Gaylin, M.D., is the president of The Hastings Center. His most recent book is *Adam and Eve and Pinocchio.* **(Charlie syndrome, Frankenstein factor, gaslight, immora, klutz factor, Q/A ratio, won)**

Barry Gifford is the author of many books, among them *Wild at Heart: The Story of Sailor and Lula.* **(drivulet)**

Todd Gitlin is the author of *The Sixties* and *Inside Prime Time.* **(mediophilia, paxophobia, rockulism)**

Elton Glaser is the author of *Tropical Depressions* and *Relics.* **(antisemantic, memorabilious, orificial, postminstrel depression, sepulchritude)**

Michael Globetti is the author of *God Save the Quarterback!* **(cosmopositeur, fauxltruism, flintimacy, plastocracy, self-agglandize, sexistence, technyokel)**

Herbert Gold is the author of *Dreaming* and *A Girl of Forty*. **(nimnut)**

Albert Goldbarth is the author of a book of essays, *A Sympathy of Souls*, and a book of poems, *Heaven and Earth*. **(androgygreed, bathosnicker, cosmetofaux, fedpo, typomort)**

Harold J. Goldberg is a professor of history at the University of the South. **(bovelousy, bovisfaction, chickty, kissinbull, saddamize)**

James Gorman is the author of *The Man with No Endorphins: And Other Reflections on Science*. **(gangst)**

Gerald Graff is a professor of English at the University of Chicago and is the author of *Professing Literature: An Institutional History*. **(careersma)**

Andrew M. Greeley is the author of many books and novels, among them *The Cardinal Sins* and *Thy Brother's Wife*. **(superglobslapcious)**

Mark Green is the New York City Consumer Affairs Commissioner. He ran for the U.S. Senate in 1986 and is the coauthor of several books, including (with John Berry) *The Challenge of Hidden Profits*. **(corpocracy, heirhead)**

Walter Griffin is a poet whose work appears regularly in leading quarterlies and journals in the United States and abroad, including *The Paris Review, Poetry,* and *The Sewanee Review*. His most recent collection, *Western Flyers,* was the 1990 winner of the University of West Florida's Panhandler Series. **(asexis)**

Allan Gurganus is the author of *White People* and *Oldest Living Confederate Widow Tells All*. **(lacktitude)**

Darren Haber is the author of the play *The Real Channel*. He is working on a new trilogy of one-act plays and completing a trilogy of novellas. **(appliction)**

Garrett Hardin is an environmentalist whose works include *Filters Against Folly: How to Survive Despite Economists, Ecologists and the Merely*

Eloquent, Stalking the Wild Taboo, and *Promethean Ethics: Living with Death, Competition, and Triage.* **(ecolacy, longage)**

   David Hare is a playwright whose works include *Plenty, A Map of the World,* and *The Secret Rapture.* **(journalize)**

   Colin Harrison is the author of *Break and Enter* and an associate editor of *Harper's Magazine.* **(volumptuous)**

   John W. Hart III's latest book is *Dugout Poems: A Poetic Encounter with the 1989 Los Angeles Dodgers.* **(ollyism)**

   Margaret H. Hazen writes historical fiction and nonfiction and is coauthor of *The Music Men.* **(diagolways)**

   Robert M. Hazen is a research scientist at the Carnegie Institution of Washington. He is coauthor of *Science Matters: Achieving Scientific Literacy.* **(expeculate)**

   Alex Heard is a free-lance writer whose work appears in *The New Republic, The Washington Post,* and *Spy* magazine. **(hathos)**

   Vicki Hearne is the author of *Adam's Task: Calling Animals by Name.* Her most recent book is *Bandit: Dossier of a Dangerous Dog.* **(unanimal)**

   Katharine Hepburn is an actress. **(galubcious)**

   E. Ward Herlands is a poet whose work has appeared in *The New York Times, Prairie Schooner, Northern New England Review,* and *Poet Lore.* **(space-poor)**

   William Herrick is the author of several books, among them *That's Life* and *Bradovich.* **(cheese-dip revolutionary, lablib)**

   Jim Heynen is the author of *You Know What Is Right, A Suitable Church, The Man Who Kept Cigars in His Cap,* and *One Hundred over 100.* **(one-downmanship)**

   Edward Hirsch is a poet whose books include *The Night Parade* and *Wild Gratitude.* His poems have appeared in *Grand Street* and *The Nation.* **(soracious)**

Jane Hirshfield is a poet and translator whose books include *Of Gravity and Angels* and *The Ink Dark Moon*. Her work has appeared in *The New Yorker* and *The Atlantic.* **(glumsiness, nex, placebitude)**

Jack Hitt is a journalist who served as editor of this dictionary. **(humediation, posation)**

Edward Hoagland is the author of many books, most recently *Heart's Desire,* a collection of essays, His essays and stories appear in *Harper's Magazine, The New Yorker,* and *The Atlantic.* **(fitch)**

Eva Hoffman is the author of *Lost in Translation.* **(contorture, horricious, technopeasant)**

Michael Holman is a filmmaker living in New York City. **(carelessful, delectatiobellum, dudeism, historywhore, ignorant, microfuture, rhythmpolitics, swoophead, unisapien)**

Charles Hood is a poet and author of *Red Sky, Red Water.* **(jizz)**

James D. Houston is the author of *The Men in My Life* and *Love Life.* **(lava)**

Geof Huth is an archivist and records manager. He is a poet and publisher of the micropress *dbqp.* **(adead, aeffective, approceive, artion, fussion, idiolexicon, idiosyntactics, incely, incerpt, massess, metaphorm, mynd, paraparadox, porthermanteauphroditic, postprototorp, pwoermd, rememory, schlaumpfkth, semiobject, spilleng, verinym, wores)**

Mark Irwin is a poet and essayist. His most recent book is *Against the Meanwhile.* **(Sambecketted)**

Molly Ivins is a columnist for the *Dallas Times Herald* newpaper and *The Progressive* magazine. **(deprovement, impravement)**

Harold Jaffe is the author of *Eros Anti-Eros* and *Madonna and Other Spectacles.* **(derviant, swethert)**

Christopher Janney is an artist-in-residence at MIT. He is the inventor of "Soundstair," a musical instrument that transforms any existing staircase into a musical stairway. **(audicon)**

Tom Jenks is the author of the novel *Our Happiness* and coeditor with Raymond Carver of the anthology *American Short Story Masterpieces.* **(slard)**

Mark D. Jones is a business executive in Virginia. **(corporonugacity)**

Lawrence E. Joseph is the author of *Gaia: The Growth of an Idea.* He is at work on his second book, *In Search of Common Sense.* **(cloin, numinition)**

Rodger Kamenetz is the author of a book of essays, *Terra Infirma,* and a book of poetry, *Nympholepsy.* **(copanoia, spousonym, technogloat)**

Karen Karbo is the author of *Trespassers Welcome Here* and *The Diamond Lane.* **(exercist, malliday, snitical)**

Margo Kaufman is a contributing editor to the *Los Angeles Times Magazine* and is also the Hollywood correspondent for *Pug Talk* magazine. **(floop, spacklebody)**

Tim Kazurinsky is an actor and screenwriter. **(aphorectum)**

Maria-Christina Keller is a writer of fiction and copy chief of *Scientific American.* **(smergdorf)**

Steven G. Kellman is a professor of comparative literature at the University of Texas at San Antonio. **(immortattle, nonymous, pandictic)**

X. J. Kennedy is the author of *Fresh Brats* and *Cross Ties, Selected Poems.* **(bank verse, blook, prosetry, story-eyed, tentatation, weenge)**

Jack Kevorkian, M.D., is a retired pathologist and the inventor of the Thanatron™—a device that allows for a doctor-assisted suicide. **(medicide, obitiatry, obitorium)**

Andrew Kimbrell is an attorney and the policy director for the Foundation on Economic Trends in Washington, D.C. He is the author of the book *Second Genesis.* **(mechanomorphism, misandrony)**

Florence King is the author of *Southern Ladies and Gentlemen, Confessions of a Failed Southern Lady,* and the forthcoming *With Charity Toward None: A Misanthropy Primer.* **(eccedentesiast)**

Larry King is a radio talk show host, and columnist for *U.S.A. Today* and *Sporting News.* **(congealiate)**

Judith Kitchen is the author of *Perennials* and *Upstairs Window.* **(acquend, traith)**

Stuart Klawans is a film critic for *The Nation.* **(heteroduck)**

Joe Klein writes about politics for *New York* magazine. **(bloatocracy, pragmyopia, soundbite)**

Wallace Knight is a professor of journalism at Marshall University. **(bubblegaffer, holastic)**

Ron Kolm is the author of *The Plastic Factory.* **(maulette)**

Hans Koning is the author of *A Walk with Love and Death, Acts of Faith,* and *Columbus: His Enterprise.* His work appears in *Harper's Magazine* and *The Atlantic.* **(world-tears)**

Joan Konner is the dean of the Columbia Journalism School. **(telecratic)**

Ted Kooser is the author of *The Blizzard Voices* and *One World at a Time.* **(mallifluous)**

Robin M. Kovat is a feature writer, a proposal developer, and a marketing strategist. Her work appears in numerous journals, among them *HealthWeek, Washington Jewish Week,* and *City Limits.* **(frue, pregnaphobia)**

Gary Krist is the author of *The Garden State.* His work has appeared in *The New Republic* and *The New York Times Book Review.* **(eloquate, media autogamy, pseudo-pseudo-lowbrowism, stelloid)**

Maxine Kumin is a poet whose books include *Nurture* and *The Microscope.* **(chacebo)**

Walter LaFeber teaches at Cornell University, and his books include *The American Age: U.S. Foreign Policy at Home and Abroad, 1750 to the Present.* **(boterium, idiowise)**

Ann Landers is a syndicated advice columnist. **(discludify)**

Louis Lasagna is dean of the Sackler School of Graduate Biomedical Sciences at Tufts University. **(libernutriphile)**

Howard Levy is a poet whose work has appeared in *The Georgia Review* and *The American Poetry Review.* **(bellie)**

Bernard Lewis is the Cleveland E. Dodge professor of Near Eastern studies emeritus at Princeton University. His most recent book is *Race and Slavery in the Middle East.* **(academagogue, autohagiographer, blundit, propagoose, trendvane)**

Marco Leyton is a writer of short stories whose work has appeared in *Rampike.* He is currently pursuing a graduate degree in psychology at Cornell University. **(decarbulate)**

Michael Lockwood is a university lecturer in philosophy at Oxford and a fellow of Green College. His most recent book is *Mind, Brain and the Quantum.* **(cosmosis, fashimite, fashist, hypocrat)**

Dan Lorber owns Down in Denver bookstore in Stephentown, New York. **(hyperbolie, patriotize, retrojealousy)**

James Lovelock is an independent scientist who developed the Gaia theory, which regards our planet as a self-regulating system that behaves as if it were a living organism. **(tromp)**

Thomas P. Luce is a business executive in Virginia. **(corporonugacity)**

John Lukacs is the author of several books, most recently *The Duel: 10 May–31 July 1940: The Eighty-Day Struggle Between Churchill and Hitler,* and a frequent contributor to *Harper's Magazine.* **(bellicist)**

Cynthia Macdonald is the author of five books of poems, the most recent of which is *Living Wills: New and Selected Poems.* She teaches in the graduate creative writing program at the University of Houston. **(amari)**

Elizabeth Macklin is a writer and author of the forthcoming collection of poetry *A Woman Kneeling in the Big City*. Her work has appeared in *The New Yorker, The Paris Review,* and *The Nation.* **(pontification point)**

Norman Mailer is the author of many novels, including *Harlot's Ghost* and *The Executioner's Song,* which won the Pulitzer Prize in 1980. **(factoid)**

Deborah Margolin is a founding member of the Split Britches theater company, a touring repertory group. She is also a playwright, poet, and performance artist. **(catamenial, yoel)**

Hans Mark is a nuclear physicist, the chancellor of the University of Texas, and the author of *The Space Station: A Personal Journey.* **(bureaucrademia)**

Michael Martone teaches creative writing at Syracuse University. He is the author of *Fort Wayne Is Seventh on Hitler's List* and *Safety Patrol.* **(table, twick)**

Lia Matera is the author of *A Radical Departure* and *The Smart Money.* **(muchismo, narcissopath, neurrotica, sisyphopath, toujours vu)**

Harry Mathews is a poet and writer whose books include *Cigarettes* and *Armenian Papers.* **(infatality, schadenschaden, tripidation)**

Eugene J. McCarthy is a former U.S. senator from Minnesota (1958–70) and a syndicated columnist. **(coallusion, couchant, iacoction, incurse, transify)**

Brian McCormick is a short story writer, poet, screenwriter, and novelist. He is the author of *The Immortality Project.* **(angster, blurbonic plague, brefecation, cliterature, conflatulations, crool, delferiority, derivasation, doremi, fantasmagorbia, fasolatido, koolish, lardist,**

masturpiece, misstery, mistery, obsolene, odeur, one-downmanship, seemius, shilldren, thanafaction, wannaBBC)

Deidre McFadyen is a journalist who served as assistant editor of this dictionary. **(garpage)**

Martha McFerren is the author of *Get Me Out of Here!* and *Contours for Ritual.* Her work has appeared in *The Georgia Review, Shenandoah,* and elsewhere. **(puremouth)**

Don McLean is a singer and composer whose recordings include "American Pie" and "Prime Time." **(chefletter, concretin)**

Steve Messina is a free-lance copy editor. He designs and publishes the Revenge & Guilt line of postcards. **(bullymia, dehumanism, domestic noninterventionism, fawnetics, holden pattern, Nintentional fallacy, schadendroid, white elephantiasis, worldorderbeat)**

Judith Michael is the pen name of Judith Barnard and Michael Fain. Their most recent book is *Sleeping Beauty.* **(ethnoid, Pablumize)**

Jessica Mitford is an investigative journalist whose books include *Poison Penmanship: The Gentle Art of Muckraking, The American Way of Death,* and *The Trial of Dr. Spock.* **(marling)**

John J. Moeling, Jr., is the publisher of *Scientific American.* **(affleurage)**

R. Bruce Moody is the author of *The Decline and Fall of Daphne Finn.* His work has appeared in *The New Yorker* and *Bottege Oscure.* **(deplhorrence)**

Francis D. Moore is the Moseley professor of surgery emeritus at Harvard Medical School and the book review editor of *The New England Journal of Medicine.* **(funktionlust, snowbird)**

Elizabeth Seydel Morgan is a poet whose collections are *Parties* and *The Governor of Desire.* **(ambidove, cogitall, febrish, genulit, zoo)**

Richard Morris is the author of eight books of scientific nonfiction and nine collections of poetry, including his most recent volume, *Assurians*. **(Shirley)**

Rodger Morrow is a copywriter living in Sewickley, Pennsylvania. **(disanthropy, euphonism)**

Carol Muske (a.k.a. Carol Muske Dukes) is the author of the novel *Dear Digby* and four books of poems. She teaches at the University of Southern California and contributes to *The New Yorker*. **(snartyr)**

Leonard Nathan is the author of *Carrying On: New and Selected Poems*. His work has appeared in *Salmagundi*. **(massdebate, theorious)**

Kent Nelson has published his short stories in many periodicals, among them *The Sewanee Review, Grand Street,* and *The Kenyon Review,* and is the author of the novel *Language in the Blood*. **(tump)**

Howard Nemerov served two terms as America's poet laureate. His work includes *War Stories: Poems About Long Ago and Now* and *The Oak in the Acorn: On Remembrance of Things Past and on Teaching Proust, Who Will Never Learn*. **(azaleate)**

Michael Novak holds the George Frederick Jewett chair in religion and public policy at the American Policy Institute, where he also serves as director of social and political studies. He is the author of many books, among them *Free Persons and the Common Good* and *This Hemisphere of Liberty*. **(sprag)**

Joyce Carol Oates is a novelist, short story writer, poet, and playwright whose work includes *Because It Is Bitter, and Because It Is My Heart* and *You Must Remember This*. **(darknatter, felifeign, partyfinesse, Silberbluster, surfeitigo, tysteria)**

Agnieszka Osiecka is a Polish novelist, playwright, and songwriter. **(bushed)**

Cynthia Ozick is the author of several novels, most recently *The Shawl,* and an essayist whose work includes the collection *Metaphor & Memory*. **(sublaudation)**

Ron Padgett is publications director of Teachers and Writers Collaborative in New York City. **(hatopia)**

Camille Paglia is the author of *Sexual Personae: Art and Decadence from Nefertiti to Emily Dickinson* and teaches humanities at the University of the Arts in Philadelphia. **(whuffle)**

Joe Nick Patoski is a senior editor of *Texas Monthly*. **(desitively)**

Jaroslav Pelikan is Sterling professor of history at Yale University and the author and editor of numerous books, among them *Jesus Through the Centuries* and the five-volume study *The Christian Tradition*. **(sourcaustic)**

Victor Perera is the author of *Rites: A Guatemalan Boyhood*. His work has appeared in *The New Yorker*, *Harper's Magazine*, and *The Atlantic*. **(nontendo)**

Fred Pfeil is a fiction writer, essayist, and reviewer whose most recent work is *Another Tale to Tell: Politics and Narration in Postmodern Culture*. **(adversize, verilude)**

Louis Phillips is the author of *Way Out* and *Scarefield*. His work has appeared in *The Georgia Review* and *The Massachusetts Review*. **(clemenvy, lachrymapotami, rectiphobia, teleminate)**

Daniel Pinkwater is a writer and radio commentator whose books include *Fishwhistle* and *Chicago Days/Hoboken Nights* **(chazzerati, literai)**

Norman Podhoretz is the author of *The Bloody Crossroads: Where Literature & Politics Meet* and is editor-in-chief of *Commentary*. **(debellicized)**

Alvin F. Poussaint is an associate professor of psychiatry at the Harvard Medical School. **(Afro-fraud, opportomist)**

Padgett Powell is the author of *Edisto, A Woman Named Drown*, and *Typical*. **(grinace)**

Lucio Pozzi is an artist living in New York City. **(arting, parchox, semot)**

Emily Prager is the author of *A Visit from the Footbinder, Clea and Zeus Divorce,* and *Eve's Tattoo.* **(bam, jetback, scud)**

Tom Prince is a senior editor of *New York* magazine. **(overling)**

Wyatt Prunty is the Carlton professor of English at the University of the South and is author of a book of poetry, *Balance as Belief,* and a book of criticism, *"Fallen from the Symboled World": Precedents for the New Formalism.* **(ovart)**

David Quammen is the author of *The Flight of the Iguana: A Sidelong View of Science and Nature* and *Blood Line: Stories of Fathers and Sons.* **(facho)**

Elliott Rabin is a former assistant editor at *Harper's Magazine.* **(digressivism)**

Howard Rabinowitz is a Hindi scholar and a screenwriter. **(poshthumous, vinylity)**

David Raksin is a composer and conductor of over 100 film scores and 450 television programs. His work includes *Laura* and *The Bad and the Beautiful.* **(minuetc, quasicaglia, quer-Schnittke, ycleptomania)**

Lou Reed is a musician whose records include "A Walk on the Wild Side," "Vicious," and, most recently (with John Cale), "Songs for Drella." **(accountout, agencide, lawshit, manacur)**

William K. Reilly is administrator of the United States Environmental Protection Agency. **(enviropreneur, planetsaurus)**

Richard Rhodes is the author of *The Making of the Atomic Bomb,* which won the Pulitzer Prize for nonfiction in 1988, and *A Hole in the World: An American Boyhood.* **(malcolmize, verity)**

Elliot Richardson is a former U.S. attorney general, and a partner in the Washington office of Milbank, Tweed, Hadley & McCloy. **(intricate, snurm)**

Donald Ritchie is the associate historian of the U.S. Senate. **(hyperbite, Nixonerate, smad)**

Roger Rosenblatt is an Editor-at-Large at *Life* magazine. **(claprehension)**

Michael Rosenblum is a video journalist living in Paris. **(dictocrat, dronage, moto, phoclo, simplicist)**

Vera Rubin is an astronomer at the Carnegie Institution of Washington. She has served on the editorial board of *Science Magazine* and is a member of the National Academy of Sciences and the American Academy of Arts and Sciences. **(multiverse)**

Witold Rybczynski is a professor at McGill University in Montreal whose books include *The Most Beautiful House in the World, Home: A Short History of an Idea,* and *Waiting for the Weekend.* **(faction)**

Kirkpatrick Sale is the author of *Dwellers in the Land: The Bioregional Vision* and *The Conquest of Paradise: Christopher Columbus and the Columbian Legacy.* **(antigaeic, deprovement, ecostery, ecuicide, stairwit)**

Scott Russell Sanders is the author of *The Paradise of Bombs* and *Secrets of the Universe.* His work appears in *Harper's Magazine.* **(adlift, autostrapper, cyber, Disney, numerocredulous, nunch, plotto, syntho, viddy)**

Luc Sante is the author of *Low Life: Lures and Snares of Old New York.* His work has appeared in *Harper's Magazine, The New Republic,* and *The New York Times Magazine.* **(unface)**

George A. Scarborough is the author of *Invitation to Kim* and *A Summer Ago.* His work has appeared in *Harper's Magazine* and *The Atlantic.* **(bodywit, irrespond, mulestool)**

Roger C. Schank is the John Evans professor of electrical engineering and computer science, a professor of psychology and education and social policy, and the director of the Institute for the

Learning Sciences at Northwestern University. **(computistic, creactive, fleducation, psychologic)**

Bill Schechter is a history teacher at Lincoln-Sudbury Regional High School in Sudbury, Massachusetts. **(doomgress)**

Edwin Schlossberg is the principal designer of Edwin Schlossberg, Inc., which specializes in the design and development of interactive entertainment and educational programs. He is an artist and an author, currently at work on an atlas of perception for Random House. **(cube, intolyte, mediate, mediatrophic, nameslug, walkie)**

Deborah Schneider is a literary agent with John Farquharson Ltd., in New York City. **(obnox)**

Daniel Schorr is a senior analyst for National Public Radio and the author of *Clearing the Air*. **(flount)**

David Schramm is the Louis Block professor in the physical sciences and author (with Michael Riordon) of *Shadows of Creation* and (with Leon Lederman) of *From Quarks to the Cosmos*. **(Big Chill, Big Crunch, gallupism)**

Grace Schulman is the author of *Marianne Moore: The Poetry of Engagement* and *Hemispheres*, and is poetry editor of *The Nation*. **(wyllth)**

James Seay is the author of *The Light as They Found It*. He has published his work in *Antaeus, The Georgia Review*, and *The Nation*. **(handsome, Saint-paul, tour-worn)**

Carole Seborovski is an artist living in New York City. **(angster, glamorose, grandigrose)**

Lore Segal is the author of *Her First American* and *The Story of King Saul and King David*. Her work has been published in *The New Yorker*. **(wowful)**

Richard Seltzer is the author of *The Name of the Hero* and *The Lizard of Oz*. He is at work on a new novel, *Sandcastles*. **(aclone, computalk, flusion, interfacelift, safeslide)**

Bob Shacochis is the author of the books *The Next New World* and *Easy in the Islands*. His work has appeared in *Harper's Magazine* and *The Paris Review*. **(academate, annilation, assoholic, massafy)**

Laurence Shames is a former ethics columnist for *Esquire* magazine. He has contributed articles and essays to *The New York Times, Playboy, Vanity Fair*, and *Manhattan, Inc.* He is the author of *The Hunger for More: Searching for Values in an Age of Greed.* **(veralgia)**

Albert Shanker is an educator who served as the president of the United Federation of Teachers from 1964 to 1985. **(antisummitism, hebdomatitism, hospitility, indignitary, trumpery)**

Walter Shapiro is a senior writer for *Time* magazine. **(skif-skaf)**

Don Share is a poet whose work has appeared in *Partisan Review, Semiotext(e), The Texas Review, The Paris Review*, and *Agni*. **(compugilist, eyelie, grite, lovedice)**

Scott Shuger is an editor of *Washington Monthly*. **(technophoria)**

Alix Kates Shulman is the author of *In Every Woman's Life . . .* , *On the Stroll*, and *Memoirs of an Ex Prom Queen*. **(affluential, easyace)**

Neil Asher Silberman is an archaeologist who has excavated in the Middle East and worked for the Israel Department of Antiquities. He is the author of *Between Past and Present: Archaeology, Ideology, and Nationalism in the Modern Middle East.* **(chronocentrism)**

Todd Silor is a visiting artist at the Computer Aided Design Laboratory of the Department of Mechanical Engineering at MIT. He is the author of *Breaking the Mind Barrier: The Artscience of Neurocosmology*. His artwork is represented by Ronald Feldman Gallery in New York City. **(factualize, processmorph, transcience)**

Edward Silver is an editor for the *Los Angeles Times*. **(corpobabble, self-unemployed)**

S. Fred Singer is director of the Science and Environmental Policy Project and author of several books, among them *Global Effects of*

Environmental Pollution and *Is There an Optimum Level of Population?* **(populution)**

Bajon Kahlil Siron-El, who has spent three-fourths of his life in jail, is now a writer and lyricist whose work ranges from church to rap to ballad to country and western. **(housin, pasminded, tempress)**

Elizabeth Anne Socolow is the author of *Laughing at Gravity: Conversations with Isaac Newton.* **(abstistic, lochsam)**

Barbara Probst Solomon is the author of several novels, among them *Arriving Where We Started, The Beat of Life,* and *Horse-Trading and Ecstasy.* **(kinket, telephonade)**

Maya Sonenberg is the author of *Cartographies,* winner of the 1989 Drue Heinz Literature Prize. **(ignoramorus)**

Gilbert Sorrentino is the author of *Misterioso, Rose Theatre,* and *Odd Number.* He is a professor of English at Stanford University. **(safirize)**

Thomas Spaccarelli is a professor of Spanish at the University of the South. **(ferversion)**

Scott Spencer is the author of several novels, among them *Endless Love, Waking the Dead,* and, most recently, *Secret Anniversaries.* **(bathosphere)**

Will Stanton has published humorous pieces in *Esquire, The Atlantic, The New Yorker, Reader's Digest, Life* magazine, *McCall's, Redbook,* and other publications. **(berrengle, bulcnaf, chimpunc, decico, dominaut, flauntlaw, hopefolly, puorgni, sexamp, sham-faced, simphobia, tautobar)**

George Starbuck is a poet whose most comprehensive collection is *The Argot Merchant Disaster,* which won the Lenore Marshall/Nation Prize as Best Poetry Book of 1983. **(scoosh)**

Fritz Stern is Seth Low professor of history at Columbia University and author of *Dreams and Delusions: National Socialism in the Drama of the German Past.* **(thoughtlet)**

Jane and Michael Stern are the authors of several books, among them *The Encyclopedia of Bad Taste, American Gourmet,* and *Roadfood.* **(horroneous)**

Robert J. Sternberg is IBM professor of psychology and education at Yale University. **(dictraitor)**

Ian Stewart is a professor at the Mathematics Institute of the University of Warwick in Coventry, England. He is the author of *Does God Play Dice?* and writes the column on mathematical recreations for *Scientific American.* **(bootscaffle, disquerify, hipposy, lepidophobia, milium, negentrope, prignant)**

John Stone is a cardiologist and dean of admissions at Emory University School of Medicine, where he is also a professor of medicine. He is the author of *In the Country of Hearts: Journeys in the Art of Medicine* and has been published in *The New York Times Magazine* and *Discover.* **(tump)**

Ronald Sukenick is the author of *Down and In* and *Blown Away.* **(iconoclysm)**

Gladys Swan is the author of *Carnival for the Gods* and three collections of short stories. Her forthcoming novel is *Ghost Dance: A Play of Voices.* **(déjà vous, keat, putsch-crow, rejectalate)**

David Swanger is the author of *The Poem as Process, Inside the Horse,* and *The Shape of Waters.* His work has appeared in *The Georgia Review, Chariton Review, Poetry Northwest,* and other literary magazines. **(inflatulate)**

Elizabeth Tallent is the author of *Time with Children, Museum Pieces,* and *In Constant Flight.* **(amaterrogate, econausea)**

Alexander Theroux is the author of *Darconville's Cat, An Adultery,* and *The Great Wheadle Tragedy.* **(boxgiggle, cathy, fusifix, rictory, Shamir, slope, wallpoodle)**

Paul Therrio is a free-lance writer. **(bridgeword, bullroar)**

Michael Thomas writes the Midas Watch column in the *New York Observer.* His most recent novel is *Hanover Place.* He is at work on a volume of commentary on the 1980s titled *Terms of Estrangement*. (**hellucyonation**)

David Thornburgh is a songwriter living in Miami Beach, Florida. (**logicate**)

George Thrush is an architect and president of George Thrush Design and director of the studio architecture program at Northeastern University. (**exfiltrate, frabble, lethargist, palindrone**)

Lionel Tiger is the Charles Darwin professor of anthropology at Rutgers University. His most recent book is *The Pursuit of Pleasure*. (**chagrim, cryptych, thinuous, updata**)

Sallie Tisdale is the author of *Stepping Westward: The Long Search for Home in the Pacific Northwest* and other books. Her prose appears in *Harper's Magazine, The New Yorker,* and other magazines. (**exercist, mimibok**)

Andrew Tobias is the author of such books as *The Only Investment Guide You'll Ever Need, The Invisible Bankers, Fire & Ice,* and *Getting by on $100,000 a Year (and Other Sad Tales)*. (**eyedropper, laudarrassment, moonshooter**)

Paul Tough is an associate editor of *Harper's Magazine*. His journalism has appeared in *Esquire* magazine. (**fandy, scuttlebutthead, zeitgeisty**)

Kathleen Kennedy Townsend is director of the Maryland Student Service Alliance. (**helmsouflage**)

James Trefil is Clarence J. Robinson professor of physics at George Mason University. He is the author of *1001 Things Everyone Should Know About Science* and coauthor of *Science Matters: Achieving Scientific Literacy*. (**gen**)

Richard Tristman is a professor of literature and language at Bennington College. (**acousticate, epistemic happiness, pleogingliasm**)

George W. S. Trow is a writer for *The New Yorker* and author of the book *In the Context of No Context*. **(ethicoterratropism, pharisant)**

Mitch Tuchman is managing editor at the Los Angeles County Museum of Art. **(pluripetasate)**

Frederick Turner is Founders professor of arts and humanities at the University of Texas at Dallas. He is the author of the epic poem *Genesis* and the books *Tempest, Flute, and Oz* and *Natural Classicism: Essays on Literature and Science*. **(convivor)**

R. Emmett Tyrrell, Jr., is editor-in-chief of *The American Spectator*. **(apodiabolosis, bidenize, black-cat story)**

Sandra Vagins is a technical editor at C.A.E.-Link Corporation in Silver Spring, Maryland. **(blandiose, Exxonecution)**

Lloyd Van Brunt is the author of *Working Firewood for the Night*, his seventh book of poems. He is working now on a memoir, *I Fall in Love with Nancy Drew*. His eighth and probably last book of poems, *La Traviata in Oklahoma, Selected and New Poems 1961–1991*, will be published in 1992. **(fatulous)**

Lesley Visser is a sportscaster for CBS Sports. Previously she wrote about sports for *The Boston Globe*. **(flustrate)**

William Walden has had eight plays produced and three published. His articles and light verse have appeared in *The New Yorker, Punch, The Atlantic,* and *The Georgia Review*, among other publications. **(scriptophile)**

Alice Walker is the author of *The Color Purple* and, most recently, *Her Blue Body Everything We Know: Earthling Poems 1965–1990 Complete*. **(womanist)**

David Foster Wallace is the author of *Girl With Curious Hair, The Broom of the System,* and (with Mark Costello) *Signifying Rappers*. **(ambiguphobe, pomoerotic)**

Paul Wallich is a science writer who works at *Scientific American*. **(logobumf, smergdorf)**

Bill Walton played basketball with the Los Angeles Clippers and the Boston Celtics. **(bridgeword, bullroar)**

Jonathan Weiner is a science writer and author of *The Next 100 Years*. He is at work on a book about evolution. **(Nooscene)**

Gerald Weissman, M.D., is a professor of medicine and director of the Division of Rheumatology at New York University Medical Center. He is the author of *The Woods Hole Cantata: Essays on Science and Society*, *The Doctor with Two Heads*, and the forthcoming *The Doctor's Dilemma*. **(derridology)**

Paul West is the author of *Lord Byron's Doctor*, *The Women of Whitechapel*, and *Jack the Ripper*. **(flaffy, mrok)**

Gahan Wilson is a cartoonist whose work appears in *The New Yorker* and *Playboy* magazines and is the author of *Eddie Deco's Last Caper* and *Everybody's Favorite Duck*. **(artifract)**

Laurie Winer is a journalist whose work has appeared in *The New York Times*, *The Wall Street Journal*, *Connoisseur*, and *New York Woman*. **(yenta envy)**

Tom Wood is a writer, and editor of *Bank Director*. **(aglyphicate)**

George T. Wright is the author of the book, *Shakespeare's Metrical Art*. He has published articles in *PMLA* and poems in *The New Yorker*, *The Sewanee Review*, and *Esquire*. **(nonswer)**

Jose Yglesias is author of *Tristan and the Hispanics* and *One German Dead*. His work has appeared in *The New Yorker*. **(oedify)**

Richard Zacks is a journalist whose work has appeared in *Life, Time, Sports Illustrated,* and *The Atlantic.* He wrote a nationally syndicated column from 1986 to 1989 and is currently at work on a screenplay. **(anchorsham, buchwald, internify, outkvetch, powerdisiac, pulprize, vindinoia)**